Commemorative Stamps
of the U.S.A.

Commemorative Stamps of the U.S.A.

An Illustrated History of Our Country

By Fred Reinfeld

BRAMHALL HOUSE • NEW YORK

For Don and Judy
who asked "why?"

383
R

DESIGN BY EDWARD A. HAMILTON

AUTHOR'S NOTE

In gathering stamps to be photographed for this volume, I was helped by the Coronet Stamp Shop of New York, which supplied almost all the stamps used. My thanks are also due to Robert Siegel, who was good enough to provide the higher values of the Columbian issue; and to Bernard D. Harmer, of the distinguished firm of H. R. Harmer, Inc., who very kindly placed at my disposal some magnificent specimens of outstanding rarities.

I am also grateful to my wife, Beatrice Reinfeld, for her patient reading of the manuscript versions and proofs and her helpful comments.

This book would not be complete without an acknowledgment of the always friendly and highly capable cooperation of members of the staff of the Thomas Y. Crowell Company.

All the photographs in this volume have been prepared in accordance with the governmental regulations which apply to such reproduction.

For the convenience of collectors, each stamp is accompanied by its Scott Catalog number. Collectors will also be interested, I believe, in the list of sources for the designs of the stamps which will be found at the end of the book.

Yea, though they should lose their lives in this action,
yet they might have comfort in the same.
. . . All great & honourable actions are accompanied
with great difficulties, and must be both
enterprised and overcome with answerable courages.

WILLIAM BRADFORD: *Of Plimoth Plantation*

Contents

Columbus in Sight of Land

230 · 1¢ blue · 1893

IT HAS been jokingly remarked that when Christopher Columbus set out on his historic voyage, he didn't know where he was going; when he arrived, he didn't know where he was; and when he returned home, he didn't know where he'd been!

Yet Columbus's seven-thousand-mile miscalculation changed the course of world history and turned a despised Genoese adventurer with holes in his cape into "the Very Magnificent Lord Cristóbal, Admiral of the Ocean Sea and Viceroy of the Islands and the Mainland."

Christopher Columbus was born in Genoa, probably in 1451, the son of a poor weaver. He went to sea at an early age, making voyages in the Mediterranean, and on the Atlantic to Africa, Ireland, and—according to some accounts—Iceland.

All our portraits of Columbus are imaginary, but we have a fair idea of what he looked like from the reports of people who knew him. He was tall, with a ruddy complexion, blue eyes, aquiline nose, and red hair. Proud, sensitive, secretive, stubborn, deeply religious, he was filled with a mysterious sense of a sublime mission.

From his experience on ships, his wide reading, and discussions with experts, Columbus became well versed in navigation and geography. There was nothing unusual in his belief that

1

Landing of Columbus

231 · 2¢ maroon · 1893

the world was round; this theory was held by most learned men of his time. Likewise they agreed that it was *theoretically* possible to reach the east coast of Asia by sailing west from Europe. What separated Columbus from the other outstanding navigators of his day was his burning conviction that such a voyage was *practicable*.

Why was Columbus alone in his belief? There were two reasons, both based on colossal miscalculations on his part. In the first place, he underestimated the circumference of the earth by about 25 per cent. Second, he thought Asia extended much further east than it actually does.

The combined effect of these errors was to give Columbus

Flagship of Columbus

232 · 3¢ green · 1893

Fleet of
Columbus

233 • 4¢ blue • 1893

the idea that he could reach Cathay (China) and Cipangu (Japan) by sailing three thousand miles. Actually the distance is in the neighborhood of eleven thousand miles—and that only by means of the Panama Canal. Luckily for the success of Columbus's first voyage, the West Indies are situated more or less where he expected to find the islands off Asia.

In those days the Portuguese were unequaled as skillful and daring navigators, and their government took an active part in promoting voyages of discovery. The King of Portugal was therefore the logical man for Columbus to approach in the hope of obtaining funds for a westward voyage.

In 1484 Columbus presented his plan to King John II. Proud and poor as he was, Columbus made far-reaching demands in return for his services and took the King's refusal as miserly and unimaginative.

As for the King, he considered Columbus a high-flown windbag. Besides, his masterly navigators were making such rewarding progress down the west coast of Africa that finding the complete eastward route to India was only a matter of time. (Three years later, in fact, Bartholomew Dias rounded the Cape of Good Hope at the southernmost tip of Africa. This brought the Portuguese into the Indian Ocean, poised to reach India.)

3

Columbus Soliciting Aid of Isabella

234 · 5¢ brown · 1893

To do King John full justice, we must remember that he submitted Columbus's proposal to a commission of Portuguese navigators and astronomers. These experts turned Columbus down because their calculations showed that the westward distance to Asia must be much greater than he claimed.

This meant the voyage would require four months—maybe more—of sailing without sight of land. The crews would be terrified, repairs would be all but impossible, food and supplies could not conceivably hold out. The routes, currents, and winds were uncharted, the instruments of that period were still crude; no doubt of it, the proposal of this Genoese was fantastic!

Certainly the judgment of the Portuguese authorities was sound. But though they were right, history proved them wrong. And though Columbus was wrong, history proved him right. Neither Columbus nor the Portuguese dreamt of the existence of a huge land mass—the Americas—lying between Europe and Asia. Nor did they guess the existence of the Pacific Ocean as a body of water distinct from the Atlantic. Thus it was pure chance—almost—that led Columbus to what later became known as the New World.

After John II's refusal, Columbus went to Spain for an audience with King Ferdinand and Queen Isabella. On his arrival

Columbus Welcomed
at Barcelona

235 · 6¢ purple · 1893

in Spain, Columbus left his little orphaned son Diego at the monastery of La Rábida. The acquaintanceship thus formed was a stroke of luck for Columbus, as the friars became his staunchest supporters and furthered his cause energetically through their influential friends at court.

Nor was this the only lucky turn for Columbus. The Spanish monarchs proved the most sympathetic listeners he had yet found. Isabella, a handsome, vivacious woman, was intelligent, learned, devout, persevering, and a first-rate administrator. Ferdinand, chiefly interested in war and devious diplomacy, was courtly, crafty, and stingy—yet sensible enough to respect his wife's superior brains.

Columbus's case was none too convincing in the absence of precedents, supporters, charts, or maps. Yet he was an eloquent speaker, and his promises inspired enthusiasm by their very vagueness. His references to the gold, precious stones, and valuable spices of the Indies were irresistible.

Unfortunately, there was a snag. Ferdinand and Isabella, preoccupied with conquering Granada (the last remaining Moorish stronghold in Spain), could spare neither time nor money.

The monarchs dallied: they could not quite bring themselves to accept, neither did they wish to dismiss Columbus. Putting

Columbus Restored
to Favor

236 • 8¢ red • 1893

off a definite decision, they submitted his plan to a commission of Spanish experts.

The years of waiting after 1486 were painful ones for Columbus. With success almost in his grasp, think of "what he had to endure from informing so many people of no understanding, although they presumed to know all about it, and replying patiently to many people who did not know him nor had any respect for his person, receiving insulting speeches which afflicted his soul." (These are the sympathetic words of his contemporary Las Casas.) Later, Columbus enjoyed the indiscreet luxury of saying, "I told you so!"

Early in 1492 the Spanish monarchs completed their conquest of the Moors. Columbus was granted another audience and this time the King and Queen were very much taken with his notion of sailing westward to find the treasure of the Indies. Nevertheless they could not bring themselves to accept Columbus's sweeping terms. And no wonder—he wanted to be knighted and given the hereditary titles of Don, Grand Admiral, and Viceroy —plus 10 per cent of all profits from the newly discovered regions, for him and his descendants.

After this last setback, Columbus left the Spanish court, determined to try his luck in another land. But a few hours later

6

Columbus Presenting Natives

237 · 10¢ brown · 1893

a royal messenger overtook him with an order to return to the Queen. His terms had been accepted after all!

Modern historians take no stock in the story that Isabella raised money on her jewels to provide the funds for Columbus's voyage. The Crown contributed part of the money; the rest came from Luis de Santángel, a high court official; from the Pinzón brothers, who were to sail with Columbus; and from Columbus himself, who must have borrowed his share.

It is likely that the three small ships provided for the voyage had the following tonnage: the *Santa María,* one hundred tons; the *Pinta,* fifty tons; the *Niña,* forty tons. The crews for all three vessels amounted to about a hundred men.

Columbus Announcing His Discovery

238 · 15¢ green · 1893

7

Columbus at La Rábida

239 · 30¢ brown · 1893

On August 3, 1492, Columbus set out on his memorable voyage from Palos, a small seaport on the southwestern coast of Spain. He reached the Canary Islands in eight days, and after waiting for needed repairs, set his course west on September 9.

With no charts and little help from celestial navigation, and the crudest of instruments, Columbus had to rely on dead reckoning to reach a destination which was only vaguely indicated on grossly inadequate maps. His safe arrival and return are convincing proof of his superb seamanship aided by that special brand of daring that often creates its own good luck.

Several days out from the Canaries, the little fleet sailed through the dense weeds of the Sargasso Sea—uncanny but harmless—without mishap. But then, as week after week went by without any sign of land, the sailors became more and more uneasy. At last, on October 9, Columbus averted mutiny only by agreeing to turn back if no land was sighted within the next three days.

Two days later, unmistakable signs of an approaching landfall turned up: a branch, a board, and a stick floating in the water. On the night of October 11-12 the tensely expectant men heard the lookout on the *Pinta* cry, *"Tierra, tierra!"*—*"Land!"* After thirty-three days at sea since his departure from the Canaries,

Recall of Columbus

240 · 50¢ blue · 1893

Columbus had at last reached his unintended goal in the Bahamas.

The next morning the Admiral and his men dressed in their best, unfurled their banners, and went ashore. After kneeling for a thanksgiving ceremony, they claimed the island for Spain. San Salvador was their name for the small island; today it is known as Watling Island.

Soon the Spaniards encountered the gentle and peaceful natives. Thinking he was in the Indies, Columbus called them Indians. Later he explored Cuba, Hispaniola (Haiti), and other islands of the region.

In January, 1493, Columbus started home, and after an exceedingly stormy voyage he was back in Palos by March 15. After sending news of his spectacular discoveries to Ferdinand and Isabella, Columbus journeyed to Barcelona to give their majesties a detailed account. Thrilled by the sight of several Indians, gaudy parrots, tropical plants, and some gold, the delighted monarchs showered honors and gifts on Columbus and confirmed the titles and claims for which he had bargained.

Columbus made three more voyages—in 1493, 1498, and 1504. He founded a colony in Hispaniola, but the problems of administration were too much for him. Serious trouble arose,

9

Isabella Pledging Her Jewels

241 · $1 salmon · 1893

Columbus made errors of judgment, and Ferdinand and Isabella lost confidence in him. Where were the gold and precious stones and spices of the Indies?

Columbus's third voyage took a promising turn, for it was on this trip that he touched the mainland for the first time; he explored the northeast coast of South America under the mistaken impression that it was the coast of Asia.

But with the Admiral's arrival at Hispaniola, disaster struck. The colony had a new governor, Francisco de Bobadilla. Instead of cooperating with Bobadilla, Columbus defied him. Thereupon the deeply offended governor put Columbus in chains and sent him home in disgrace.

Ferdinand and Isabella were affable to the Admiral on his return to Spain and restored most of his honors—but he never regained his old posts as Governor and Viceroy. Sick and embittered, Columbus continued to believe to the day of his death that he had found the Indies. He never realized—or at least never admitted—that what he had actually found was a huge land mass previously unknown to Europe.

On his fourth and last voyage in 1504 Columbus explored the eastern coast of Central America in his search for a strait to the Spice Islands. Increasingly ridiculed and discredited and

Columbus in Chains

242 · $2 red · 1893

entangled in aggravating lawsuits, Columbus was now a broken man. "They all made fun of my plan then; now even tailors wish to discover," he wrote contemptuously of the men who were reaping glory from his pioneering efforts. He died in 1506.

Amerigo Vespucci, also an Italian, voyaged westward in 1499, 1500, and 1503. Unlike Columbus, Vespucci finally came to realize that the "Indies" were nowhere near Asia, but were truly a New World. After a while geographers who were impressed by his arguments began to call the New World "America." Thus Columbus lost even the honor of having the New World named for him.

Though he was not fully appreciated in his lifetime, Colum-

Columbus Describing the Third Voyage

243 · $3 green · 1893

11

Isabella and Columbus

244 · $4 carmine · 1893

bus has since been recognized as the man who changed the course of world history by his memorable voyage. The whole mighty epic of exploration and settlement of the Americas rests on the steadfast faith and toil of one man who triumphed over every obstacle that fate placed in his way.

The Columbian stamps, the first ever issued by the United States for commemorative purposes, appeared in connection with the Columbian Exposition held at Chicago in 1893. That is why the stamps were issued in 1893, although the four-hundredth anniversary of Columbus's first voyage occurred in 1892. In the opinion of many collectors, the Columbian stamps are the handsomest and most desirable of all the commemoratives.

Columbus

(America to left, Liberty to right)

245 · $5 black · 1893

Marquette on the Mississippi

285 · 1¢ green · 1898

IN 1898, almost fifty years after the wild California Gold Rush brought many thousands of pioneers to the West, the city of Omaha staged its Trans-Mississippi Exposition. "Trans-Mississippi" means "across the Mississippi," a phrase which compactly sums up the western migrations that turned the United States into a vast subcontinent.

For almost two centuries after Columbus unknowingly discovered the New World, the Mississippi remained a mystery to Europeans. The Indians told wild tales of a "Great River" guarded by demons, monsters, and wild tribesmen. Did the river really exist? And if it did, where did it flow?—south? or perhaps west, out into the Pacific Ocean?

At last, in 1672, the Governor of New France selected Louis Joliet, a fur trapper and expert woodsman, to trace the course of the fabled river. Joliet was to be accompanied by five *voyageurs* (skilled canoemen) and Father Jacques Marquette (1637-1675), one of those resolute yet gentle Jesuit missionaries who were doctors, diplomats, and explorers as well as priests.

Traveling in two birchbark canoes, the tiny expedition descended the Mississippi as far as the mouth of the Arkansas River (seven hundred miles north of New Orleans), and then turned back to Canada. In four months Marquette and Joliet

13

Farming
in the West

286 · 2¢ red · 1898

covered some twenty-seven hundred miles. This fearless advance into the unknown was the first step in the settlement of the West.

In those days the buffalo was still the monarch of the plains. It is estimated that in 1492 there were forty-five million buffaloes; in 1889, five hundred and forty-one!

To the Plains Indians nothing was more delectable than juicy buffalo steaks roasted on a spit. Dried and pounded with plums or berries and mixed with fat, the meat was known as pemmican—perhaps the most nutritious food ever prepared by man.

But the buffalo was more than food; it was a way of life. Its hide was used for coats, robes, tepees, moccasins, and bowstrings. From the bones, tools and arrow points were fashioned. Lariats were made from the hair, thread from the tendons, rattles from the hoofs.

There were no horses in the New World when the first Europeans arrived. Until then the Indians hunted the buffalo on foot with bow and arrow. Their bows were powerful enough to drive an arrow right through a buffalo's massive shoulders with fatal effect. The migrations of huge buffalo herds in search of fodder turned the Plains Indians into wanderers as well.

14

Indian
Hunting Buffalo

287 • 4¢ orange • 1898

Once the Indians obtained mounts, the buffalo hunts became much more efficient. They were marvelous riders and trainers. Before they had firearms, they often stampeded the buffaloes into stockades or over cliffs. Buffalo Jump-Off, in the Yellowstone River Valley, Montana, is the best-known of these primitive slaughterhouses.

Where the Indian had killed sparingly and reverently, appeasing the spirits of the dead buffaloes, the white man slaughtered senselessly. By 1820 there were no buffaloes left east of the Mississippi, and by 1850 their numbers had dwindled to twenty million; by 1870 to five and a half million. In the 1870's travelers still reported seeing herds eight miles long. Sometimes the animals stopped trains, or else, swimming a river, blocked a steamboat's progress.

The steady stream of western migration and the invention of the repeating rifle meant the virtual extinction of the buffalo and of the Indians who were dependent on the beasts. By killing off the herds, the white men forced the Indians into the reservations and deprived them of the gloriously free life they had enjoyed for centuries. Confronted with this disaster in the 1850's, the Indians fought back as hard as they could; but they fought for a lost cause.

15

Frémont on the Rocky Mountains

288 · 5¢ blue · 1898

The westward traffic that crushed the Indians had its head-quarters at St. Louis, founded in 1762 and destined to become the world's leading market for raw furs. The mountain men brought their pelts from the Missouri Valley and Rocky Mountain country to St. Louis and purchased supplies there for their next trip. Traders on the old Santa Fe Trail worked out of St. Louis, taking trade goods in their covered wagons and bringing back furs, gold and silver, and horses. Profits of 50 per cent were not unusual.

Through St. Louis passed pioneers bound for Texas, for the California gold diggings, for Pikes Peak, for the Oregon Trail, for the Great Plains grasslands. The old buffalo trails became covered-wagon routes which later served the stagecoaches. The first railway west of St. Louis was the Pacific Railroad—later the Missouri Pacific—on which construction started in 1851.

Few men played a more important role in the settlement of the West than John Charles Frémont (1813-1890), known as the Pathfinder. By means of his explorations of the Rocky Mountain passes in the 1840's, Frémont acted as a publicity agent for the attractions of the Far West. Frémont's accounts of his daring expeditions brought thousands of emigrants in search of fertile farm land.

Troops Guarding Train

289 · 8¢ lilac · 1898

Unfortunately for Frémont, his impetuous, ambitious temperament was not seasoned with sound judgment. After running up a fortune of ten million dollars in California gold mines and real estate, he died practically a pauper.

It is all too easy to get a misleading picture of pioneer life by reading about such dashing figures as Frémont and his favorite scout Kit Carson. Years earlier, William Cobbett, an English visitor, was appalled by the harsh conditions of frontier life —"the rugged roads, the dirty hovels, the fire in the woods to sleep by, the pathless ways through the wilderness, the dangerous crossings of the rivers."

But the hardships of migration to the Far West were much worse. The settlers had a saying that "the cowards never started and the weak ones died on the way." It was tragically true: the trails were marked by many a grave.

There was always danger from the Indians, especially when small parties were involved. Thirst could be agonizing, and the broiling sun, dust, and wind were cruel to the eyes. Bad drinking water brought on dysentery; some of the travelers succumbed to cholera.

Swamps, quicksands, and sandy soil often trapped the Conestoga wagons. Sometimes wheels cracked or wagon tongues split,

Hardships of Emigration

290 · 10¢ slate · 1898

or else the wagons overturned on steep grades or capsized in the swift currents of rivers.

When animals strayed off, valuable time was lost chasing them. Again, they might become so weary that precious articles had to be thrown aside to lighten the load. One group of forty-niners during a period of twenty-four hours counted seventeen abandoned prairie schooners, twenty-seven dead animals, eight dead bodies.

The wagon trains were often guarded by detachments of United States cavalry from one of the forts that dotted the West. Some of these wagon trains were fifteen miles long. The body of a wagon was generally painted blue, the wheels red. The thick white canvas top was waterproof, and each wagon was drawn by a team of oxen—as few as six, as many as sixteen.

When supply trains encamped at night, the men loosened the animals and drove them into a corral made by placing the wagons in a circle with the tongues pointing outward. This was the best protection against Indians. The men slept on the ground, wrapped in their blankets, and took turns standing guard against surprise attack.

The animals were hitched to the wagon in pairs, with the strongest pair directly next to the wagon. It was not unusual

Western Mining Prospector

291 · 50¢ olive · 1898

for oxen and even horses and mules to break loose from a wagon train and run off with a buffalo stampede. Such wild rushes were dangerous as well as costly.

From 1849 until well into the 1890's many of the emigrants sought quick riches by mining precious metals. The California Gold Rush (see stamp 954) was followed by gold strikes in Nevada (stamp 999), Idaho (stamp 896), Colorado (stamp 1001), Montana (stamp 858), Alaska (stamp 800), the Black Hills (stamp 858), and Arizona.

A few men became wealthy but the vast majority found only hardship and keen disappointment and back-breaking toil. Such names as Poverty Gulch and Blue Monday Butte tell their own story. But high prices, primitive conditions, and pervasive lawlessness failed to disillusion the optimists. The lone prospector with his pack mule was a familiar and pathetic sight in the West long after the great days were over.

Many mining settlements became ghost towns once the profitable veins of ore were exhausted. Others retained an unsavory reputation for years. Tombstone, Arizona, was one of the toughest until it was cleaned up by Wyatt Earp, the courageous United States marshal. Deadwood, which sprang up overnight when gold was discovered in the Black Hills in 1874, prided

Western Cattle
in Storm

292 · $1 black · 1898

itself on being a wide-open town. The killing of Wild Bill
Hickok by a shot in the back was a typical incident.

Farming on the prairies seems tame by comparison, but it
involved so many privations that in 1862 the Homestead Act
gave a hundred and sixty acres outright to settlers on condition
that they built a house and cultivated the land for five years.

As the country's population grew, the demand for wheat was
greatly stimulated. The invention of Cyrus McCormick's reaper
(page 187), the arrival of large numbers of immigrant farmers,
the improved shipping facilities of the ever multiplying railroad
networks all helped to meet that demand.

There were other problems too: frost, fungus, and drought
often proved disastrous to the wheatlands. Here the Department
of Agriculture helped farmers by encouraging research to discover the hardiest strains of wheat. Investigators traveled to
Turkey, Russia, and China to find the best varieties, and
American farmers benefited by their studies.

The development of cattle-raising was even more remarkable.
Back in 1521 the Spaniards had brought to Mexico the ancestors of the Texas longhorns. By 1830 Texas had a hundred
thousand of them. For a time they were public property and
anyone could brand them and claim them as his own.

Mississippi River Bridge at St. Louis

293 • $2 brown • 1898

In the 1870's the number of cattle raised for the market rose into the millions, and the carefree and independent cowpuncher became a hero to Americans and Europeans who lived humdrum lives. Actually a cowboy's life was often lonely, full of hard work and routine, some dangers, and few pleasures.

Once a year the cattlemen rounded up their herds, branded and counted them, and set off for Abilene or Dodge City or some other cattle town where the steers were loaded into box cars. A steer that was worth three dollars in Texas might fetch as much as thirty at Abilene. The Chisholm Trail was a favorite route— about eight hundred miles long, and taking from three to five months to negotiate.

About fifteen cowmen might accompany the herd to keep it intact, protect it from rustlers and Indian attacks, and head off stampedes. A storm or high wind could easily disrupt the whole herd.

Today the Old West exists mostly in books. The ox-drawn covered wagon and rickety stagecoach have given way to the railroad, the automobile, and the airplane. Huge dams are repairing the ravages of centuries. Towns, factories, and farms abound in a region that was once a solitude where the thud of buffalo hoofs could be heard miles away.

21

Fast Lake Navigation

294 · 1¢ green and black · 1901

In 1901 Buffalo's Pan-American Exposition paid tribute to the progress made in North and South America during the nineteenth century. The commemorative stamps issued for this occasion stress the century's improvements in communication.

Two stamps of the series remind us that the Great Lakes are the most valuable inland waterway in the world. This has been especially true since 1855 when the Sault Sainte Marie Canal was built to link Lake Superior with Lake Huron. The canal uses five locks to save vessels from the dangers of the St. Marys River rapids.

Great Lakes freighters are known as "bulk carriers." They are specially designed to carry large cargoes and make loading and unloading easy. Millions of tons of iron ore are shipped from the shores of Lake Superior to Ohio lake ports and then by rail to the steel mills of Ohio and Pennsylvania. The same freighters carry back millions of tons of coal which comes from the mines of West Virginia, Pennsylvania, and Ohio and is destined for use by Canadian railroads.

Canada supplies 60 per cent of the world's newsprint. Freighters bring the logs to pulp and paper mills which in turn ship to Chicago, Detroit, Cleveland, and other large cities.

Much of the grain from Canada's Port Arthur and Fort William (the world's leading grain-shipping port) goes to Buf-

Fast Express

295 · 2¢ red and black · 1901

falo, with its huge grain elevators that have a capacity of fifty million bushels. Port Huron, also located in Canada, has the largest oil refinery in the British Commonwealth; some of the Great Lakes tankers carry over a hundred thousand barrels in a single shipment. Detroit sends out thousands of cars on Lake freighters every day, and receives thousands of tons of machinery and materials through the same source.

Storm and fog are no longer the menaces they once were on the Great Lakes. Radio, depth finders, radar, and detailed and accurate weather reports from Canada and the United States have made navigation much safer.

American contacts with Canada have become steadily more important in other ways as well. For example, the growth of commerce and tourist travel between the two countries has resulted in no less than nine bridges over the Niagara River, six of them directly linking the United States and Canada. The bridge pictured on the 5¢ stamp is a steel arch structure 1,240 feet long with an arch span of 840 feet. It accommodates railroad trains and motor vehicles and was completed in 1897.

On the other hand, improvements in oceanic communication have come more slowly. Thus, in 1901 ocean steamship design still awaited many improvements. John Ericsson's screw propeller, introduced in the 1840's, was much safer and far more

Automobile

296 · 4¢ brown and black · 1901

powerful than the clumsy old-style paddle wheels. Yet it was not until about 1890 that paddle wheels died out and sail really surrendered to steam.

By 1850 regular sailing schedules were coming into effect. The ever larger waves of emigration to America and the importance of fast mail service between the Old World and the New led to one improvement after another in steamship design. Wooden hulls gave way to iron, which was in turn ousted by steel. Wood was finally replaced by coal as a far more satisfactory fuel.

But the most spectacular improvements came after the turn of the century. The steam turbine made machinery less bulky, gave more power, and reduced vibration. Oil became the preferred fuel. The invention of wireless saved many lives.

The international rivalry in building luxury liners led eventually to the American superliner *United States,* which crossed the Atlantic on its maiden voyage in 1952 in the record time of three days and eleven hours. This vessel is built of aluminum, is fireproof and air-conditioned throughout, has every known electronic aid to navigation, and even makes its own supply of fresh water by an ingenious process. Carrying two thousand passengers and a crew of a thousand, the *United States* was the last word in comfort and safety at the time of its launching.

Bridge at
Niagara Falls

297 · 5¢ blue and black · 1901

While the steamship had a hard time overcoming popular prejudice, the steam locomotive had a phenomenally rapid acceptance. There was good reason: by 1830 America's territorial expansion and the needs of business activity called for sharp improvement in transportation methods. Shipping was time-wasting, cumbersome, unreliable, and often led to spoilage or loss. The invention of the locomotive in England solved the problem.

Americans wanted locomotives like Puffing Billy and The Rocket, as some of the early models were called. Soon the Delaware and Hudson Canal Company imported a locomotive named the Stourbridge Lion because of the fierce lion's face on its front.

Peter Cooper's tiny American-built locomotive Tom Thumb raced along madly at fifteen miles an hour. After their first spell of skepticism people accepted the railroads as perfectly practical. The earliest railroad lines were short—some no more than ten miles—and this proved the bane of railroad travel. To ride from Rochester to Boston, for example, required ten train changes.

Each road was locally owned and determined the width of its own tracks without paying any attention to other lines. Later on, when the systems began to be linked up, passengers and freight had to be transferred from line to line. The delay and expense

Canal Locks at
Sault Sainte Marie

298 · 8¢ lilac and black · 1901

involved gradually led to the use of standard-size equipment and the formation of long-distance trunk lines.

The Pullman car appeared in 1858; the diner was a later refinement. Freight cars gradually became highly specialized, their design determined by the nature of the freight. Brakes went through a long process of development until the Westinghouse air brake offered a satisfactory solution. The amount of railroad track rose from nine thousand miles in 1850 to thirty thousand in 1860 and by the end of the century it had risen to one hundred seventy thousand.

Unlike the railroad, the automobile was in its infancy in 1901. For centuries men had dreamed of a vehicle that would move by itself—the literal meaning of *automobile*. Even the great Sir Isaac Newton had dabbled with the idea. But the earlier models were all powered by steam, which required too much space for the engine. The miserable quality of oldtime roads was another discouragement to inventors.

In 1769 Nicholas Cugnot's three-wheeled "automobile," using a steam engine, ran three miles an hour. Unfortunately, it had to stop every fifteen minutes to get up more steam.

During the nineteenth century there were many steam coaches in England—huge, clumsy affairs that belched smoke. Many people thought them hideous, and dangerous as well. In

26

Fast Ocean Navigation

299 · 10¢ brown and black · 1901

1865 the opposition forced a law through Parliament providing that these vehicles be preceded by a man on horseback waving a red flag to warn passers-by. The law was eventually repealed.

A German named Gottfried Daimler solved one problem in the 1880's by designing a light, practical internal-combustion engine that used gasoline. In the United States, Henry Ford put together his first "horseless carriage" in the 1890's. Its engine was at the rear, and the contraption ran on bicycle tires. It had two speeds, but no reverse and no brakes. Like all the early automobiles, it made a fearful racket, gave off irritating fumes, raised a small dust storm, and broke down frequently.

The evolution of this comical-looking horseless buggy into the sleek cars of today took many years and the work of many men. Ford's "tin Lizzie" was a favorite subject for jokes, yet by 1927 he had turned out his fifty-millionth car and become one of the richest men in the world.

The United States was now covered by a network of thousands of miles of fine roads; the manufacture of automobiles became the country's leading industry; and the automobile had revolutionized American life. Back in 1901, however, these developments were reserved for the remote future; the man who included the automobile among the Pan-American stamps was something of a prophet.

Robert R. Livingston

(1746-1813)

323 · 1¢ green · 1904

THOMAS JEFFERSON prided himself on three achievements: his writing of the Declaration of Independence and of the Statute of Virginia for Religious Freedom, as well as his founding of the University of Virginia. He had many other accomplishments; he was a lawyer, statesman, gentleman farmer, architect, engineer, musician, inventor, philosopher, scientist—and also President of the United States.

Jefferson's two terms as President from 1801 to 1809 called for all his wisdom and tact and patience. Neither England nor France was disposed to deal fairly with the infant Republic. At home the pressures of party politics intensified his problems.

In those days the United States sprawled like an awkward giant from the Atlantic coast to the Mississippi River. Railroads were still unknown, canals were scarce, and even ordinary roads were few in number and wretched in quality. The Appalachian Mountain chain split off the frontier communities from the seaboard states.

To dispose of their produce, the frontiersmen had to rely on water-borne traffic. The tough, roistering rivermen, "half horse and half alligator," brought the products of the frontier down the Ohio and Mississippi rivers on flatboats and barges to New Orleans. There they sold or bartered their cargoes.

Thomas Jefferson
(1743-1826)

324 · 2¢ red · 1904

New Orleans, at the mouth of the Mississippi on the Gulf of Mexico, was the frontiersmen's door to the great world. But unfortunately New Orleans was also the capital of the vast Spanish-held Louisiana Territory west of the Mississippi. The hinterlands of the Territory were a mystery even to the Spaniards; they knew only that it was a wilderness of forests, grasslands, Indians, and wild beasts.

Jefferson was well aware of the dangers arising from American dependence on New Orleans. For every foreign ship there were five American vessels in the port, "through which," as he pointed out, "the produce of three-eighths of our territory must pass to market." And to Robert Livingston, the American Minister to France, Jefferson wrote, "There is on this globe one single spot the possessor of which is our natural and habitual enemy. It is New Orleans."

The situation was even more alarming for the United States than was generally realized, for in 1800 Napoleon Bonaparte, the virtual dictator of France, had secretly obtained the Louisiana Territory from Spain. When Jefferson heard of this arrangement, he authorized Livingston to buy New Orleans and some land east of the city.

It was fortunate for the United States that the prolonged

James Monroe
(1758-1831)

325 • 3¢ purple • 1904

and tiresome negotiations had been entrusted to Livingston. As a member of one of the most prominent and influential colonial families, Livingston had been one of the outstanding members of the Continental Congress.

Under the Articles of Confederation, Livingston became Secretary of Foreign Affairs. He played an important part in preparing the Treaty of Paris which ended the Revolutionary War in 1783. It was chiefly due to Livingston's efforts that New York ratified the Constitution in 1788.

Though Livingston was an experienced negotiator, the ensuing months of sparring and haggling with Talleyrand, Napoleon's bland, hypocritical minister, seemed to lead nowhere. During the negotiations Spain—still nominally in control of the Territory—issued an order barring the port of New Orleans to Americans.

The enraged frontiersmen threatened to secede from the Union or march on New Orleans if the objectionable order were not rescinded. To quiet their clamor and give Livingston some moral support, Jefferson sent his good friend James Monroe to France as Minister Extraordinary. About the time of Monroe's arrival the French executed an amazing about-face and agreed to sell not only New Orleans but the whole Louisiana Territory

William B. McKinley
(1843-1901)

326 · 5¢ blue · 1904

to the United States. Why the French changed their minds is explained on page 316.

Modern historians describe the Louisiana Purchase as the most important event in American history during the first half of the nineteenth century. Yet in 1803 no one realized that the Americans were buying the most valuable undeveloped resources in the whole world. Not only were they doubling their national area at one stroke—and a peaceful one at that—but they were setting the stage for the future expansion of the United States to the Pacific coast.

By purchasing roughly nine hundred thousand square miles or six hundred million acres for fifteen million dollars, the United States acquired all the land of the future states of Missouri (1821), Arkansas (1836), Iowa (1846), Nebraska (1867), North and South Dakota (1889), and part of the land of Louisiana (1812), Minnesota (1858), Kansas (1861), Colorado (1876), Montana (1889), Wyoming (1890), and Oklahoma (1907). The dates in parentheses give the year of statehood.

As we have seen, Americans had only the vaguest ideas about the extent of the Louisiana Territory. To dispel some of the mystery, Jefferson sent out an expedition under Captain Meriwether Lewis and Lieutenant William Clark. During the years

Map Showing
Louisiana Purchase

327 · 10¢ brown · 1904

1804-1806 these explorers covered eight thousand miles, getting as far as the headwaters of the Columbia River and returning with much valuable information.

After journeying up the Missouri in 1804, Lewis and Clark and their men spent the winter at Indian villages in North Dakota. They then came to the most difficult phase of the expedition, approaching and crossing the Rockies. Sacajawea, their able Indian woman guide, had a remarkable knowledge of this terrain.

The nature of the country they found is dramatically presented in the side panels that flank Livingston's portrait on the 1¢ commemorative stamp. On the left we see the land that Livingston was sent to buy: a Florida swamp with palm trees and Spanish moss. On the right is a scene alluding to the land he actually bought: a covered wagon approaches a wooded and snow-capped mountain.

Livingston, Jefferson, and Monroe, the architects of the Louisiana Purchase, all appear in the set of commemorative stamps. So does President William B. McKinley, who shortly before his death signed the bills authorizing the Federal government's participation in the Louisiana Purchase Exposition of 1904, held to celebrate "the most stupendous bargain of all time."

Captain John Smith

(1580-1631)

328 · *1¢ green* · *1907*

AFTER EARLIER attempts to found an English colony in the New World had proved unsuccessful, the Virginia Company of London sent out a group of settlers who landed at Jamestown in May, 1607.

The 2¢ stamp shows the colonists landing to take possession of Virginia in the name of James I. The leader carries an English banner and in the background we see the tiny fleet anchored in the James River. At the left is a tobacco plant, the source of Virginia's later wealth; at the right is a stalk of Indian maize, the food that kept the settlers alive during Jamestown's darkest days.

It seemed doubtful that the new settlement would last very long. The site was a poor one, marshy, mosquito-infested, and lacking good drinking water. Disease took a heavy toll.

The colonists were "gentlemen" who had never done a day's work, or else city-bred people to whom farming was a mystery. For years the threat of famine hung over Jamestown. The men who came there expected to find gold and return home millionaires; they were not interested in planting crops and settling permanently in the New World.

Their "beastial slothfullnesse" was aggravated by factional disputes. Jealousy and the resultant bickering made progress

Founding of
Jamestown

329 · 2¢ red · 1907

almost impossible. Recurring conflicts with the Indians drained the colony's vitality and resources.

From time to time new colonists arrived, but supplies remained scanty for years. In fact, the dreadful winter of 1609-1610, when five out of every six settlers perished, has gone down in history as the Starving Time.

Somehow Jamestown managed to endure, despite all these misfortunes. Perhaps some of the credit belongs to that doughty fighting man Captain John Smith. After a lively career as a soldier of fortune in the Old World, Smith came to Virginia in search of adventure and fame. He was a brave and resourceful leader, but his explosive temper and boastful tendencies made him a hard man to get on with.

Interestingly enough, some scholars accept Smith's remarkable tale of how he killed three Turks in individual combat, in full sight of the Hungarian and Turkish armies!

Smith, who has been called our greatest colonial hero and the world's biggest liar, appears on the 1¢ stamp. In the upper corners are copies of medallions of Chief Powhatan and his favorite daughter Matoaka, better known as Pocahontas. She was about thirteen years old when, according to Smith's account, she saved his life by putting her arms around him as her father's braves advanced to beat their bound captive to death.

34

Pocahontas

(1595?-1617)

330 • 5¢ blue • 1907

Pocahontas was a saucy and fun-loving girl. When she grew up, she was converted to Christianity and baptized as Rebecca. She became the wife of John Rolfe, a Jamestown planter, who brought her to England, where she was much admired. The dignified and graceful bearing of this Indian princess made an especially favorable impression when she was presented at court.

Pocahontas died quite young, but a portrait painted in England has preserved her likeness for us. The portrait, which appears on the 5¢ stamp, shows her wearing a hat of the period, with a fashionable starched ruff and a dress of stiff brocade. Her husband, John Rolfe, is remembered for his romantic marriage, and for a more prosaic reason: he was the pioneer tobacco grower of Virginia.

In time tobacco became more valuable than gold, providing the Virginia planters with beautiful mansions and handsome furniture and table silver, as well as elegant clothes, art masterpieces, and exquisitely bound books. Tobacco became the source of Virginia's wealth and aristocracy. The distinguished society of Virginia gave America such men as George Washington, who led the Revolutionary Army to victory; Thomas Jefferson, who wrote the Declaration of Independence; and James Madison, who was known as the Father of the Constitution.

Centennial of Lincoln's Birth

367 · 2¢ red · 1909

No OTHER President had a childhood as poverty-stricken as Abe Lincoln's. When he was seven he started doing the work of a full-grown man, chopping down trees to make a clearing for a farm and prepare logs for a cabin.

The Lincoln family moved from Kentucky to Indiana and later to Illinois. The hard conditions of frontier life left little room for education, and Abe enjoyed only about a year of systematic schooling. He had few books, but his genuine love for them was carefully fostered by his affectionate stepmother. The boy spent many an evening sprawled on the cabin floor, reading by the light of the fireplace.

In his youth Lincoln tried his hand at many kinds of work: he was a field hand, ran a ferry, kept a store, chopped wood, worked in a tannery, became a surveyor and later a postmaster. He took a long time to get his career under way.

At last, in his middle twenties, Lincoln started studying law. He became a lawyer when he was twenty-eight. Unexcelled as a storyteller, he won many a case on the strength of his gift for making an important legal point through some whimsical story or tall tale of the kind that the pioneers greatly relished. How he achieved his position of national prominence is told on page 197.

William H. Seward

(1801-1872)

370 · 2¢ red · 1909

IN 1741 Peter the Great commissioned Vitus Bering, a Danish sea captain in Russian service, to explore the north Pacific region. This was the beginning of Russian expansion in Alaska, although the first formal Russian claim to it did not come until 1799.

Because the Russians were mainly interested in huge profits from the fur trade, they colonized Alaska very thinly. By 1850 their profits were declining and they were quite ready to part with Alaska.

William H. Seward, Secretary of State from 1861 to 1869 under Abraham Lincoln and Andrew Johnson, negotiated the purchase of Alaska for $7,200,000. The treaty was signed on March 20, 1867, which is celebrated in Alaska as Seward Day.

At the time of the purchase, very little was known about Alaska, and many Americans scoffingly referred to it as "Seward's folly" or "Seward's icebox." Yet from 1867 to 1937 the exploitation of Alaska's resources yielded about two billion dollars.

The commemorative stamp appeared in connection with the Alaska-Yukon-Pacific Exposition held at Seattle in 1909 to celebrate the purchase of Alaska, the development of the Yukon region, and the beginning of scheduled steamship travel to Alaska.

The *Clermont*
and the *Half Moon*

372 · *2¢ red* · *1909*

By BUILDING the first commercially successful steamboat, the *Clermont,* Robert Fulton (1765-1815) freed navigation from its thousands of years of dependence on the whims of the weather. The *Clermont* was completed in August, 1807, and moored to a dock in the Hudson River. As a large crowd looked on, the boat set off on its maiden voyage.

But soon the *Clermont* slowed to a halt. Had Fulton failed? No, for after a minor repair the steamboat continued up the Hudson, past the Palisades, Yonkers, Tarrytown, West Point, and all the way to Albany. People came from miles away to see and hear this "monster moving on the water, defying the winds and tide, and breathing flames and smoke—the horrible creature which was marching on the tides and lighting its path by the fires which it vomited."

The hundred-and-fifty-mile trip took thirty-two hours and was a complete success; the age of steam navigation had at last arrived.

The Hudson-Fulton stamp celebrates the centennial of the *Clermont's* voyage, as well as the three-hundredth anniversary of Hudson's discovery of the river named after him. On this stamp we see the *Clermont,* Hudson's ship the *Half Moon,* and the Indian canoes that preceded them.

Vasco Núñez de Balboa
(1475-1517)

397 · 1¢ green · 1913

NOWHERE WAS the completion of the Panama Canal awaited more eagerly than in California. For many years Californians had been looking forward to the days when voyages from coast to coast would be shortened considerably.

To celebrate the opening of the canal, the city of San Francisco planned the Panama-Pacific Exposition scheduled to begin in 1915. Two years before the opening, there appeared a series of commemorative stamps that called attention to the exposition.

On the 1¢ stamp we see a portrait of Vasco Núñez de Balboa, wearing the armor of a Spanish nobleman of the sixteenth century. Palm trees appear on each side of the stamp, with a branch of wheat on the left, a branch of rye on the right.

Balboa was a Spanish stowaway who became the leading conquistador in the first Spanish mainland settlement in the New World—the Isthmus of Panama. He had the leadership qualities for forging ahead in a world of shipwreck, massacre, starvation, disease, greed, and treachery; a world where cruelty and courage were equally commonplace.

When an Indian guide saw how the Spaniards became excited over a gold ornament, he said contemptuously, "Why quarrel over such trifles?" He promised to lead them to the vast ocean

Panama Canal

398 · 2¢ carmine · 1913

that would serve as the highway to the undreamt-of riches of the Incas.

Accordingly, in 1513 Balboa headed a small force across the jungles and mountains of the isthmus. They were the first Europeans to behold the shores of the Pacific from the New World. Because they were looking southward, they called it the South Sea.

Four centuries later, almost to the very day, the first vessel entered the Panama Canal on September 26, 1913. The first complete trip through the canal took place on January 7, 1914, and on August 15, 1914, the "Big Ditch" was officially open for traffic.

The building of the Panama Canal was one of the most remarkable engineering projects of all time. Construction lasted from 1904 to 1914, employing about thirty-five thousand men and costing three hundred and sixty million dollars. The chief credit belongs to Colonel George Goethals (see stamp 856) and to William C. Gorgas, Surgeon-General of the United States Army, who supervised the heroic work of draining the swamps and safeguarding the canal workers against malaria and yellow fever.

The operation of the canal, which is forty miles long from shore to shore, is a miracle of mechanical skill. The water level

Golden Gate

399 · 5¢ blue · 1913

at the Atlantic end is lower than the Pacific level. Ships entering the canal from the Atlantic are raised; those entering from
the other side are lowered.

The canal is divided into six locks—large concrete basins.
(The Pedro Miguel locks appear on the 2¢ stamp.) When a ship
enters from the Atlantic side, the gates of the first lock are
closed and water is forced into the lock. This causes the vessel
to rise.

Then the ship passes through other locks, where the process
is repeated. Vessels entering from the Pacific side are gradually
lowered as they progress through the canal. Actually, ships do
not pass through the "Big Ditch" on their own power; they are
drawn by electric "mules" attached to each vessel by four steel
cables, two on each side of the ship.

The two remaining stamps have Californian subjects. The
Golden Gate, which appears on the 5¢ stamp, is a narrow chan-
nel about four miles long and deep enough to accommodate
ocean-going vessels. This strait, which connects the Pacific
Ocean with San Francisco Bay, gets its name from the indescrib-
ably beautiful sunset glow of its waters. General John Charles
Frémont (see stamp 288) is credited with naming the Golden
Gate in 1846, but the name may be much older.

Strangely enough, explorers sailed along the California coast

Discovery of
San Francisco Bay

400 · 10¢ orange · 1913

for two centuries without daring to enter the Golden Gate. Not realizing that the channel was deep enough for their ships, the navigators feared that shoals would ground them. The ironic result was that San Francisco Bay, generally considered the finest harbor in the world, was eventually discovered from the landward side.

The 10¢ stamp depicts the discovery of San Francisco Bay on November 2, 1769, by a Spanish expedition under José Ortega. The bay, which has an area of four hundred and fifty square miles, is almost completely landlocked. To the west it is shielded from coastal storms by the twin peninsulas which are separated by the Golden Gate.

In 1775 the Spanish ship *San Carlos* sailed through the Golden Gate into the bay—the first vessel to make the trip. A year later the Spaniards built a fort on the southern peninsula. This structure, the *Presidio,* became the nucleus of the later city of San Francisco.

As late as 1847 the city was a sleepy little settlement of less than a thousand inhabitants. The great days of the port of San Francisco began with the Gold Rush two years later. It is tantalizing to think of the proportions the gold stampede would have taken on if the Panama Canal had been in existence in those days.

Liberty Victorious

537 · 3¢ purple · 1919

WHEN WAR broke out in Europe in 1914, most Americans hoped that their country would be spared the horrors of fighting. But this was the first war on a world-wide scale, and even neutrality could not save America from the ravages of unrestricted German submarine warfare. Our relations with Germany became more and more unfriendly until finally the United States declared war on April 6, 1917.

At once President Wilson set up a Council of National Defense to gear industrial production to the war effort and operate the railroads and steamship lines. To finance the war, the government increased taxes and sold Liberty Bonds.

Although half a million men volunteered within two months after the declaration of war, many more were needed. The United States had to adopt conscription—the draft. In June, 1917, over nine million men in the age group from twenty-one to thirty registered for military service. The Army established thirty-two military camps to train soldiers, and by the war's end had landed two million fighting men in France.

The commemorative stamp pictures Liberty Victorious holding a sword in her right hand and scales of justice in her left. The United States flag, directly in back of the goddess, is flanked by those of her allies: the British and Belgian flags at the left of the stamp, and the French and Italian flags at the right.

The *Mayflower*

548 · 1¢ green · 1920

FROM THE time of the founding of the Church of England by Henry VIII during the sixteenth century, the royal ministers and the bishops of the Established Church were in open conflict with several religious groups that wanted to worship God in their own way and objected to elaborate ceremonial.

The disobedient sects included the Puritans, who continued to be members of the Church but sought to "purify" it; and the Separatists, who refused to have anything to do with the Established Church. Harried by brutal persecution, some Separatists escaped to Holland, where they met with a friendly reception.

After a few years these exiles began to fear that their children would grow up as Hollanders, forgetting their English speech, their English ways, and their religion. In 1617 the group decided to seek a haven in the New World where it could keep its traditions alive. It was this group that became known—but not until almost two centuries later—as the Pilgrims.

They were not wealthy people, and to finance their voyage they needed the help of the Second Virginia Company of Merchant Adventurers, who supplied the necessary funds, provided a charter for a colony in the New World, and obtained the King's permission to found a settlement. The Pilgrims under-

Landing of the Pilgrims

549 · 2¢ red · 1920

took to repay the loan with furs and other products of the New World.

After returning to England, the Pilgrims sailed from Plymouth on September 6, 1620, on the *Mayflower,* a stout, broad-beamed vessel of a hundred and eighty tons, almost a hundred feet long, with three masts and square-rigged sails.

Only about a third of the one hundred and two passengers were Pilgrims. The rest were indentured servants, hired hands, and "Strangers"—people who did not share the Pilgrims' religious beliefs, but who hoped to make a better living in the New World than they had in England. The redoubtable Captain Myles Standish was a "Stranger" and not a Pilgrim. However, William Bradford and William Brewster, the two outstanding members of the group, were Pilgrims.

At first the weather was pleasant, but soon furious north Atlantic gales lashed the *Mayflower* so that it tossed on the mountainous billows like a toy. After a while the buffeting seas forced water through the seams, but these were satisfactorily calked. The seasick, cooped-up passengers were terrified, but at last the roaring winds died down, and on November 11 they sighted land.

The Pilgrims first went ashore not at Plymouth, as tradition

45

Signing of the
Mayflower Compact

550 · 5¢ blue · 1920

has it, but at Provincetown. Before leaving the ship, they drew up the *Mayflower* Compact, which reads in part:

"In the name of God, Amen . . . We whose names are under-written . . . doe by these presents solemnly & mutualy in ye presence of God, and one of another, covenant & combine our-selves togeather into a civill body politick . . . and by vertue hearof, to enacte, constitute and frame just and equall laws . . . as shall be thought most meete and convenient for ye generall good of ye Colonie, unto which we promise all due submission and obedience."

The signers of the document then proceeded to elect John Carver governor of the new colony—the first instance of self-government and free election of a governor in American history. Aside from these democratic features, the compact had the additional purpose of quelling any dissension in the group. On December 21 (later celebrated as Forefathers' Day) the pas-sengers landed at Plymouth Rock to found their settlement.

On all three stamps of this issue there is a border of haw-thorn blossoms (the English mayflower) on the left, and a border of trailing arbutus (the American mayflower) on the right. A curious feature of these stamps is that they are in no way identi-fied as American postage.

Warren Gamaliel Harding
(1865-1923)

610 · 2¢ black · 1923

As THE publisher of the Marion *Star,* one of the most influential newspapers in Ohio, Warren Gamaliel Harding became a leading political figure in that state.

After serving as a member of the state legislature and as lieutenant-governor, he was elected to the United States Senate in 1914. Though his record in the Senate was not out of the ordinary, he was nominated for President on the Republican ticket in 1920 and won the election in a landslide victory.

A genial, strikingly handsome man of distinguished appearance, Harding lacked the background and forceful leadership that are the hallmarks of an exceptional President. Nevertheless, his administration had some constructive features.

President Harding made an important contribution to efficiency in government by founding the Bureau of the Budget. He also called a Naval Conference which was held at Washington in 1922-1923. His Secretary of State, Charles Evans Hughes, was able to secure reductions in the navies of the great powers.

Unfortunately, President Harding's administration was discredited by the Teapot Dome scandals. The strain proved too much for him, and after being stricken with pneumonia during an exhausting speaking tour, he died at San Francisco on August 2, 1923.

47

The New Netherland

614 · 1¢ green · 1924

DURING THE sixteenth century, fierce civil wars raged in France between the Catholics and the Huguenots (French Protestants). In 1562 Admiral Gaspard de Coligny, leader of the Huguenots, sent an expedition to the New World to establish a haven for people of his faith. The fleet reached Florida and sailed up the St. Johns River. Here the French built Fort Caroline, one of the earliest European settlements within the present area of the United States.

However, the colony did not prosper. As often happened during the early colonization efforts, the settlers refused to work. They bickered constantly; they antagonized the Indians; they were attacked by disease, and soon found themselves on the edge of starvation.

One particularly discontented group went off to found a colony at Port Royal (South Carolina), but this infant settlement did not last very long. In 1565 reinforcements reached the Florida colony from France, but it was already too late. For the Spaniards, who considered Florida their special preserve, had learned of the presence of the French—their religious as well as commercial enemies.

Determined to crush their rivals, the Spaniards sent out a force under Pedro Menéndez de Avilés, their most capable mili-

Landing at Fort Orange

615 • 2¢ red • 1924

tary leader. On his arrival in Florida Menéndez founded St. Augustine, the oldest existing European settlement within the present area of the United States. A short time later he attacked the Huguenots, defeated them, and put the survivors to the sword.

Thus ended this pioneering colonizing attempt, which is commemorated by a monument erected on the site at Mayport, Florida, by the Daughters of the American Revolution on May 1, 1924.

The Walloons had better luck with their colonizing efforts. They were French-speaking Protestants who lived in northeastern France and southwestern Belgium. Persecution drove them to Holland, where they were on good terms with the Pilgrims. After the Pilgrims settled in the New World in 1620, the Walloons were eager to follow their example.

And so, in 1623 a group of thirty families, most of them Walloons, sailed on the two-hundred-and-sixty-ton Dutch ship *New Netherland* to the Dutch trading posts in the New World. Eight artisans and farmers were left on Manhattan Island; two families settled in Connecticut and four in Delaware; the rest sailed up the Hudson to Fort Orange (later Albany). Around the fort they founded the settlement of Beverwijk (Home of the

49

Monument at Mayport, Florida

616 · 5¢ blue · 1924

Beaver) and in time this location became the most important fur-trading center in the Thirteen Colonies.

One of these settlers wrote home: "We were much gratified on arriving in this country. Here we found beautiful rivers, bubbling fountains flowing down into the valley; agreeable fruits in the woods, such as strawberries, walnuts, and wild grapes. The woods abound with venison. There is considerable fish in the rivers; good tillage land. Here there is, especially, free coming and going, without fear of the natives of the country."

The first white child born in the Dutch settlements was of Walloon ancestry. The minister of the Dutch Reformed Church on Manhattan Island preached some of his sermons in French for the benefit of the Walloons; even as late as 1661 half the colony was of Walloon extraction.

Peter Minuit, the first governor of New Netherland, was a Walloon. In 1626 he bought Manhattan from the Indians for sixty guilders' worth of hatchets, beads, and assorted gewgaws.

Thus the Huguenots were responsible for one of the earliest settlements within the present boundaries of the United States, while the Walloons played a major role in founding the leading fur-trading center as well as the colony that later became one of the great commercial and cultural capitals of the world.

Washington at Cambridge

617 · 1¢ green · 1925

THE END of the French and Indian War in 1763 sharpened the struggle between England and the American colonies over the issue of no taxation without representation.

Anticipating trouble, the British stationed large numbers of troops in Boston, the fountainhead of American resistance. The presence of the hated troops led to incidents, with provocation given by both sides.

From 1773 on, events moved rapidly. In December of that year Bostonians dumped three hundred and forty-two chests of tea from a British vessel anchored in the harbor—the famous Boston Tea Party. England hit back with the Boston Port Bill, closing the port to all shipping.

In September, 1774, the First Continental Congress met at Philadelphia to unite all the colonies in resisting the British.

About the same time, Massachusetts set up a Provincial Congress, an illegal organization as far as England was concerned. The Congress called for a militia of twelve thousand men, another illegal organization. These were the famous minutemen, pledged to gather for battle at a minute's notice. (Daniel Chester French's magnificent conception of the *Minuteman* appears on the 5¢ stamp and is described in detail on page 183.)

The British tried to cripple colonial resistance by outlawing

Birth of Liberty

618 · 2¢ red · 1925

John Hancock and Samuel Adams, the ringleaders. The two proscribed men went into hiding, continuing to organize the patriots and assemble military stores for the time when they would be needed.

On April 18, 1775, the minutemen learned that a British force was setting out that night to capture Hancock and Adams at Lexington and then go on to Concord to destroy the military supplies stored there.

The minutemen lost no time: they sent Paul Revere and other couriers to ride through the countryside and rouse the farmers to oppose the British expedition.

Hancock and Adams, warned just in time, had a narrow escape to safety. When the British arrived at Lexington at dawn, they found a small force of minutemen lined up by the road. The regulars fired directly into this group, killing and wounding several.

At Concord it was a different story. Minutemen streamed from the fields and villages to drive back the British with heavy losses. In the words of Ralph Waldo Emerson's stirring *Concord Hymn:*

> By the rude bridge that arched the flood,
> Their flag to April's breeze unfurled,

The *Minuteman*

619 · 5¢ blue · 1925

> Here once the embattled farmers stood,
> And fired the shot heard round the world.

It was war at last. One could no longer speak of "disaffection" or "disobedience" or "the King's unruly subjects." News of what had happened at Lexington and Concord spread swiftly through Massachusetts and the other colonies. In groups of ten or half a dozen, patriots streamed into Cambridge, an army without a commander. These groups became the nucleus of the Continental Army.

Two months later the Continental Congress named George Washington Commander in Chief of the American army. On July 3 he reviewed his troops, according to the traditional accounts, under a majestic elm near Boston Common. (The tree, which lived on until 1923, is shown on the 1¢ stamp.)

Washington was soon disillusioned about his army. There were no uniforms, no cannon. Discipline was unheard of. Troops showed up drunk at morning inspection, officers shaved their men, "resigning" or deserting was all too frequent. Washington introduced order and discipline, won the confidence of his troops, and obtained supplies. It was these men, and others like them, who fought and died for Washington to achieve independence.

53

The *Restaurationen*

620 • 2¢ black and red • 1925

A NORWEGIAN named Kleug Peerson visited the United States in 1821. After returning to his native land, he sang the praises of the New World enthusiastically.

Peerson's countrymen were so impressed that in 1825 the first group of Norwegian emigrants set out for New York. Fifty-two strong, they sailed in the sloop *Restaurationen*. After landing at New York on October 10, 1825, they settled in Orleans County in New York State. Thus began a wave of immigration that was to bring two hundred thousand Norwegian men, women, and children to the United States in the next fifty years.

Most of the Norwegian pioneers settled in the Midwest; fertile farming land was their goal. Life was hard, especially at the beginning, but relatives and friends from "the old country" eased the newcomers' burden of finding a new home in a strange land.

A great help to the newcomers was Ole Rynnig's work entitled *A True Account of America For the Information and Help of Peasant and Commoner*. That cumbersome title soon went by the board; to the Norwegians who read it avidly it was simply "the American Book."

Rynnig had settled in Illinois in 1837. His guidebook was rich in valuable practical advice to the would-be pioneers. It told them the best time of the year for sailing; what food,

Viking Ship

621 · 5¢ black and blue · 1925

medicines, and other supplies they would need for the voyage; what tools to take along; and what articles would bring a good price in America.

For many a Norwegian emigrant Ole Rynnig's advice softened the sorrow of departure and overcame the bewilderment that often makes new surroundings uncomfortable.

It is one of history's ironies that these peaceful, hard-working farmers were descendants of the ruthless vikings, or Norsemen, who terrorized the coasts of Europe with their audacious raids during the Middle Ages.

About 875 the vikings reached out across the uncharted seas to settle in Iceland; a century later they reached Greenland. The Norse epics tell us how Leif Ericson sailed from Norway for Greenland in the year 999 and arrived instead in a region the vikings called Vinland.

It is generally believed that Vinland was on the mainland of North America—perhaps Nova Scotia or Labrador, even Massachusetts or Rhode Island. Several years later Leif Ericson led another expedition to Vinland and spent some time there before returning to Greenland.

The 5¢ commemorative stamp carries a picture of one of the beautiful viking ships, flanked by a Norwegian shield on the left and an American shield on the right.

Sharon Vaught

Liberty Bell

627 · 2¢ red · 1926

THE MEETINGS of the Continental Congress took place in the State House in Philadelphia, which had been constructed in 1735 as the home of the colonial government of Pennsylvania and did not become known as Independence Hall until many years after the Revolution.

In 1745 a tower was added to the State House to contain a bell for announcing important events and calling Assembly members to meetings. Cast in London, the bell weighed a ton. It was five feet high and had a diameter of five feet at the bottom. On it was inscribed a stirring Biblical phrase: "Proclaim Liberty throughout all the land unto all the inhabitants thereof."

The bell was hung in the State House in August, 1752. A few days later it cracked and the following June it was reinforced with copper.

Years later, on July 8, 1776, the State House bell tolled to assemble the people of Philadelphia for the first public reading of the Declaration of Independence.

Since that day of joyous celebration the bell has been known to all Americans as the Liberty Bell. After cracking again in 1835—you can see the crack on the commemorative stamp!— it was never repaired. To this day it remains one of the most precious relics of American freedom.

John Ericsson

(1803-1889)

628 · 5¢ blue · 1926

THE SWEDISH-BORN inventor John Erics-son displayed his mechanical aptitude at an amazingly early age. The most valu-able of his early inventions was the screw propeller (1835) which enabled steam to take the place of sail.

In order to exploit this invention more profitably, Ericsson came to the United States, where he was naturalized in 1848. Shortly after the outbreak of the Civil War, when all Northern warships were at the mercy of the Confederate ironclad *Merri-mac*, Ericsson came to the rescue of the Union by presenting the plans of his *Monitor* to the Navy Department.

Ericsson's "cheesebox on a raft" was a nine-hundred-ton ironclad, one hundred and seventy-two feet long, with side armor five inches thick and two formidable guns in a revolving turret. The *Monitor* was launched early in 1862, just in time to fight its famous duel with the *Merrimac* and prevent the South from smashing the Federal blockade.

In refusing payment for saving the Union from disaster, Ericsson proudly declared: "Nothing could induce me to accept remuneration from the United States for the Monitor invention, once presented by me as my contribution to the glorious Union cause, the triumph of which freed four million bondmen."

Hamilton's
Gun Crew

629 · 2¢ red · 1926

THE RESOURCEFUL retreat of the American army from Long Island to Manhattan on August 29, 1776 (see stamp 1003), soon led to another American rout. It was one of the few occasions when Washington lost his temper in public. One of his aides reports him as throwing his hat on the ground in a fury and yelling, "Are these the men with whom I am to defend America?"

Order was gradually restored to the American ranks, and Washington luckily had time to establish his army behind strong fortifications in the hills and forests of White Plains. He disposed his men effectively, giving them ample mobility on interior lines so they could shift quickly to threatened points.

On October 26 the British broke through with greatly superior numbers. This time the Americans fell back in good order. An important role in the rear-guard action was played by a battery commanded by nineteen-year-old Captain Alexander Hamilton. Later he was to become one of the most brilliant statesmen of the young republic.

Hamilton and his gun crew appear on the White Plains commemorative stamp. Their banner is not the flag traditionally credited to Betsy Ross (see stamp 1004); the official American flag was not in use until 1777. Hamilton's battery had a regimental flag with a crossed sword and staff as well as a liberty cap and Patrick Henry's ringing words—"Liberty or death."

The Spirit of St. Louis

C 10 · 1927

10¢ blue

AFTER WORLD WAR I, there was a great upsurge of interest in the peacetime development of aviation. One of the signs of the times was Raymond Orteig's offer of twenty-five thousand dollars, made in 1919, for the first nonstop flight from New York to Paris.

By 1926 the prize was still unclaimed. Three unsuccessful flights had cost the lives of six brave men. Charles A. Lindbergh, a young army airmail pilot, decided to attempt the trip. Despite the extreme risk involved, he was determined to use only one motor and to fly solo. In that way he would lighten the plane's burden and thus assure himself enough fuel to complete the journey.

On the morning of May 20, 1927, Lindbergh took off at Roosevelt Field in Long Island. For a good part of the trip he had to contend with poor visibility because of fog and clouds. Nevertheless, he arrived at Le Bourget Field in Paris after flying thirty-six hundred miles in thirty-three and a half hours. This historic trip had the practical value of blazing the way for regularly scheduled trans-Atlantic travel.

Lindbergh's plane *The Spirit of St. Louis* appears on the commemorative stamp, together with a map showing the course of his historic flight. The plane is one of the most popular exhibits at the Smithsonian Institution.

Battle of
Bennington

643 · 2¢ red · 1927

THOUGH VERMONT was not one of the original thirteen colonies, its Green Mountain Boys struck two of the most powerful blows for freedom during the American Revolution.

When George Washington took over the command of the ill-equipped American army, it lacked even a single cannon. But after Vermont's Ethan Allen seized Fort Ticonderoga, he sent down the captured fieldpieces. It was enough for Washington to mount these weapons to force the British to withdraw from Boston.

In 1777 General Burgoyne marched his army southward from Canada as part of the British master plan to split the thirteen colonies. After recapturing Ticonderoga without any trouble, he assigned a force of Hessians, Tories, Indians, and Canadians to head towards Bennington, Vermont, for horses and supplies.

On August 16 this expedition was stopped in its tracks by the Green Mountain Boys. At their head was Colonel John Stark, a Bunker Hill veteran who had grimly told his men: "We beat them today, or Molly Stark's a widow."

Burgoyne's disaster at Bennington led to his greater disaster at Saratoga (see stamp 644). That is why the commemorative stamp pays tribute to a sturdy buckskin-dressed Green Mountain Boy.

60

Surrender
of Burgoyne

644 · 2¢ red · 1927

WHEN "GENTLEMAN JOHNNY" BURGOYNE set out from Quebec on June 17, 1777, with a force of ten thousand men, he intended to march south and split off New England from the other colonies.

But Burgoyne was no fighter. He was lazy, pleasure-loving, and unfamiliar with forest fighting; nor did he get the support he expected.

As Burgoyne's men plodded through the pathless wilderness, they frittered away precious time building roads and bridges on which to drag their heavy cannon. Soon food and supplies began to run short, and the uncanny woods bristled with unseen enemies.

Worried about the supply problem, Burgoyne committed the deadly blunder of sending off sizable detachments to round up provisions. At Oriskany, Fort Stanwix, and, above all, Bennington (see stamp 643), these forces were clawed so badly that thousands of his men deserted.

The Battle of Saratoga was the final blow. Burgoyne could no longer offer resistance to the American farmers and backwoodsmen he despised so heartily. On October 17, 1777, he surrendered. His defeat gave the Continental cause new vigor, and encouraged France to help the Americans win their freedom.

Washington
Kneeling in Prayer

645 · 2¢ red · 1928

DURING THE Revolutionary War, winter was always the most dreadful time of year for the Continental Army.

After losing the battles of the Brandywine and Germantown in the late fall of 1777, Washington had to look on helplessly as the British set up comfortable winter quarters in Philadelphia. For his own army he chose Valley Forge, about twenty-seven miles northwest of the city and situated on high ground with a commanding view of the countryside.

When Washington encamped there, he had about eleven thousand men. They sheltered themselves as best they could in wigwams of twisted boughs and in skimpy huts.

Soon the winter of despair began to take its toll of these barefoot, half-naked men. They starved, sickened, froze. Thousands died. Thousands deserted.

But even in that time of need the Americans had friends. Lafayette and Steuben came thousands of miles from Europe to share the hardships at Valley Forge. Slowly, the ordeal neared its end with the approach of spring. And in May, 1778, the Americans had word that patient, weary, old Ben Franklin had at last negotiated the French alliance. The hardships of the long winter were forgotten in the shouts of jubilation. Hope had replaced despair.

Overprint on
Regular Postal Issue

646 · 2¢ red · 1928

ON JUNE 18, 1778, the British army left Philadelphia and headed for New York. Washington's army set out in grim pursuit during an abnormally hot and humid spell. The chase went on for ten days.

The two armies finally clashed at Monmouth Court House in New Jersey on June 28—one of the hottest days of which we have record. It is said there were more casualties from the blazing sun than from the fighting. That is why many a soldier blessed the name of Molly Pitcher on Monmouth battlefield.

Molly's real name was Mary Ludwig Hays. To be with her soldier husband, Molly stayed with the army to tend the wounded.

While wounded men lay helpless and moaned through cracked lips for water, Molly went back and forth to a nearby spring to fetch water for them. The grateful cry, "Here's Molly with the pitcher!" gave her the nickname by which she is remembered.

Monmouth was a victory for the American troops, though the British were able to slip away after nightfall. But for most Americans what is memorable about Monmouth is the figure of a heroic woman repeatedly risking her life to relieve the sufferings of wounded men.

63

Overprint on
Regular Postal Issue

647 · 2¢ red · 1928

IN 1776 the British Admiralty sent Captain James Cook on the third and last of his remarkable voyages of exploration. Cook, the finest navigator in the British Navy, was to sail along the Pacific coast of North America in the hope of finding the Northwest Passage that was supposed to link the Atlantic with the Pacific.

Cook had many claims to fame. Though he had hardly any schooling, he taught himself mathematics and astronomy after joining the Royal Navy. His charts of the St. Lawrence River were so accurate that they enabled the British to bring their fleet up the river in 1759 to storm the heights of Quebec. In later years his explorations took him to Australia, New Zealand, Tasmania, Tahiti, and many other far-off lands.

But Cook was not only capable; he was kind. He avoided the extremes of discipline and treated his crews considerately. Cook was one of the first to realize the importance of fresh fruit and vegetables in avoiding the dread disease known as scurvy.

Though Americans and Englishmen were at war, Benjamin Franklin called on American vessels to refrain from attacking Cook's ship. Franklin was one of the leaders in the struggle for American independence, yet he admired Cook so deeply that he could not think of him as an enemy.

Overprint on
Regular Postal Issue

648 · 5¢ blue · 1928

While sailing across the Pacific, Cook's expedition reached the Hawaiian Islands in January, 1778; the arrival marks the official discovery of the archipelago. We do not know just when the islands were originally settled, but Hawaiian legends tell of a migration of Polynesian peoples in far-off times. In their long outrigger canoes they ventured thousands of miles across the uncharted vastness of the Pacific until they came to the Hawaiian Islands.

Cook was a naturally friendly man who got on famously with the natives of exotic regions by treating them without any feeling of condescension. The Hawaiians, he noted in his journal, "seemed to be mild and goodnatured; and were furnished with no arms of any kind except some small stones which they had manifestly brought for their own defense; and these they threw into the sea when they found there was no occasion for them."

Cook named the islands the Sandwich Islands in honor of the Earl of Sandwich, First Lord of the Admiralty. Through a tragic misunderstanding which infuriated the natives, Cook was killed by them in a violent outburst when he returned to the islands early in 1779.

In 1928 the issue of two overprinted stamps commemorated Cook's discovery of the Hawaiian Islands.

Wright Brothers'
Biplane

649 • 2¢ red • 1928

IN 1928 President Coolidge called an International Civil Aeronautics Conference at Washington in celebration of the twenty-fifth anniversary of the Wright brothers' flight at Kittyhawk, North Carolina on December 17, 1903 (see stamp C 45 and C 47). This was man's first flight in a heavier-than-air, power-driven machine.

In a relatively short time the Wrights had achieved the success that had eluded experimenters for four hundred years, beginning with the pioneering research of Leonardo da Vinci. Interestingly enough, the Wrights' successful flight took place only six days after the failure of Professor Samuel Langley's model. After slight modification, Langley's machine proved practicable in 1914.

During 1904 the Wright brothers made 105 flights, two of them covering three miles in five minutes, or at the rate of thirty-five miles an hour. However, the elation of the brothers quickly turned to disappointment when the Army unexpectedly turned down the airplane on the ground that it had not reached a "stage of practical operation."

In 1908, after the Wrights had built twenty-four additional experimental models, the Army finally signed a contract with them. For some time to come, however, the development of the

66

1928-Type Monoplane

650 · 5¢ blue · 1928

airplane was held back by patent suits which discouraged new firms from coming into the field.

In 1907 an Aeronautical Division came into existence as part of the United States Signal Corps. The division had one officer, two enlisted men—and no planes. In 1918 it became a separate organization within the army. Renamed the Air Service, it had a personnel of a hundred thousand men, thirty-five hundred American planes, and five thousand foreign planes in the closing months of the war.

Airmail service started in 1918, and airlines with regularly scheduled flights began operating the following year. By 1928 they were flying along 14,155 route-miles, and transoceanic and transcontinental nonstop flights had shown that long-distance service was feasible.

Delegates from forty countries attended the conference—a telling indication of the importance that aviation had achieved in a few years.

The 2¢ stamp of this issue features the first Wright biplane in flight as the pilot lies flat on the bottom wing. Note the propeller in the rear. On the 5¢ stamp we see a monoplane of 1928 vintage in flight. On both stamps the Washington Monument appears on the left, the Capitol on the right.

Surrender of Fort Sackville

651 · 1929
2¢ black and red

IN THESE days of wars fought by mass armies, it seems almost unbelievable that Colonel George Rogers Clark (1752-1818) conquered the Northwest Territory with a force that never numbered more than two hundred men. From this area of more than half the size of the original thirteen colonies, the states of Ohio, Indiana, Michigan, Illinois, Wisconsin, and part of Minnesota were eventually created.

Clark was only twenty-five when he conceived the audacious plan of seizing the vast Northwest from the British and their Indian allies. For this superb leader, men were willing to make forced marches in single file through forests, plod through miles of slimy swamps, row on flood-swollen rivers, wade in icy waters, and even go without food for several days before fighting against much larger and better-equipped enemy forces.

Despite these privations, Clark succeeded in capturing the British fort at Kaskaskia in the Illinois country and Fort Sackville near Vincennes on the banks of the Wabash. During the negotiations which led up to the Treaty of Paris in 1783, at the end of the Revolutionary War, possession of these key fortresses won the Northwest Territory for the United States.

Invention of the Electric Lamp

654 · 2¢ red · 1929

IN THE popular mind, the electric light will always be associated with the name of Thomas Edison—rightly so, because it cost him more ingenuity and patience than any of his other inventions. The idea of an incandescent electric lamp did not originate with Edison, but the credit for perfecting it is his.

The problem was to devise a lamp that would be bright, long-lasting, and cheap. To the earlier inventors, this combination seemed hopeless. In Edison's case, however, the difficulties only stiffened his determination.

Finally, on October 21, 1879, Edison developed a working model using carbonized cotton for the filament. After he had hooked up the lamp to an electric current, the filament worked perfectly for forty hours. Still unsatisfied, Edison experimented with over six thousand varieties of vegetable fiber for the ideal filament. The earliest manufactured electric lamps used bamboo, but later on cellulose proved more satisfactory.

Meanwhile, on New Year's Eve, 1879, Edison gave a public display of the operation of the incandescent electric lamp powered from a central station. The demonstration, a sensational success, is commemorated on this stamp.

Major-General John Sullivan

(1740-1795)

657 · 2¢ red · 1929

NOWADAYS THE tranquil Mohawk Valley in upstate New York is a region of fertile farms and busy factories. In earlier times, however, it was known as the Bloody Mohawk. For almost two centuries after the French explorers made deadly enemies of the Iroquois Indians in 1608, the valley was the scene of scalping raids, massacres, and fiendish tortures.

During the American Revolution, the Mohawk Valley was one of the chief sources of food for the American army. By inciting the Iroquois to raid American settlements in the valley, the British created a serious problem for the "rebels."

In 1778 the bloodthirsty Indian raids provoked an outcry that could no longer be ignored. General Washington decided on a large-scale expedition that would safeguard the frontier permanently by crushing the Tories and Indians in the valley. Major-General John Sullivan, who is pictured on the commemorative stamp, headed the invading army.

On August 22, 1779, Sullivan's troops began their retaliatory burning of one Indian village after another, ruining cornfields and vegetable patches just before harvest time, axing fruit trees and butchering livestock. It was a cruel tactic in a time of crisis. With the end of the war the Indians lost their lands and tranquillity settled down at last in the Bloody Mohawk.

135th Anniversary

680 · 2¢ red · 1929

IN 1791 President Washington ordered "Mad" Anthony Wayne (1745-1796) to Ohio to curb the Indian menace. Though General Wayne had a reputation for rashness and bluster, few could equal him when it came to methodical planning. He took almost three years to raise troops and drill them to perfection as he advanced warily into Indian country, building a string of forts along his route.

On the scene of an earlier defeat, Wayne built Fort Recovery, and here, on June 30, 1794, his army was attacked by a large and well-armed Indian force. Wayne drove off the Indians, and almost two months later, on August 20, the two armies came to grips at Fallen Timbers, a tangled forest area full of trees felled by a tornado.

Wayne defeated the Indians so badly that their fighting spirit was at last broken. A year later the Treaty of Greenville made large-scale settlement reasonably safe. Ohio's population grew rapidly from then on, and in less than ten years the Territory was admitted into the Union (page 314).

On the commemorative stamp we see a memorial statue of General Wayne, with an Indian on the left and a frontiersman on the right. The statue was set up on the battlefield one hundred and thirty-five years after Wayne's memorable victory.

Ohio River Lock

681 · 2¢ red · 1929

FEW AMERICAN rivers have grander historical associations than the Ohio, the waterway on which the pioneers streamed into the West by canoe, flatboat, and later by steamboat.

However, the Ohio had many navigational hazards as it wound nearly a thousand miles from Pittsburgh to Cairo, Illinois, where it empties into the Mississippi. In 1875 the Federal government decided to "canalize" the Ohio all the way, to give it a uniform depth. After a promising start, the work was dropped because the river had lost almost all its freight traffic to the railroads.

World War I revived river traffic because of the wartime strain on the railroads. As a result, Congress authorized enough funds in 1922 to complete the canalization of the Ohio. Army engineers finished the project in 1929 after constructing forty-two movable dams and four fixed dams with locks. The commemorative stamp shows a ship entering an Ohio River lock.

Canalization of the Ohio proved vital to victory in World War II. Over a thousand vessels—harbor tugs, mine layers, mine sweepers, LST's, and even naval drydocks—went down to New Orleans. Thus, the Ohio, once the favored waterway of Indians, fur traders, and pioneers, has continued to be immensely useful in the age of world wars.

72

Colonial Seal

682 · 2¢ red · 1930

IN THE 1620's, as the struggle between the Stuart monarchy and the Puritan group in Parliament became ever more intense, many Puritans began to look to the New World for the site of a "Godly commonwealth." Massachusetts seemed a logical place for a colony, as the Pilgrim settlement at Plymouth was prospering despite difficulties and hardships.

Headed by John Endicott and John Winthrop, the first great wave of Puritan migration arrived in the Massachusetts Bay Colony in 1630. Eleven ships brought a thousand colonists, three times as many as Plymouth had had in ten years. In that first year the Puritans founded Boston, and by 1643 the Massachusetts Bay Colony had sixteen thousand settlers.

The Puritan communities elected their officers in democratic town meetings. They were equally progressive in educational affairs, founding Boston Public Latin School in 1635 and Harvard College in 1636. In religious matters, however, the Puritans were too severe for freedom-loving people whom they drove away from their settlements (see stamps 772 and 777).

The commemorative stamp shows a colonial seal with the figure of an Indian. In one hand he holds a bow, in the other an arrow. On either side is a small pine tree, favorite symbol of Massachusetts.

Founding of Charleston and Carolina

683 · 2¢ red · 1930

IN 1663 Charles II of England granted the region lying between Virginia and Florida to eight courtiers. They called the grant Carolina, after Charles I.

The Lords Proprietors began colonizing Carolina in 1670, and ten years later they founded Charles Town. Though menaced by Indians, Spaniards, and pirates, the colony flourished. Its fertile soil was rich in rice and indigo, it had an abundance of game and fish, and the British Navy prized its naval stores—timber, hemp, turpentine, tar, pitch, and resin.

The colony had other attractions: religious tolerance, a representative assembly, sizable grants to indentured servants who had gained their freedom. Quakers, Huguenots, Swiss, Germans, and discontented Dutch settlers from New York flocked to Carolina.

In time, Charles Town became the leading seaport and most populous city in the South. Its brilliant sunshine and charming architecture gave it an elegant character all its own.

Carolina split up into South and North Carolina in 1729, and about sixty years later Charles Town became Charleston. The commemorative stamp shows a colonial governor and an Indian on a beach, with two vessels in the background. Sprays of rice and indigo decorate the borders.

74

175th Anniversary

688 · 2¢ red · 1930

AT THE outbreak of the French and Indian War in 1754, General Edward Braddock was assigned command of the British forces in North America. He had an army of about fourteen hundred British regulars and half as many colonial troops with which to capture the French Fort Duquesne at the forks of the Ohio—the present site of Pittsburgh.

After starting from Virginia, Braddock's army had to advance through miles of wilderness. Braddock, who was accustomed to European fighting on flat terrain, scoffed at warnings about Indian methods of fighting from cover. Thus his men in their bright scarlet uniforms presented perfect targets to sharpshooters well screened against reprisals.

As Braddock's force was crossing the Monongahela River, an enemy force of less than a thousand men, mostly Indians, opened a withering fire on the redcoats. Hidden in ravines and behind trees, the ambush attackers killed or wounded two-thirds of the invaders. The rest broke and ran for their lives.

Despite serious illness, Colonel George Washington was in the thick of the fighting. Four bullets passed through his clothes without harm, and two horses were shot from under him. The commemorative stamp features a statue of young Washington to honor his heroic conduct during the battle.

Baron Friedrich
von Steuben
(1730-1794)

689 · 2¢ red · 1930

It is one of history's pleasantest oddities that a man with the high-sounding name of Baron Friedrich Wilhelm August Heinrich Ferdinand von Steuben was willing to join George Washington's revolutionary "rabble."

Steuben had distinguished himself in the Prussian army of Frederick the Great during the Seven Years' War (1756-1763). Unemployed in peacetime, the Baron tried in vain to secure a commission elsewhere. Years went by, until at last there was a war that offered Steuben a useful role in the struggle for American independence.

The Baron had a Prussian love of system. Drilling his men constantly, he instilled discipline and hammered away at the essentials of strategy. At the same time he introduced the American soldiers to the most effective methods that had been developed in centuries of European warfare.

Impressed by Steuben's love of order and efficiency, Washington appointed him Inspector-General of the American army. Eventually Steuben became an American citizen and spent the rest of his life in the United States. After the Revolution, Congress voted him a fair-sized pension, a well-earned reward for "the drillmaster of the Continental Army" who enlisted in the cause in its darkest hour.

Count Casimir Pulaski

(1748-1799)

690 • *2¢ red* • *1931*

AT THE age of twenty-one, Count Casimir Pulaski led the Polish partisans in an insurrection to free Poland from Russian domination. The rising was crushed mercilessly and Pulaski fled to Turkey.

In 1776 he made his way to Paris, where Benjamin Franklin welcomed the ardent young patriot and sent him on to America. Washington had Pulaski appointed a brigadier-general to head the American cavalry. While in service, Pulaski prepared a book of regulations which was used by the American army until well into the twentieth century.

This brave and dashing soldier did not shrink from sharing the hardships of Valley Forge, and he distinguished himself in some of the most desperate battles of the war. Finally, he organized a cavalry legion and spent fifty thousand dollars of his own money to equip it. While heading an impetuous charge at the Battle of Savannah, Pulaski was fatally wounded in the stomach by a burst of shrapnel. He died two days later in agony.

Towns in Tennessee, Virginia, and Wisconsin have been named for Pulaski, as well as Fort Pulaski near the scene of his death. These are only a few of the ways in which Americans honor Pulaski as one of that band of devoted men who came to America to fight for freedom.

50th Anniversary

702 · 2¢ black and red · 1931

THOUGH THE Red Cross is a private organization, the President of the United States is its nominal head, and its accounts are audited by the War Department. Anyone living in the United States can be a member of the Red Cross. It is financed by voluntary contributions.

The Red Cross was originally founded for wartime service (page 312), and its work in the two World Wars was on a truly heroic scale. International treaties permit it to cooperate with army and navy doctors. It also assembles and distributes blood plasma and performs a variety of other invaluable tasks.

The peacetime work of the Red Cross is even more diversified. It has extended an efficient helping hand to sufferers in thousands of disasters—storms, famines, mine explosions, droughts, earthquakes, and hurricanes. The Johnstown flood of 1889, the San Francisco fire of 1906, the New England hurricane of 1938 are spectacular examples of disasters in which the Red Cross helped thousands of helpless and homeless victims. Its cooperation with the United States Health Service is perhaps the most important of its many other peacetime services.

The commemorative stamp shows a Red Cross nurse kneeling before the globe with outstretched hands.

Comte de Rochambeau
(1722-1807)

George Washington
(1732-1799)

Comte de Grasse
(1722-1788)

703 · 2¢ red and black · 1931

YORKTOWN IS a magic name to Americans. Here a combined American and French force trapped and captured a large British army under Lord Cornwallis in 1781.

Alarmed by his losses in men and supplies in the southern campaigns (see stamp 785), Cornwallis had entrenched his forces at Yorktown, where the York River empties into Chesapeake Bay. Here he awaited the arrival of a British fleet that would carry his men from the peninsula to safety.

But Admiral de Grasse soon stationed a powerful French fleet at the entrance to the bay and drove away a British rescue fleet. The trap at Yorktown had snapped tight; there was no escape for the invaders.

Meanwhile, Washington's army, stationed in New York, stole away and headed for Yorktown. French forces likewise marched southward.

On September 14 the reinforcements arrived at Yorktown. The ring around the British was complete. With only seventy-five hundred men against thirty-one thousand French soldiers and sailors and nine thousand Americans, they could not hope to hold out very long. On October 19, 1781, they surrendered. American independence was at last assured.

Painting by
Charles Willson Peale

704 • ½¢ brown • 1932

GEORGE WASHINGTON appears more often on our stamps than any other American. The expression we see on that pock-marked and deeply lined face is stern, lonely, aloof. This is the man Frederick the Great of Prussia called "the greatest military genius of his age." The British historian John Richard Green described Washington as "the noblest figure that ever stood in the forefront of a nation's life."

"Frozen dignity" and "marble statue" are some of the terms that biographers have used about Washington. His own dignity and the awe of his fellow men combined to turn him into a curiously remote figure. The legends of Parson Weems and other Washington-worshipers have intensified this unreal impression.

The fact is, though, that Washington had very human qualities. Far from being strait-laced, he was passionately fond of dancing and fox hunting. We think of him as a superb soldier and statesman, but what he really loved was farming. That famous self-possessed air is likewise deceptive. Washington had a blazing temper which he tried very hard—on the whole, successfully—to curb.

Washington's shyness was another handicap that he never

Profile Bust by
Jean Antoine Houdon

705 · 1¢ green · 1932

quite conquered. It is on record that on more than one occasion public praise made him so bashful that he was at a loss for words. This happened to him, for example, when the Virginia House of Burgesses gave him an ovation for his outstanding military services in the French and Indian War. Many years later he remarked just before his inauguration, "I approach the chair of government with feelings not unlike those of a culprit who is going to his execution."

The fact that Washington suffered from bad teeth—raging toothaches and poorly fitted false teeth—may also partly account for his stern expression. During the siege of Yorktown (see stamp 703), he suffered agonies from his teeth, which hardly left him in the joyous frame of mind the occasion called for.

What was the wellspring of Washington's actions? He had a deep sense of what was honorable and what it meant to be a gentleman. To him, "honorable" and "gentleman" were not empty words. They represented ideals that guided his conduct. He wanted to do the right thing, to be thought well of by other people, to be famous—but only by honorable means.

It was part of Washington's code to seek out responsibilities that were not always pleasant, to take on duties that were not always welcome. He tried harder than most men—and succeeded

Painting by
Charles Willson Peale

706 · 1½¢ brown · 1932

better than most—to be patient, fair, conciliatory. Washington's abiding integrity enabled him to endure where other men would have collapsed. These are the qualities that endowed him with a more than life-size nobility and grandeur.

As a schoolboy, he had to copy and memorize the one hundred and ten *Rules of Civility and Decent Behaviour in Company and Conversation,* made up by a French monk in 1595. The last item in the copybook was, "Labour to keep alive in your breast that little spark of celestial fire called conscience." These precepts made a strong impression on the boy, and as a grown man he tried faithfully to carry them out.

While young George was fond of books, he was even more devoted to hunting and other sports. Unusually tall and powerfully built, he was a magnificent horseman and accustomed to command even as a youngster. His love of life in the open blended nicely with his skill as a surveyor and was a useful preparation for his later military career. When he was twenty-two, he became a rich man by inheriting the Mount Vernon estate from his half-brother Lawrence Washington.

But even before that, he had already shown his mettle as a soldier. In 1747 some of the most prominent men of his colony organized the Ohio Company of Virginia. Two years later they

Painting by
Gilbert Stuart

707 · 2¢ red · 1932

received a royal charter granting them half a million acres on both sides of the Ohio River. Both France and England claimed this area, but while the French had several skimpy settlements there, the British had none.

By 1753, Washington, though only twenty-one, was already a major in the Virginia militia. Despite his youth, he was sent by Governor Dinwiddie on a mission which took him five hundred miles into the wilderness to investigate French activity in the disputed territory. Following instructions, Washington warned the French in courtly language to clear out. They naturally refused to do anything of the sort, but Dinwiddie was deeply impressed by this serious and ruggedly persevering young man.

A year passed as a major conflict shaped up. The French captured Fort Prince George at the forks of the Ohio, where the Allegheny and Monongahela Rivers join—the present site of Pittsburgh. When Virginia sent another force to challenge the French at Fort Duquesne—the new name for Fort Prince George—Washington (now a lieutenant-colonel) was second in command.

Outnumbered three to one, the colonists retreated and built Fort Necessity, where they soon had to surrender. The first

Painting by
Charles Willson Peale

708 · 3¢ purple · 1932

shots in the wilderness solitude had started a conflict that was to rage in Canada, Europe, and India—the struggle known in its American phase as the French and Indian War.

After his release, Washington returned home and was given a high post in General Braddock's unfortunate expedition (see stamp 688). Washington's early fighting experience was perfect training for the grim task of leading inadequate numbers of poorly equipped men on hopeless ventures.

In 1759 Fort Duquesne finally passed to the British, and the Americans started the long, slow, dangerous trek into Ohio and Kentucky. As for young Colonel Washington, he retired from military service—for good, so it seemed—to devote himself to his eight-thousand-acre estate at Mount Vernon. He was not one of those wealthy landowners to whom a farm, no matter how extensive, is merely a plaything. With his love of farming, he was keenly interested in all the latest and best methods.

Washington rotated his crops at a time when few farmers realized how this increased the yield and avoided exhaustion of the soil. In his quest for new and better varieties, he was always importing shrubs, trees, and plants from Europe. He bred superior cattle and doubled the wool clip from his sheep. A

84

Painting by
Charles Peale Polk

709 · 4¢ brown · 1932

garden of kitchen herbs added variety and relish to his meals.

Right up to the end of his life Washington made a point of riding around his vast estate daily to keep every part of it in good condition. When he was at odds with Thomas Jefferson over political doctrine, they still corresponded avidly about improved techniques and tools.

Life at Mount Vernon was pleasant—too pleasant to last. The discontent of the colonists mounted steadily. Unlike such hotheads as Patrick Henry and Sam Adams, Washington was at first a reluctant rebel. But once he joined the fight, he took the leading part in it.

Washington's task as Commander in Chief of the Continental Army was a heartbreaking one. Though the colonies had a population of two million, there were never more than twenty thousand men in his forces. Few Americans thought of their country as a *nation*. They were anxious about their crops, homesick for farm and family. They were reluctant to fight outside their own colony; their patriotism was local or at best sectional.

But Washington was cruelly hampered in other ways. He found himself in the crossfire of the conflicting jealousies and vanities of generals, governors, and delegates to the Continental

Painting by
Charles Willson Peale

710 · 5¢ blue · 1932

Congress. Repeatedly smoothing the ruffled feathers of these people in public, he was constantly exasperated in private.

After the Battles of Long Island and White Plains in 1776 (see stamps 1003 and 629), Washington saw his army melting away with the approach of winter. Beset by harrowing doubts and a morbid fear of failure, he confided to a friend:

"I know that without men, without arms, without ammunition, without anything fit for the accommodation of a soldier, that little is to be done—and, what is more mortifying, I know that I cannot stand justified to the world, without exposing my own weakness, and injuring the cause by declaring my wants, which I am determined not to do, further than unavoidable necessity brings every man acquainted with them."

And Washington kept his word. One observer during those desperate days wrote admiringly that he "showed himself to his harassed and enfeebled army with a serene, unembarrassed countenance." Shortly before the lightning stab against Trenton, Tom Paine penned these words: "I love a man that can smile in trouble, that can gather strength from distress and grow brave from reflection."

On that cheerless Christmas Eve of 1776, Washington saved the Revolution from extinction. As his poorly clothed troops

Painting by
John Trumbull

711 · 6¢ orange · 1932

marched knee-deep in snow to the Delaware River, penetrating winds blew sleet against their chilled faces and bodies. Crossing the river through the ice blocks took nine hours, until at 4 A.M. the last boatload was landed.

Through it all, Washington remained superbly calm. There still remained a six-mile march to Trenton in the snow. The muskets were too wet to be used—only bayonets would do. At last they were in Trenton—no more need for silence. Shouts broke from their throats as they fixed bayonets and charged the enemy's quarters. The bewildered Hessians, drunk, sleepy, half-dressed, were helpless. Some two hundred were killed or wounded, the remaining thousand or so surrendered.

That brilliant victory saved the Revolution and heartened every patriot—but for how long? In two bleak winter months Washington's force sank to eight hundred men. When he asked the Continental Congress for $150 in silver to pay his spies, the best it could do was to scrape up $124 for him!

But this was only a foretaste of the dread winter of 1777-1778 —the winter of Valley Forge (page 62). An army doctor wrote despairingly in his diary:

"Poor food—hard lodgings—Cold Weather—fatigue—Nasty Cloaths—nasty Cookery—Vomit half my time—smoak'd out of

Painting by
John Trumbull

712 · 7¢ black · 1932

my senses—the Devil's in't—I cant endure it—smoke and Cold—hunger and filthyness—A pox on my bad luck."

Historians have quibbled over whether or not Washington was a great general. One thing is certain—the man who held that army together was a great man. He was great not only in the means he used, but in the ends he worked for. Idolized by his men, he could have become a king had he wanted to. When one army faction proposed kingship to him in 1782, he described it as "the greatest mischief that can befall my country."

And Washington went on: "If I am not deceived in the knowledge of myself, you could not have found a person to whom your scheme were more disagreeable." Nor was this the reply of a cold, priggish perfectionist. A year later, when Washington took leave of his officers at Fraunces Tavern, there was "such a scene of sorrow and weeping I had never before witnessed and hope I may never be called upon to witness again." So it was recorded by Benjamin Tallmadge, a trusted aide of Washington.

When at last the weary years of the war for independence were over, Washington was able to retire to his beloved Mount Vernon. A little later he was offered one hundred and fifty shares in two Virginia canal development companies "as a mode

88

Crayon Drawing by
Charles Saint Memin

713 · 8¢ green · 1932

of adding something substantial to the many honorary awards bestowed on him." He declined the gift, but there is a delightfully human touch in his plaintive confession to Madison that he "disliked the appearance of ostentatious disinterestedness." In other words, he did not want people to think he was publicly parading his honesty.

There are many glimpses in Washington's correspondence that reveal the man behind the stern, aloof expression. In calling on Madison for advice, he writes with disarming humility: "I am very troublesome but you must excuse me. Ascribe it to friendship and confidence."

And later, as President, he writes playfully to John Jay: "If Mr. Jay proposes going to church, the President would be obliged to him for a seat in his carriage."

The thought Washington gave to the problem of re-election shows how eager he always was to be esteemed by his fellow men: "A declaration to retire not only carries with it the appearance of vanity and self-importance but it may be construed into a move to be invited to remain. And on the other hand to say nothing, implies consent."

Yet with all his self-doubts, Washington's achievements as President were second only to his generalship in the Revolution.

Pastel Portrait by
W. Williams

714 · 9¢ pink · 1932

His administration saw the beginnings of the Cabinet, the creation of the Federal judiciary, the funding of the Revolutionary
debts, the establishment of the first United States Bank, the
introduction of a protective tariff. Above all, Washington maintained a difficult neutral course between England and France,
and sought a middle ground in the bickerings between Alexander Hamilton and Thomas Jefferson.

This was the last and perhaps the greatest of all the sacrifices
that George Washington made for his country—that he gave
up the longed-for leisure of his old age to help build a brave
new world for those who would inhabit it after his lifetime
was spent.

Painting by
Gilbert Stuart

715 · 10¢ yellow · 1932

90

Ski Jumper

716 · 2¢ red · 1932

OUR MODERN Olympic Games can be traced back to the ancient athletic festivals at Olympia in southwestern Greece. Among the ancient Greeks these games started in legendary times and had religious meaning. The earliest Olympic Games of which we have authentic record took place in 776 B.C.

At first the games consisted of foot races. Later, other types of contests were added: chariot racing, wrestling, boxing, jumping, discus throwing, and the like.

Scoring an Olympic victory was one of the greatest honors to which a Greek could aspire. Victors were crowned with olive wreaths; Pindar and other great poets wrote odes in their honor; Phidias and other sculptors made statues of them.

The Olympic stadium seated over forty-five thousand spectators, and people came from all over Greece to watch the games. If a war was in progress, it had to stop during the festival. The games took place regularly until Roman Emperor Theodosius I prohibited them in 394 A.D.

For many centuries no Olympic Games took place. But when Heinrich Schliemann, the famous explorer of ancient ruins, dug up a stadium in 1878, the discovery aroused world-wide interest. This led in turn to the idea of reviving the Olympic Games in modern form.

91

Olympic Runner

718 · 3¢ purple · 1932

The first modern Olympic Games took place, quite appropriately, at Athens in 1896. Since then the games have been held at Paris (1900), St. Louis (1904), Athens (1906), London (1908), Stockholm (1912), Antwerp (1920), Paris (1924), Amsterdam (1928), Los Angeles (1932), Berlin (1936), London (1948), and Helsinki (1952).

In addition to the standard track and field events, other events have been included in modern Olympic competition. These include swimming, rowing, horsemanship, cycling, shooting, fencing, soccer, and winter sports.

One of the most thrilling events of the modern games is the marathon race, held in memory of the magnificent victory of the greatly outnumbered Greeks over the Persian host of Darius at Marathon in 490 B.C. Pheidippides, the finest runner of his day, was sent from the battlefield to carry the good news to Athens. After running eight leagues (about twenty-four miles), Pheidippides arrived in the market place, gasped, "Rejoice, we conquer!" and fell dead.

The Winter Olympic Games of 1932 were held at Lake Placid, New York, in February, with entrants from nineteen countries taking part in hockey, curling, speed-skating, dog-sled, bobsled, figure-skating, ski-racing, and ski-jumping contests.

The Discus Thrower

719 · 5¢ blue · 1932

A new indoor rink, with nine miles of brine pipes, was constructed for the skating events. Costly improvements in the bobsled run included a steep stone-lined trench a mile and a half long. Three major curves and twenty-two minor ones created exciting hazards for the five-hundred-pound Olympic bobsleds. During one of the races the German team, hurtling down at sixty-five miles an hour, shot off eighty-five feet into a gully.

The United States won the Winter Games by a comfortable margin. Among individual performers a young Norwegian girl named Sonja Henie was lifted to stardom by her brilliant victory in the figure-skating contest.

The Summer Olympic Games took place in July and August of 1932 at Los Angeles. Two thousand athletes came from thirty-nine countries and were housed in the cottages of Olympic Village, which was provided with its own post office. A special Olympic Stadium was constructed for the occasion, with a seating capacity of one hundred and five thousand. The United States won most of the track and field events.

A special issue of three stamps commemorated the Olympic Games. In the upper corners of the 2¢ and 5¢ stamps one may find the Olympic torch, which is lit at the beginning of each Olympiad and kept burning until the final event is over.

Centennial of
Julius Sterling Morton

717 · 2¢ red · 1932

IN 1858, when Julius Sterling Morton (1832-1902) became sec-retary of the Nebraska Territory, it was known as the great American desert. The pioneers had cleared the forests for plant-ing, for lumber to build homes, and for firewood. They had done so thorough a job that a man could ride for miles without seeing a tree.

Well aware of the value of trees, Morton suggested in 1872 that a special day be set aside for planting trees and thus trans-forming the great American desert into the flourishing land of farms and orchards that we know today.

The people of Nebraska gladly accepted Morton's wise pro-posal. In the next sixty years they planted about eight hundred million trees. In 1895 the Nebraska legislature gave the state the official title of Tree Planter's State. (It has since been changed to Cornhusker State.) New York celebrated its first Arbor Day in 1888, and within ten years school children had planted 200,000 trees.

Many other states have adopted Arbor Day as an occasion for planting trees and impressing children with the importance of trees. By picturing a boy and a girl planting a tree, the com-memorative stamp conveys the idea that trees planted now will benefit the generations that live after our time.

94

Founding of Philadelphia
250th Anniversary

724 · 3¢ purple · 1932

WILLIAM PENN (1644-1718), the son of a distinguished British admiral, fearlessly risked disgrace by becoming a Quaker. After being jailed several times and threatened with life imprisonment, his staunch reaction was: "My prison will be my grave before I will budge a jot. For I owe obedience to the Conscience of no mortal man."

The Quakers' belief in the universal brotherhood of man caused them to be hated in many quarters. Imprisonment, flogging, heavy fines and confiscations were often their lot.

Penn's father was a rich man, and the son's inheritance included a claim on the British Crown for sixteen thousand pounds. In 1681 William Penn persuaded the King to satisfy the debt by chartering the colony of Pennsylvania, with a view to settling thousands of Quakers and other persecuted people there. The following year Penn sailed with a large group of Quakers to found Philadelphia, the "City of Brotherly Love."

Complete religious toleration was only one of the many enlightened features of Pennsylvania's government. In time, Penn spent almost all his fortune on the colony. But it was money well spent, for helping distressed people came to absorb all the energies of this sincere, truly goodhearted man. The American tradition of freedom of worship owes much to William Penn.

Daniel Webster

(1782-1852)

725 · 3¢ purple · 1932

DANIEL WEBSTER is considered by many the finest orator America has produced. To this day his eloquence continues to inspire New England legends and tall tales.

Webster gained wealth and prestige from his law practice. With his rough-hewn face, flashing black eyes, and thrilling voice, he was equally effective when it came to swaying a crowd. His gift for colorful imagery, backed by a superb memory, attracted huge audiences. Aside from the years when he served as Secretary of State, Webster was a senator from Massachusetts from 1828 until his death.

In 1830 Webster delivered what is generally considered the finest speech ever made in the United States Senate. Hayne of South Carolina had described the Union as a confederation of states which could obey or disobey Federal laws as they thought best.

In reply, Webster dramatically prophesied that this principle of "nullification" would in time lead to civil war. After describing the benefits that every American received from a strong Federal Union, Webster concluded with his immortal phrase: "Liberty and Union, now and forever, one and inseparable!"

Thirty years later this exciting debate was reopened—with bullets instead of words—in the war between the states.

96

Founding of Georgia

726 · 3¢ purple · 1933

JAMES EDWARD OGLETHORPE (1696-1785), who founded Georgia, the last of the thirteen colonies, was one of the most enlightened men of his time.

As a member of Parliament, Oglethorpe denounced the laws which made it a crime for a man to be unable to pay his debts. Instead of being given a chance to earn the money to satisfy his creditors, the debtor was thrown into jail—and allowed to rot there until he was able to pay.

He also tried to influence people to stamp out the slave trade with its horrors. "Impressing" (kidnaping) men into the Royal Navy was another evil Oglethorpe fought.

Oglethorpe's interest in helping unfortunate people gave him the idea of colonizing the region between English Carolina and Spanish Florida. In 1732 Oglethorpe obtained a royal charter from George II to found a colony called Georgia, after the King. The charter authorized Oglethorpe and nineteen other trustees to run the colony. The following year Oglethorpe brought the first settlers—thirty-five families—to found the city of Savannah.

Oglethorpe was a man of action as well as a man of good will —a pioneer who blazed the way for the successful reforms of later statesmen. It took them more than a century to catch up with his ideas.

97

Newburgh
Proclamation

727 · 3¢ purple · 1933

THOUGH THE capture of Yorktown (see stamp 703) virtually ended the fighting in the Revolutionary War, the state of hostilities dragged on for almost two years. During this period General Washington maintained his headquarters at the Hasbrouck House—pictured on the commemorative stamp—at Newburgh, New York.

The troops were bored, eager for discharge, and smoldering with resentment over the arrears in their pay. The officers were angry at the shabby way they were treated by Congress. The states were busy quarreling over boundaries and tariffs. The country seemed headed for anarchy.

On April 19, 1783, the anniversary of the Battles of Lexington and Concord (see stamp 618), Washington issued a general order proclaiming the coming of peace. With humility and awe he wrote about "the stupendous fabrick of freedom and empire on the broad basis of independency." He asked his soldiers, "those gallant and persevering men," to "close the drama with applause"—to retire and let the United States form a sound government.

In this thoughtful address Washington rendered his country a precious service. To be the architect of victory was not enough; he did not want the country's newly gained freedom to perish in vengeful disputes.

98

Fort Dearborn

728 · 1¢ green · 1933

CHICAGO, the second largest city in the United States and the fifth largest in the world, owes its phenomenal development to its strategic location. It was this location that made Chicago the world's leading grain market, the largest meat distributor, and the greatest railroad center. In 1950 the value of Chicago's industrial production was eight billion dollars. Long before that, it had become the leading machine manufacturing center of the United States.

But in 1679 there was only a small trading post established by the French on the future site of Chicago, along the portage route between Lake Michigan and the tributaries of the upper Mississippi. For many years the region remained Indian country; white settlers did not appear in appreciable numbers until the end of the eighteenth century.

Fort Dearborn, the forerunner of Chicago, was built by the United States Army in 1803. The fort did not serve its purpose very well, for in 1812 the Indians razed it and massacred the helpless pioneers. The fort was rebuilt in 1816; twenty years later, when the Indian menace was gone, it was abandoned.

In the 1820's the introduction of the steamboat and the building of canals strongly stimulated westward migration. By 1830 speculators were laying out the first town lots of Chicago at prices of forty to sixty dollars apiece. Three years later Chicago

Federal Building
at the World's Fair

729 · 3¢ purple · 1933

had a population of three hundred and fifty and was officially incorporated; this was the beginning of its "Century of Progress."

Land values rose sensationally, only to collapse in the panic of 1837. But this did not keep newcomers away, and Chicago's population rose steadily to forty-five hundred by 1840 and thirty thousand by 1850.

The decade just before the Civil War was a period of enormous railroad development. Chicago became a vast terminus for the produce of the surrounding prairies, shipments on the Great Lakes, and for east-west traffic. In this decade the city achieved its pre-eminence in grain, meat, and lumber handling.

We do not know whether Mrs. O'Leary's cow started the great fire of 1871 by kicking over a lighted lantern, but there is no doubt about the devastation: three hundred people lost their lives, ninety thousand were left homeless, and the property loss amounted to two hundred million dollars.

Yet the destroyed city was quickly replaced by a new city of stone and steel. Chicago's architects were equal to the challenge, and it was then that the skyscraper originated. The arrival of many nationalities aided Chicago's turbulent and strident development, and by 1890 Chicago's rapidly growing population topped the million mark. (In the next sixty years the popu-

The Graf
Zeppelin

C 18 · 1933
50¢ green

lation was to rise to three million six hundred thousand.)

Chicago has had two strikingly lavish fairs to celebrate its progress. The first of these was the Columbian Exposition of 1893 (page 12); the second was the World's Fair which observed a "Century of Progress" in 1933 and paid tribute to the machine age.

The strikingly beautiful buildings constructed for the 1893 fair started new trends in architecture. Electricity, still a novelty to many people in those days, lit up the exhibits at night like a veritable fairyland.

At the 1933 fair, the three tall towers of the Federal Building stood out prominently against a vista of long, low buildings that included the U-shaped Hall of Science, the Travel and Transportation Building, and the million-dollar General Motors assembly plant. One of the many features was the special transatlantic flight of the dirigible *Graf Zeppelin* to the fair.

Three stamps commemorated the World's Fair of 1933: the 1¢ stamp with a view of Fort Dearborn; the 3¢ stamp picturing the Federal Building; and the 50¢ airmail stamp depicting the *Graf Zeppelin*, with the Federal Building on the left and the hangar at Friedrichshafen, Germany, on the right. The contrast between the log stockade and the airship vividly highlights the old and the new in Chicago's Century of Progress.

101

"In a Common Determination"

732 · 3¢ purple · 1933

IN MAY, 1933, when the National Industrial Recovery Act went into effect, the NRA Blue Eagle became the favorite symbol of the New Deal's efforts to revive business and reduce unemployment.

The National Recovery Administration was set up to create jobs, shorten hours of work, raise hourly wage rates, end child labor, and guarantee the right of collective bargaining. More than seven hundred industries with twenty-three million employees were allowed to prepare fair-trade codes for their members.

Hugh Johnson, a retired brigadier-general, was the first NRA administrator. Colorful and forceful and a master of all the arts of publicity, Johnson organized NRA parades in leading cities and had Blue Eagle placards displayed in millions of store windows.

In May, 1935, a New York poultry firm successfully fought the law before the Supreme Court, arguing that commerce within a state could not be regulated by the Federal government. The high court agreed, and held the NRA unconstitutional.

The commemorative stamp shows a farmer, a businessman, an industrial worker, and a woman employee marching together "in a common determination."

Map of Byrd Expeditions

733 · 3¢ blue · 1933

THE AIRPLANE has given man more knowledge of the polar regions since 1927 than he obtained in thousands of years before the Air Age. Richard E. Byrd, born in 1888, was the pioneer of this aerial progress.

The Antarctic region, a bleak waste almost as large as North America, has mountains of ice that tower as high as fifteen thousand feet, and flat icebergs that are forty miles long in some cases. This desolate area, which is much colder than the Arctic, has no human inhabitants. It is rich in minerals. Oddly enough, it had a semitropical climate in prehistoric times.

On his first expedition to the Antarctic in 1929, Byrd flew to the South Pole through passes in the icy mountains—a short trip but one full of risks and thrills. During the second expedition he narrowly escaped death by carbon monoxide poisoning.

The Little America commemorative stamp was issued to celebrate Byrd's second expedition to the Antarctic. The stamp shows a map of the world with dotted lines tracing Byrd's previous flights and proposed explorations. A solid dot indicates the position of Little America, Byrd's headquarters on an ice shelf of the Ross Barrier. This stamp was not issued to the general public, but was used only for mail carried on Byrd's second expedition.

150th Anniversary
of Kosciuszko's
American Citizenship

734 · 5¢ blue · 1933

WHEN THE American Revolution broke out, Thaddeus Kosciuszko (1746-1817), the liberty-loving Polish patriot leader, saw a chance to strike a valiant blow for freedom. After his arrival in the United States in 1776, the Continental Congress commissioned him a colonel of engineers.

Thad Kosci, as the Americans called him for convenience, soon made a name for himself as an exceptionally skillful designer and builder of fortifications. His commanders—and the British as well!—commented admiringly on his redoubts, batteries, parapets, ditches, and underground passages.

Kosciuszko's masterpiece was his fortification and landscaping of West Point, which he turned into the most inaccessible and valuable fortress of the Revolutionary War. The work, which took over two years, was highly praised by the most exacting experts; it explains why the British were willing to pay Benedict Arnold twenty thousand pounds for the plans to West Point. Later on, during the southern campaign of General Greene, Kosciuszko was kept busy building camps, bridges, and forts.

After the Revolution, Kosciuszko went back to his native Poland to fight against Russian tyranny. His efforts failed, but his gallant struggle against hopeless odds made him an admired figure throughout the civilized world.

The *Ark* and the *Dove*

736 · 3¢ red · 1934

IN 1632 King Charles I of England gave George Calvert, Lord Baltimore, a royal charter for a large grant of land in the New World. They named the region Maryland in honor of the Queen, Henrietta Maria. Baltimore hoped to create a haven for persecuted fellow Catholics, but he died before he could carry out the project.

Late in the following year his elder son, Cecil Calvert, second Lord Baltimore, outfitted two vessels, the *Ark* and the *Dove,* and sent several hundred colonists to found a settlement. Most of the colonists were Catholics.

Unlike the early settlers at Jamestown in Virginia, the Maryland colonists were not plagued by disease and starvation; and they wisely remained on friendly terms with the Indians.

Despite their legal position as proprietors of the colony, the judicious Baltimores avoided the pitfalls of absolutist rule. From the start, the freemen of the colony were allowed to propose laws and assist the governor and the council.

In line with this liberal trend, the Maryland Assembly passed the famous Toleration Act in 1649, providing that every Christian "shall be nowise troubled or molested for or in respect of his religion, nor in the free exercise thereof, within this province."

Whistler's "Portrait of My Mother"

737 · 3¢ purple · 1934

THE CELEBRATION of Mother's Day began on May 9, 1914, when President Wilson set aside the second Sunday in May "as a public expression of our love and reverence for the mothers of our country."

In store windows and elsewhere, the universal symbol of Mother's Day is the painting we call "Whistler's Mother," though the artist himself gave it the cold-sounding name of *Arrangement in Grey and Black.*

By calling the picture an arrangement, Whistler was stressing the relationship of the color values: gray wall, green curtain, black dress, and white cap, cuffs, and handkerchief. Despite all the insistence on technique, the painter was careful to give his mother a sweet, tender expression. His emphasis on technique did not wholly rule out sentiment.

Whistler first exhibited the portrait at the Royal Academy in London in 1872. At first the painting was sent down to the cellar, but after a great deal of wrangling it was hung at the annual exhibition.

In 1878 Whistler had to pawn the portrait when he went bankrupt. Thirteen years later the French government bought the painting for a mere four thousand francs. One of the world's most famous paintings, it now hangs in the Louvre.

Nicolet's Landing on the Shores of Green Bay

739 · 3¢ purple · 1934

WHAT THE French accomplished in their settlement of the New World seems miraculous when we consider how few colonists they had. What they lacked in numbers, they made up in daring, endurance, finesse, and woodcraft.

In 1634 Samuel de Champlain, the "Father of New France," decided to send one of his best *coureurs de bois* ("woods-runners") to search for the Northwest Passage to the Indies. Champlain's choice, Jean Nicolet (1598?-1642) set out on the Great Lakes with seven Indians.

Nicolet had no fear of the hardships of the western wilderness. According to an old chronicle, he had "undergone such fatigues as none but eyewitnesses can conceive; he often passed seven or eight days without food, and once full seven weeks with only bark from the trees for nourishment."

Confident that he would meet Chinese, Nicolet took along a ceremonial robe of "Chinese damask, all strewn with flowers and birds of many colors."

In the course of his trip Nicolet discovered Lake Michigan and became the first white man to enter the Wisconsin country. He failed, of course, to find the route to the Indies, but he made useful treaties with the Indians and greatly increased the scope of the highly profitable fur trade.

107

Yosemite
National Park

740 · 1¢ green · 1934

SIXTY MILLION years ago the Sierra Nevada ("Snowy") Mountains, much lower than they are today, were in a moist, fairly warm area. Underground upheavals raised them for thousands of centuries, forcing the mountain streams to dizzy heights and creating some of the most beautiful waterfalls in the world.

Snow on the peaks froze into glaciers during the Ice Age. Giant glaciers, some of them three thousand feet thick, pushed their way through the Yosemite canyons. The glaciers that melted after the Ice Age turned into swift-running streams and lakes that are far above sea level.

The Yosemite Falls pour down, with interruptions, a total of 2,425 feet, and the park has other falls that dwarf Niagara's mere 165 feet. Yosemite's forests contain hundreds of giant sequoia trees, some of them 3,800 years old, with a thickness of 34 feet. Yosemite has seven hundred miles of forest trails.

El Capitan, a fantastic mass of granite that towers 3,600 feet above the valley floor, appears on the commemorative stamp.

The Grand Canyon of the Colorado River, one of the wonders of the world, is two hundred and seventeen miles long, with a width of from four to eighteen miles, and a height that reaches

Grand Canyon National Park

741 · 2¢ red · 1934

nine thousand feet in some parts. Grand Canyon National Park, located in northern Arizona and opened by the United States government in 1919, includes about half of this vast, steep, and wide natural gorge.

It took millions of years for the Grand Canyon to come into existence. This magnificent laboratory of nature is the world's most picturesque example of erosion (the gradual wearing away of rocks and soil).

The erosion is in large part the work of the swift-flowing Colorado River, one of the longest in the United States. In its seventeen hundred and fifty miles there are rapids that rush along at twenty-five miles an hour. Every twenty-four hours the river carries down a million tons of silt—soil, sand, and gravel. That is why the Spaniards called it *colorado* ("reddish").

The sides of the canyon have cliffs and terraces that are made up of successive layers, each dating back to a different geological period. Each layer has its special color and all are rich in fossils.

The variety of colors—among them gray, purple, red, black, green, brown, and blue—gives the canyon the final touch of grandeur that attracts upwards of half a million tourists each year. Now hazy, now brilliant, the colors change with the shifting intensity of the sunlight.

Mount Rainier National Park

742 · 3¢ purple · 1934

Ages ago many of the rocks were formed into fantastic shapes that have received fanciful names. The commemorative stamp, for example, shows the "temples" of Deva, Brahma, and Zoroaster, as well as Bright Angel Canyon.

In 1792 the British explorer Captain George Vancouver discovered a lofty snow-capped peak in what is now the state of Washington. He named the mountain after his friend Rear Admiral Peter Rainier of the British Navy.

Once an active volcano, Mount Rainier has been dormant since 1870. It is the fourth highest mountain in the United States, towering 14,408 feet and being visible 200 miles away in clear weather. To the Indians, Rainier was "the home of the gods," perhaps because of its volcanic character.

Today Mount Rainier attracts thousands of visitors who come to ski and toboggan on its snowy slopes. The mountain is covered with many glaciers—some of them the largest in the United States. Their erosive action is imperceptibly grinding down the mountainside.

Mount Rainier is densely wooded for the first four thousand feet or so. At higher levels the trees thin out and become shorter because of the powerful winds that buffet them. Mount Rainier National Park, established in 1899, has many miles of attractive

Mesa Verde
National Park

743 · 4¢ brown · 1934

woodland trails. The commemorative stamp presents a view of Mirror Lake, with the snow-capped mountain in the background.

In 1888 two cowboys searching for strayed cattle looked down from the rim of a canyon and discovered a "cliff palace." Here they found over two hundred rooms built of stone, and many remains of an ancient Pueblo civilization.

Mesa Verde ("Green Table") National Park, a plateau twenty miles long and eighteen miles wide, rises two thousand feet above the surrounding country in some places. It has numerous canyons where the cliff dwellers built their homes.

The park, which came into existence in 1906, is in the southwestern corner of Colorado, near the point where Colorado, Utah, New Mexico, and Arizona meet. The chief reason for establishing the park was to preserve the magnificent relics of a culture that disappeared centuries ago.

Archaeologists who have studied the region tell us that the Pueblo Indians settled on the mesa almost two thousand years ago. Cliff Palace, which appears on the commemorative stamp, was the largest dwelling. It looks quite like a modern apartment house.

Yellowstone is sixty-two miles long and fifty-six miles wide,

Yellowstone National Park

744 · 5¢ blue · 1934

the largest of all the national parks. Almost all of it is in Wyoming, with a small strip overlapping into Montana and Idaho. An extensive plateau, averaging eight thousand feet above sea level, it is surrounded by mountain peaks that tower about three thousand feet higher.

The most famous feature of Yellowstone is its three thousand or so geysers and hot springs. Some of these shoot streams of water as high as two hundred feet in the air. Old Faithful, by no means the largest or showiest of the geysers, has always been Yellowstone's chief attraction because of the regularity and frequency with which it erupts—about once an hour. Old Faithful appears on the commemorative stamp.

But Yellowstone has many other wonders, such as mountains thrown up by earthquakes; one of these is a mountain of obsidian (natural glass). There is a living forest that stands on top of twelve layers of petrified forests. Yellowstone Lake, largest of the park's thirty-six lakes, is eight thousand feet above sea level and has a perimeter of a hundred miles. The falls of the Yellowstone River tumble three hundred feet, almost twice as far as Niagara. A little farther on is the Grand Canyon of the Yellowstone, twenty miles long, with gorgeously colored walls that are

Crater Lake
National Park

745 · 6¢ blue · 1934

a thousand feet deep and separated by a chasm almost twice as wide.

Two hundred clear, cold mountain streams provide some of the finest fishing in the United States, but hunting has been banned since 1894. The herd of a thousand buffalo is the largest in the country, and the wildlife includes large numbers of moose, elk, deer, antelope, bears, and mountain sheep.

Half a million visitors enjoy Yellowstone every year. In the opinion of many, it is still the most beautiful national park.

Beautiful as Crater Lake is, many other national parks are no less attractive. But Crater Lake has a geological history that sets it apart from all others.

Millions of years ago there was an active volcano, about fourteen thousand feet high, in southern Oregon. During the Ice Age this mountain was covered with glaciers. Frozen outside, it seethed under the surface at fantastically high temperatures.

Finally there came an explosion of such force that it flung up a huge pile of debris and hurled it many miles. The tremendous thrust of the explosion caved in the top seven thousand feet of the mountain.

When the collapsed glaciers melted in the crater, they formed a lake with an area of twenty square miles and a depth of two

Acadia
National Park

746 · 7¢ black · 1934

thousand feet. Today this lake, six thousand feet above sea level, is lined with brilliantly colored lava cliffs. No less remarkable is the color of the waters of Crater Lake—the "bluest" blue of any lake in the world.

This awesome sight is part of Crater Lake National Park, which has an area of roughly two hundred and fifty square miles and was established in 1902. The commemorative stamp offers a view of the lake, including Wizard Island, a cone-shaped crater thrust seven hundred and fifty feet above the surface of the lake a thousand years ago by another earthquake.

Of all our national parks, only one is on the seacoast, where the surf thunders against jagged rocks. This is Acadia National Park, most of which is located on Mount Desert Island off the northern coast of Maine.

Acadia was a region that took in part of what is now northeast Maine and southeast Canada. The Acadians were peaceful French farmers and fishermen who, despite their lack of interest in politics and wars, were torn from their homes in 1713 during Queen Anne's War. These were the people whose somber story of exile was related by Longfellow in *Evangeline*.

The park is a picturesque combination of cliffs and caves, forest land and inlets, with the sea hammering away at the rocks

114

Zion
National Park

747 · 8¢ green · 1934

as it has for thousands of years. Another attractive feature of the island is that it is a way station for great throngs of birds that migrate in the fall to warmer climes and several months later wing their way north in springtime.

Great Head, a rocky outcropping on the ocean shore, appears on the commemorative stamp.

The Mormon pioneers discovered Zion Canyon in 1858. About fifteen miles long, this canyon has steep walls that are half a mile high and anywhere from twenty feet to half a mile apart.

In 1909 Zion Canyon was set aside as a national monument. Ten years later, together with Great West Canyon and Parunuweap Canyon, it became Zion National Park. All three canyons have been formed over a period of millions of years by the erosive action of the Virgin River cutting through their soft sandstone content.

Centuries ago, Indian cliff dwellers lived here, presumably to be safe from attack. Even today tourists do not have an easy time of it as they negotiate the steep, winding trails.

The alternation of dazzling red and white sandstone layers in the canyons has created a spectacular color scheme. Over the

Glacier
National Park

748 · 9¢ pink · 1934

centuries, nature has carved the rocks into striking shapes. The most impressive of these sights is the Great White Throne, pictured on the commemorative stamp. This awe-inspiring rock towers more than two thousand feet, completely detached from the canyon walls through the process of erosion.

Millions of years ago the Glacier National Park area held shallow seas filled with mud from nearby rivers. Over the centuries the land rose until the seas disappeared and mountains towered in their stead. There were so many earthquakes that in some places rocks that are twenty million years old are covered by other rocks four times as old. To these upheavals we owe sights that are not easy to match for sheer grandeur.

Later on, the rivers at the highest altitudes froze into glaciers. Grinding against each other and slowly melting, they were reduced to their present comparatively small size.

Among the park's many attractions are its two hundred and fifty lakes nestling among mountains that include several peaks of ten thousand feet or more. The trails that wind through the steep mountains are much safer than they were in Indian days.

Glacier National Park, the third largest of our national parks, was established in 1910. It is located in northwestern Montana, on the Canadian border, and has an area of about fifteen hun-

Great Smoky Mountains National Park

749 · 10¢ gray · 1934

dred square miles. The commemorative stamp offers a view of Two Medicine Lake, with Mount Rockwell in the background.

In early times the Great Smoky region on the boundary of Tennessee and North Carolina was the heart of the Cherokee country. The bluish-gray mist that envelops the mountains most of the time is the source of their name. The unusually moist atmosphere, the heavy rainfall, the action of hot sun on damp ground—all these factors contribute to the haze around the Great Smoky Mountains.

Great Smoky National Park, largest in the East, is fifty-four miles long and nineteen wide. North Carolina and Tennessee raised half the money needed to buy the land. The balance was furnished by John D. Rockefeller, Jr.

It is said that the Great Smoky region has more virgin forest than all the rest of the eastern United States, and it has more kinds of trees than can be found in all of Europe. Mount LeConte, pictured on the commemorative stamp, is noted for the colorful variety of its plant life. The views from the peak are so stunning that it is known as "the grandstand of the Smokies."

117

Charter Oak

772 · 3¢ lilac · 1935

In 1686 King James II of England, a strong believer in the "divine right" of kings to rule as they pleased, revoked the charters of all the New England colonies. Combining them into the Dominion of New England, he installed the tyrannical Sir Edmund Andros as governor. Thus, the colonists lost all their cherished rights of self-government.

Andros arrived in Hartford in October, 1687, with an armed force and demanded the surrender of Connecticut's charter. According to legend, the colonists created one delay after another until darkness came; then they spirited the charter out of the council chamber and hid it in a hollow of a large white oak seven feet thick—the celebrated Charter Oak.

A year later, the "Glorious Revolution" drove James II from the throne, and the colonists recovered their rights.

The commemorative stamp, which features a picture of the Charter Oak, was issued for the three-hundredth anniversary of the founding of Hartford in 1635 by settlers led by Reverend Thomas Hooker. Like Roger Williams and his followers (see stamp 777), Hooker and his congregation had found life in the Massachusetts Bay Colony too strict. As the later story of the Charter Oak suggests, these freedom-loving people and their descendants set a high value on their hard-won liberties.

View of
Exposition Grounds

773 · 3¢ purple · 1935

THOUGH SAN DIEGO is a bustling airplane manufacturing center and contains extensive Navy, Marine, and Coast Guard installations, it still has traces of the old leisurely Spanish mission days.

It was on this site, quite near the present Mexican border, that the Spaniards founded their first permanent settlement in Upper California in 1769. The harbor, one of the finest in the world, had been known to them long before; Juan Rodríguez Cabrillo entered it in 1542.

San Diego became California's capital in 1825 under Mexican rule. It was here that the American flag was first raised when California revolted in 1846.

San Diego's California Pacific International Exposition, attractively set out in beautiful Balboa Park, opened in 1935. Thirty-two foreign governments contributed to the House of Pacific Relations, and the United States, Standard Oil, and Ford buildings also housed notable exhibits. An item of great interest to Californians was the gold spike which Leland Stanford used to join the Union Pacific and Central Pacific in 1869 (see stamp 922).

The commemorative stamp gives a comprehensive view of the exposition grounds, with Point Loma and San Diego Bay in the background.

119

River Gorge
Above and Below
Construction Work

774 · 3¢ purple · 1935

EVERYTHING ABOUT Boulder Dam is on a heroic scale. Built of 3,200,000,000 cubic yards of concrete, this massive structure is 1,200 feet long and 660 feet thick. Its height of 726 feet, equivalent to a 60-story skyscraper, makes it the tallest dam in the world. It irrigates a million acres in California, Arizona, and Nevada, and has doubled the agricultural production of those states. The dam also generates electricity to supply the power needs of the Pacific Southwest.

Boulder Dam is located on the boundary line between Arizona and Nevada, about 25 miles southeast of Las Vegas, Nevada. Behind it is Lake Mead, the largest artificially created body of water in the world. This reservoir, 115 miles long and 589 feet deep, has a storage capacity of ten trillion gallons.

Originally named Hoover Dam in 1930, the towering structure became Boulder Dam in 1935, and Hoover Dam again in 1947. Huge as the dam is, it is only a part of the Boulder Canyon Project, computed to cost $485,000,000. Aside from irrigating arid land and providing electricity, the project was planned to control the floods of the turbulent Colorado River and to hold back the enormous quantities of silt carried along by its swift current (see stamp 741).

State Seal

775 · 3¢ purple · 1935

FRENCH EXPLORERS, traders, and missionaries played an important part in the early history of Michigan. After the French and Indian War, France lost the Michigan country to England, which in turn lost it to the United States by the terms of the Treaty of Paris in 1783.

In 1787 the United States established Michigan as part of the Northwest Territory. However, the British forces, with headquarters in Canada, disregarded the treaty terms and refused to leave Michigan. The United States was too weak to drive the British out, and they remained in control of Michigan until 1796. In that year General Anthony Wayne formally took possession of Michigan for the United States.

In 1805 Michigan became a Territory—the first step toward statehood. During the War of 1812, it was one of the chief battlegrounds. After the war, when public lands were offered at attractive prices, settlers began to stream into Michigan in considerable numbers.

The first steamboat appeared on the Great Lakes in 1818, and the opening of the Erie Canal in 1825 contributed to Michigan's rapid growth. By 1830 Michigan had thirty thousand inhabitants, and five years later it was ready for statehood and was admitted to the Union.

Sam Houston
(1793-1863)
Stephen F. Austin
(1793-1843)

776 · 3¢ purple · 1936

APPROPRIATELY ENOUGH, this commemorative stamp displays the portraits of Stephen F. Austin, who founded the first American settlement in Texas in 1821, and Sam Houston, who played the leading role in achieving Texan independence.

In 1835 Austin tried to negotiate Texan home rule under the Mexican constitution, but his mission failed. Thereupon, the Texans revolted and set up a provisional government with Sam Houston as head of their army.

The Texans gained badly needed time for organizing their resistance through the heroic defense of the Alamo by one hundred and eighty-seven greatly outnumbered Texans. Rather than surrender, the Texans fought on until all were killed. The Alamo, which is pictured on the commemorative stamp, is known as "the cradle of Texan liberty."

On March 2, 1836, Texas declared its independence of Mexico. Six weeks later, Houston's force, outnumbered three to one, surprised the Mexican army at San Jacinto during siesta time. Attacking savagely with shouts of "Remember the Alamo!" the Texans killed half the enemy troops and captured almost all the rest. The battle, which lasted less than half an hour, gave Texas its independence. A handsome monument commemorates the battle site.

Roger Williams
(1603?-1683)

777 • 3¢ purple • 1936

IN 1631, when persecution of his fellow Puritans was at its height, Roger Williams saw that there was no future for him in England. Seeking freedom in the New World, he settled in Massachusetts. Here he taught and preached, and traded with the Indians.

Soon Williams was at odds with the Puritan elders on many points—above all his belief that everyone should have the right to practice his religion as long as he did no harm to his fellow citizens. This was dangerous doctrine in a community that punished unorthodoxy by public whipping, locking in the stocks, branding, or lopping off ears. In the winter of 1635-1636 the elders drove Williams from the colony.

Without the help of friendly Indians, Williams would have perished in the wilderness. In the spring he founded Providence Plantations, which prospered because its democratic government attracted newcomers.

Williams welcomed Quakers, Jews, and others who were systematically persecuted in those days, and he extended rights to women that were not generally granted them for several centuries. We owe some of the best elements of the American tradition to this fearless and enlightened man.

State Capitols

782 · 3¢ purple · 1936

THE SPANISH explorer Hernando de Soto was the first white man to set foot in Arkansas. His expedition arrived there in 1541 and spent about ten months in the region. During its wanderings the Spanish expedition visited the remarkable "Hot Springs" which hundreds of years later became a Federal reservation in 1832 and a National Park in 1921.

In 1682 René Robert de La Salle claimed the Mississippi valley, including Arkansas, for France. Four years later he sent Henri de Tonty, known as "the father of Arkansas," to found Arkansas Post, the first white settlement in the Louisiana Territory.

At the time of the Louisiana Purchase in 1803, Arkansas was still very thinly settled, having less than a thousand inhabitants. The Arkansas *Gazette,* founded at Arkansas Post in 1819, is the oldest existing newspaper west of the Mississippi. During the 1820's the government began to build military roads in the region, and steamboats appeared on the Arkansas River.

In 1836 Arkansas became the twenty-fifth state, entering the Union as a slave state because it had been settled mainly by Southerners who raised cotton. The commemorative stamp pictures Arkansas Post as well as the first State House and the present Capitol.

Map of the Oregon Territory

783 · 3¢ purple · 1936

DURING THE first half of the nineteenth century Great Britain and the United States had many heated arguments over their disputed claims to the Oregon country. It was a prize worth arguing about, for it contained the future states of Oregon, Washington, Idaho, and small parts of Montana and Wyoming.

Some Americans were indifferent to the Oregon question. A senator from New Jersey pointed out in 1824 that it would take an Oregon congressman a whole year just to travel from Oregon to the national capital and home again.

Unfortunately, the senator could not foresee the remarkable experience of Ezra Meeker, who was twenty-one when he went to the Pacific coast in 1852 by way of the Oregon Trail. The trip took six months, the normal traveling time for the route. In 1924 Meeker covered the same distance by airplane—in one day.

In the left panel of the commemorative stamp we see a mounted Indian looking off in the distance, with tepees in the foreground and trees and mountains in the background. The right panel shows a covered wagon coming out of a mountain pass. The central part of the design is given over to a map that gives us a vivid idea of the extent of the Oregon Territory as compared with that of modern Oregon.

125

Ratification of the Nineteenth Amendment— Sixteenth Anniversary

784 · 3¢ purple · 1936

SUSAN B. ANTHONY (1820-1906), who did more than anyone else to obtain voting rights for women, was the ideal choice for this commemorative stamp.

When she began teaching school at the age of seventeen for board and five dollars a month, she soon found that men were paid much more for the same work. Then and there she decided to devote her life to fighting for women's rights. Though she loved children, she never married; a family would have hampered her lifework.

Despite the constant danger of mob violence, she spoke out fearlessly against Negro slavery. On one occasion the Mayor of Albany, with drawn pistol, protected her right to speak. She did not shirk such menial jobs as selling tickets or sweeping halls. When her women's suffrage magazine failed with debts of ten thousand dollars, she worked for six years to pay off every penny.

Some men were so baffled by her ready wit and logical thinking that they were reduced to cruel insults. Recognition and universal respect came to her only in old age. A man who disagreed with her views but could not help admiring her integrity once wrote: "I don't believe in woman suffrage, but I do believe in Susan B. Anthony."

George Washington
(1732-1799)
Nathanael Greene
(1742-1786)

785 • 1¢ green • 1936

As A practicing Quaker, Nathanael Greene knew nothing about war until he enlisted as a private to fight in the Revolutionary army. Then came an amazing turn in his fortunes. The Continental Congress, anxious to curry favor with his native Rhode Island, promoted Greene to brigadier-general! This appointment of an inexperienced young man might easily have been one of the worst political blunders of the Revolution.

Luckily, Greene was superbly qualified to be a military commander in that age of gifted amateurs. He hurriedly read two books on war, and all the rest of his knowledge was picked up on the battlefield. Nevertheless, he impressed Washington from the very start. Throughout the Revolution the commander in chief gave Greene difficult assignments which the younger man carried out admirably.

In 1780 Washington showed his confidence in Greene by turning over to him the southern Continental army, which was outnumbered almost ten to one by the British forces under Cornwallis. Relying on a combination of brilliant strategy and swift mobility, Greene fought five battles that forced the British to retreat to Yorktown (see stamp 703). Thus Greene laid the groundwork for the decisive American victory of the Revolution.

Andrew Jackson
(1767-1845)
Winfield T. Scott
(1786-1866)

786 · 2¢ red · 1937

WINFIELD T. SCOTT ("Old Fuss and Feathers") was vain, testy, tactless, pompous, quarrelsome—but he was also courageous and honorable and rated the outstanding general in the period between George Washington and Robert E. Lee.

Scott became a national hero during the War of 1812. Many years later, as an old man, he carried out a masterly campaign during the Mexican War. Landing at Vera Cruz, his army followed the historic invasion route traced by Hernando Cortés in his conquest of Mexico three centuries earlier.

Andrew Jackson ("Old Hickory") was pugnacious, impulsive, peppery, and stubborn. He earned his nickname as a relentless fighter against the Indians.

Jackson was idolized for his victory at New Orleans where he led an unorthodox force of regulars, militiamen, slaves, and smugglers against seasoned British troops. The Battle of New Orleans was really a series of actions, with the last one starting at dawn on January 8, 1815. In one hour the British lost two thousand men, while the defenders suffered trifling losses.

Jackson's popularity brought him in time to the White House, where he served two stormy terms. He spent his remaining years at his beloved home, pictured on the commemorative stamp.

Philip H. Sheridan
(1831-1888)

Ulysses S. Grant
(1822-1885)

William T. Sherman
(1820-1891)

787 · 3¢ purple · 1937

"LITTLE PHIL," as Sheridan was called by his troops, hastened Northern victory by his hammer blows at the Confederate cavalry. In 1864 he ravaged the Shenandoah region so ruthlessly in a reprisal raid that he boasted: "The crow that flies over the Valley of Virginia must henceforth carry his rations with him."

Sherman is remembered for his march through Georgia, which brilliantly achieved its objective of breaking the back of the Confederacy—though at the cost of inflicting intense hardship on Southern civilians. To Sherman's way of thinking, this was a lesser evil than letting the war drag on.

Grant's capture of Fort Donelson in Tennessee in 1862 was the North's first substantial victory. On July 4, 1863, Grant took Vicksburg after a grueling siege and thereby smashed the Confederate hold on the Mississippi. President Lincoln, recognizing Grant's merit, placed him in command of all the Union armies. It took Grant more than a year of pitiless battering and heavy losses to force Lee's surrender.

Thus these three men, by their determination, their generalship, and their devotion to the Union cause, brought to an end the most devastating war ever waged within the United States.

129

Robert E. Lee
(1807-1870)
Thomas J. Jackson
(1824-1863)

788 · 4¢ gray · 1937

THIS STAMP honors the memory of two men who both opposed secession and yet became the two outstanding generals of the Confederacy.

Robert E. Lee (see stamp 982) belonged to Virginia's most distinguished family. On the commemorative stamp we see a picture of his ancestral home, Stratford Hall, in its day the largest and most elegant residence in all the United States.

As for Thomas Jonathan Jackson, he came of a poor family totally lacking in social distinction. Jackson was a bearded, hawk-nosed, grim-looking man with gray-blue eyes. Though he received the nickname of "Stonewall" at Bull Run, the first battle of the Civil War, his men referred to him affectionately as "Old Jack" or "Deacon Jackson"—this last because of his deeply religious nature.

During Jackson's Shenandoah and Maryland campaigns, he terrorized the Northern armies with his lightning marches and surprise raids. He was accidentally shot by his own men during the twilight hours after the Battle of Chancellorsville, and died eight days later of pneumonia brought on by exposure and shock. His premature death cast a pall over the Southern cause and gave Southerners their first depressing intimation of coming defeat.

United States Military Academy

789 · 5¢ blue · 1937

In 1802 Congress authorized the establishment of the United States Military Academy to train commissioned officers for the regular Army. The school has fifteen thousand acres at West Point on the Hudson River. In Revolutionary times, there was a fortress here which Benedict Arnold tried to turn over to the British during his infamous betrayal negotiations.

The number of cadets is limited to twenty-five hundred with about seven hundred and fifty openings available each year. Candidates are selected from a variety of sources, including nominations by senators and congressmen. These candidates must pass rigorous physical and mental tests. On graduating, a cadet becomes a second lieutenant in the regular Army or the Air Force.

Ever since its founding, the Military Academy has stressed strict discipline, character training, and development of the capacity for leadership. The distinguished service of West Point graduates in all the wars of the United States has given the Military Academy imperishable prestige.

In the foreground of the commemorative stamp we see Washington Hall at the left and the North Cadet Barracks at the right. The chapel appears at the upper right, while the upper left gives a view of the old observatory as seen from a distance.

131

John Barry
(1745-1803)
John Paul Jones
(1747-1792)

790 · 1¢ green · 1936

JOHN BARRY and John Paul Jones were unsurpassed for daring, resourcefulness, and fighting spirit. Each has been called the Father of the American Navy.

While commanding the brig *Lexington*, Barry had the distinction of taking the first naval prize of the Revolution when he captured the British vessel *Edward*. Later on he was assigned the *Alliance*. During his memorable homeward voyage from France in 1781 in this ship, he twice gave battle to pairs of British vessels and forced all four enemy vessels to strike their colors.

Jones never had the pleasure of commanding a first-class ship; his *Bonhomme Richard* was an aged craft retired from French service in East Indian waters. Her timbers were rotten, her guns in no state to stand the force of a recoil.

In 1779 Jones had his famous three-hour duel with the British frigate *Serapis*. Asked if he was surrendering his badly riddled ship, Jones gave the legendary reply: "I have not yet begun to fight!"

At last, Jones managed to get the two ships lashed together, and his men boarded the *Serapis* in a savage attack that brought them victory. This gallant struggle has always formed one of the most inspiring traditions of the American Navy.

Stephen Decatur
(1779-1820)
Thomas MacDonough
(1783-1825)

791 · 2¢ red · 1937

IN 1804, during the war with the Barbary Pirates, the frigate *Philadelphia* ran aground in the harbor of Tripoli and all her crew was captured. Under cover of darkness Stephen Decatur led a small force of volunteers into the heavily fortified harbor, overpowered the guards, and destroyed the beautiful frigate. Of this exploit Horatio Nelson, the great British admiral, said, " 'Tis the most bold and daring act of the age."

Decatur added to his laurels in the War of 1812, and in 1815 he broke the power of the Barbary Pirates and ended their custom of exacting tribute from the United States. He is still remembered for his fervent toast: "Our country: in her intercourse with foreign nations may she always be in the right; but our country, right or wrong."

Thomas MacDonough was in command of the Lake Champlain Squadron when the British attacked it in greatly superior force in September, 1814. MacDonough, a first-rate combat commander, scored a decisive victory that had far-reaching effects. The British dropped their invasion plans and scaled down their peremptory demands in the peace negotiations that were then going on in Ghent, Belgium. Thus, the United States emerged creditably from a war in which it had not shown to much advantage.

133

David G. Farragut
(1801-1870)
David Dixon Porter
(1813-1891)

792 · 3¢ purple · 1937

DAVID GLASGOW FARRAGUT, one of the most attractive figures in American naval history, became a midshipman at the age of nine and was assigned command of a captured British whaler when he was barely twelve.

Though a Southerner, Farragut remained loyal to the Union when the Civil War broke out. In 1862 the South was feverishly building ironclads to break the Northern blockade. Farragut succeeded in destroying the ironclads at New Orleans by running his ships through a narrow channel under the crossfire from two fortresses and smashing a barrier of huge logs and sunken vessels.

At Mobile Bay the following year, Farragut faced even more formidable ironclads in a harbor heavily mined with barrels loaded with gunpowder. Lashed to the rigging to get a better view of the battle, Farragut gave the famous command, "Damn the torpedoes! Go ahead!" after his best ship was blown up. Again, he was victorious.

Farragut's foster brother David Dixon Porter gave him valuable aid at New Orleans. Later, Porter helped Grant crush Vicksburg into submission—giving the North full control of the Mississippi and as a result leaving the Confederacy in a desperate situation.

George Dewey
(1837-1917)

William T. Sampson
(1840-1902)

Winfield S. Schley
(1839-1911)

793 · 4¢ gray · 1937

THE SINKING of the *Maine* in Havana harbor on February 15, 1898, made war between the United States and Spain a certainty—though to this day the cause of the disaster remains a mystery.

On the outbreak of hostilities, Commodore Dewey of the Asiatic Squadron received orders to engage the Spanish fleet in the Philippines: "You must capture vessels or destroy." Dewey's fleet steamed into Manila Bay at night, undetected by the Spanish harbor batteries. Opening fire on the Spanish fleet at dawn, the Americans sank or damaged every enemy ship.

On the other side of the world, Admiral Sampson and Commodore Schley blockaded Admiral Cervera's fleet in the harbor of Santiago, Cuba. Meanwhile the *Oregon,* pride of the American Navy, raced sixteen thousand miles from Seattle to Santiago by way of Cape Horn. The *Oregon* arrived in time to assist in demolishing Cervera's fleet when the Spaniards tried to slip past the blockade.

Brief though it was, the Spanish-American War firmly reinforced the concept of a two-ocean navy in the minds of American strategists. That is why construction of the Panama Canal, linking the Atlantic and the Pacific, got under way only a few years later.

United States
Naval Academy

794 · 5¢ blue · 1937

ALTHOUGH THE United States Military Academy came into existence in 1802, the Navy lacked a similar training school for its
future officers for many years. The coming of steam and the
continuous improvements in gunnery made technical knowledge essential. In 1815 Congress provided for schoolmasters on
warships, but these civilian teachers had little authority.

At last the Naval Academy became a reality in 1845 at
Annapolis, Maryland. (During the Civil War years the school
was temporarily moved to Newport, Rhode Island.) Candidates
are selected in much the same way as for the Military Academy
(see stamp 789). The cadets follow a four-year course of studies
and are known as midshipmen; they graduate with a bachelor
of science degree and a commission of ensign in the Navy or
second lieutenant in the Marine Corps.

The program of studies offers a well-rounded combination
of general and technical subjects, stressing seamanship and navigation, ordnance and gunnery, marine engineering, and practical experience gained from summertime cruises on battleships,
airplane carriers, and destroyers.

The commemorative stamp features the official seal of the
Naval Academy, flanked by two cadets, one in a uniform of
1845, the other in a modern uniform.

Rufus Putnam
(1738-1824)
Manasseh Cutler
(1742-1823)

795 · 3¢ purple · 1937

In 1786 General Rufus Putnam, a distinguished Revolutionary soldier, formed the Ohio Company of Associates in Boston. The thousand members, all war veterans, each contributed one thousand dollars in Continental currency and ten dollars in gold and silver. (A Continental dollar was worth about eight cents.)

The Ohio Company's purchasing agent, the Reverend Manasseh Cutler, succeeded in buying a huge tract of some of the choicest public lands in Ohio on extremely favorable terms for the veterans.

While dealing with the Continental Congress, Cutler also recommended some of the admirable provisions of the Ordinance of 1787. The basic principle of this document was that the Northwest Territory was to be protected and developed and then made a part of the United States on an equal footing with the original thirteen states.

The ordinance guaranteed freedom of speech, press, and assembly, as well as universal male suffrage. It provided for the establishment of public schools, churches, and state universities, and forbade slavery.

In time, the Northwest Territory was carved up into the states of Ohio, Indiana, Michigan, Illinois, Wisconsin, and part of Minnesota.

350th Anniversary

796 · *5¢ blue* · *1937*

IN 1584 Sir Walter Raleigh took out a royal charter to found the first English colony in the New World. The expedition sent out by him landed at Roanoke Island, off the coast of North Carolina, and brought back enticing reports of "fruitfull and wholsome soil."

Three years later, Raleigh sent three vessels with one hundred and thirty colonists to settle on Roanoke Island. On August 18, 1587, Virginia Dare was born at Roanoke. She was the granddaughter of John White, governor of the colony, and she is believed to have been the first child of English parentage born in the New World.

When serious shortages developed at Roanoke, White decided to sail to England for aid. It was 1590 before he was able to return to Roanoke. When he did come back, he could find no trace of the colony.

Some historians have guessed that the colonists were massacred by Indians or went off somewhere and perished in the wilderness from exposure or disease. Others believe that the colony was wiped out by the jealous Spaniards, who had settlements not too far away. But no one knows for sure: to this day Roanoke remains the Lost Colony.

Signing of the Constitution

798 · 3¢ purple · 1937

AFTER THE American colonies declared their independence, the newly created states were exceedingly jealous of their freedoms and powers. They therefore devised a feeble compromise national government based on the Articles of Confederation.

The articles purposely left out a President and a judicial system. Power remained with the states. Congress could levy taxes but could not collect them. It could declare war but could not raise an army. No article could be changed without the unanimous consent of the states.

The Federal Constitution created by the Philadelphia Convention of 1787 was a vast improvement. It divided Congress into a Senate with equal representation for all states, and a House of Representatives with members elected on the basis of population. The new Constitution provided for a President to carry out the laws passed by Congress, and a judiciary to interpret the laws. Changes in the Constitution were possible by means of later amendments.

And so there was a happy ending to all the bickering. No wonder Thomas Jefferson spoke jubilantly of "changing a constitution by assembling the wise men of the state, instead of assembling armies."

Hawaiian Islands: Kamehameha I

799 · 3¢ purple · 1937

ABOUT 1780, a local chieftain named Kamehameha began extending his power throughout the islands of the Hawaiian Archipelago until he welded them into a single kingdom. He is remembered as Kamehameha the Great.

During the next century, the dynasty he founded was steadily weakened by outside influences. From 1820 on, American missionaries came to live on the islands, building schools, starting a newspaper, and translating the Bible into the Hawaiian language. The first sugar crop was grown in 1835, and, later on, the large-scale cultivation of pineapple and other fruits assured the prosperity of the islands.

The United States, Great Britain, and Germany were all interested in annexing Hawaii because of its strategic position in the Pacific. After some unrest in the islands, the United States annexed them in 1898 and gave them the status of a Territory two years later.

Few Americans realized the importance of Hawaii as a naval base until the Japanese attack on Pearl Harbor plunged the United States into World War II. In 1953 a bill was introduced in Congress proposing statehood for Hawaii. This bill was consolidated with the Alaska statehood bill in the Senate.

Alaska:
Mount McKinley

800 · 3¢ purple · 1937

WITH AN area of 586,400 square miles, Alaska is one-fifth the size of the United States and twice the size of Texas. As only 3 per cent of the area is always under snow and ice, Alaska's climate is milder than is generally believed. Much of the region is mountainous, and Mount McKinley, the highest point in North America, is 20,300 feet above sea level.

Alaska is one of the chief sources of furs for the American market. The rocky Pribilof Islands off the coast are the greatest seal breeding grounds in the world. For years the animals were butchered indiscriminately until the signing of an international treaty in 1911. Since then the seals have increased from one hundred thousand to well over two million.

The Yukon and Klondike gold rushes, toward the end of the nineteenth century, yielded some remarkably profitable claims. The Territory is also rich in many other kinds of minerals as well as timber and fisheries.

During World War II, Alaska took on great strategic importance with the building of the Alcan Highway and the construction of military bases. In 1953 a bill was introduced in Congress proposing statehood for Alaska. In the Senate, the bill was consolidated with the Hawaiian statehood bill at the insistence of the supporters of Alaskan statehood.

141

Puerto Rico: La Fortaleza

801 · 3¢ purple · 1937

PUERTO RICO is one of the most beautiful islands in the West Indies, though poverty and overpopulation have created some ugly slums.

Columbus visited the island on his second voyage in 1493. Some years later, the Spanish explorer Juan Ponce de León discovered gold on the island, and perhaps for that reason named his first settlement Puerto Rico ("Rich Port"). The Spaniards soon enslaved all the natives, and by the end of the sixteenth century there were no Indians left. The Spaniards then began importing Negro slaves from Africa.

Centuries of Spanish misrule led to the ruin of Puerto Rico's once rich soil and reduced most of the inhabitants to poverty. Like the people of nearby Cuba, they clamored for freedom and conspired against the government. During the Spanish-American War, U. S. forces quickly conquered the island.

After the Spanish-American War, Puerto Rico became an American Territory, with a governor appointed by the President. American citizenship rights were extended to all Puerto Ricans in 1917. How Puerto Rico achieved self-government is described in the discussion of stamp 983.

La Fortaleza, the governor's palace in San Juan, built by the Spaniards in 1529, appears on the commemorative stamp.

Virgin Islands: Charlotte Amalie

802 · 3¢ purple · 1937

THE VIRGIN ISLANDS, a group of sixty-eight islands in the Caribbean, were discovered and named by Columbus on his second voyage in 1493. They have had a picturesque colonial history, belonging at one time or another to France, England, and the Knights of Malta. In 1671 they came under Danish rule.

American statesmen were interested in the islands even before the Civil War. In 1867 Secretary of State Seward signed a treaty to buy the islands for seven and a half million dollars, a sum greater than the purchase price of Alaska. But within a month, an earthquake, a hurricane, and a tidal wave influenced the Senate against the deal. The treaty draft and two later ones were rejected.

Not until World War I, when the U-boat menace had become critical, did the purchase go through. But by then the price had gone up to twenty-five million dollars.

As the United States purchased the Virgin Islands for their strategic value in the Caribbean, they first came under the supervision of the Navy Department. In 1931 they were transferred to the Department of the Interior. Five years later the islands obtained a measure of self-government.

The commemorative stamp offers a view of the splendid harbor of Charlotte Amalie, the capital of the islands.

Colonial-Type Courthouse

835 · 3¢ purple · 1938

UNDER THE Articles of Confederation (see stamp 798), the new United States Constitution, prepared in 1787, had to be approved by the existing Congress and then ratified by all the states. This requirement spelled disaster, for the states were determined to hold on to their powers.

The Founding Fathers, well aware of these difficulties, suggested a radically different procedure. Each state was to approve or reject the Constitution through a specially elected ratifying convention. To by-pass the requirements for unanimous voting, the Constitutional Convention ruled that the new document should go into effect as soon as nine states had ratified it.

For months there was excited campaigning for and against the Constitution. The commemorative stamp gives us the feeling of those agitated times in its picture of two messengers leaving a colonial courthouse to spread the news that another state has ratified the Constitution.

On June 21, 1788, New Hampshire became the ninth state to ratify the Constitution, bringing the new government into existence. Virginia and New York soon added their favorable votes, but North Carolina and Rhode Island stubbornly held out. The threat of boycott finally brought them into the Union after Washington's inauguration in 1789.

Landing of the Swedes and Finns

836 · 3¢ purple · 1938

IN 1638 a small Swedish expedition arrived in the New World. Sailing up the Delaware River, the colonists built Fort Christina on the present site of Wilmington, Delaware. Though their settlement was destined to be a failure, the Swedes made a very valuable contribution to American pioneer life by introducing the log cabin, which had previously been unknown to the New World.

Throughout the life of the colony, the Swedes bickered with the Dutch over land claims. New Sweden never had much prospect of permanence; the homeland was too deeply involved in European wars and diplomatic maneuvers. While a fair number of Finns arrived in New Sweden, the Swedes were lukewarm about emigrating.

Under the circumstances, New Sweden's four hundred pound governor, Johan Printz, did a good job in maintaining the sparsely populated colony. In 1655 this colorful, shrewd, strong-willed leader had to bow to the superior Dutch forces of Peter Stuyvesant.

A few Swedes settled in Pennsylvania, and when William Penn founded Philadelphia in 1682, he found three Swedes living in the area. This is one of the many interesting sidelights of New Sweden's story of failure.

Statue by
Gutzon Borglum

837 · 3¢ purple · 1938

GENERAL RUFUS PUTNAM and the Reverend Manasseh Cutler (see stamp 795), the moving spirits of the Ohio Company of Associates, played a leading role in the founding of the first settlements in the Ohio Valley.

In April, 1788, Putnam led forty-eight men on flatboats to the mouth of the Muskingum River, on the Ohio. The group, which included surveyors and carpenters, built a stockade on this site, and the settlement was named Marietta, after the French Queen Marie Antoinette.

Three months later, Marietta became the first capital of the newly formed Northwest Territory, with General Arthur St. Clair as its first governor. Later on, Marietta developed into one of the most important shipping points on the Ohio River.

In the early days of the first settlements, life was very hard on the Ohio frontier. The possibility of an Indian raid was always present, and a peaceful farm might be transformed into a fortress at a moment's notice. Gutzon Borglum's statue, which appears on the commemorative stamp, is a tribute to the pioneers who braved these hardships.

General Anthony Wayne's victory at Fallen Timbers in 1794 (stamp 680) crushed the Indians. From then on, more and more settlers poured into the now peaceful Ohio region.

Territorial
Capitol

838 · 3¢ purple · 1938

IOWA is so famous for the extraordinary fertility of its soil that the slow pace of its early settlement seems puzzling at first sight. The explanation lies in the fact that the first white men who came to Iowa were not farmers.

René Robert de La Salle claimed the Iowa region for France in 1682. Yet for the next one hundred and twenty years it remained Indian country; the French were interested in furs, not farming. Julien Dubuque, generally considered the first permanent white settler in Iowa, came there in 1788 to mine lead. At the time of the Louisiana Purchase in 1803, Iowa had less than fifty white men.

From 1820 on, the factors favoring settlement gradually asserted themselves. Steamboats began to ply the Missouri River. The Black Hawk War of 1832 broke the power of the Indians, and white settlement became reasonably safe.

By 1836 there were ten thousand pioneers living in Iowa. A steady stream of settlers was heading for the region, and many new towns were being founded. In 1838 Iowa became a territory, with its capital first at Burlington and then at Iowa City. A public school system began in 1839, and colleges and universities were also founded with remarkable rapidity. The capitol building appears on the commemorative stamp.

147

Tower of the Sun

852 · 3¢ purple · 1939

THE GOLDEN GATE INTERNATIONAL EX-
POSITION opened in 1939 to celebrate the
completion of the Golden Gate Bridge
and San Francisco-Oakland Bay Bridge.
The bridge that crosses the Golden Gate is the highest in the
world; it towers to the height of a 65-story building. The Golden
Gate Bridge has an over-all length of 8,940 feet, and its over-
water span of 4200 feet is the world's longest.

The San Francisco-Oakland Bay Bridge is the most difficult
and complex bridge ever built and the most expensive ($77,-
200,000). It is actually a series of bridges with a total length
of over eight miles.

To house the Golden Gate Exposition, San Francisco built
Treasure Island, a 400-acre man-made island in San Francisco
Bay. When the Exposition was over, the island was converted
into an airport.

About twenty countries bordering on the Pacific took part
in the exposition, which was distinguished for its picturesque
architecture, brilliant lighting, and handsome masses of flowers.
The special stamp, which has been called the most artistic of
the whole commemorative series, features the 400-foot Tower of
the Sun, the exposition's distinctive landmark.

148

Trylon and Perisphere

853 · *3¢ purple* · *1939*

MOST EXPOSITIONS have been held to celebrate a period of power and prosperity.
The New York World's Fair, however,
was conceived to bring the city out of the
psychological doldrums of the Great Depression. The fair slogan
was "The World of Tomorrow with the Tools of Today."

Sprawling over twelve hundred acres at Flushing Meadows
on Long Island, the fair took two years to build at a cost of
$156,000,000. Thirty-three nations, plus Puerto Rico, were
represented, and foreign countries issued about one hundred
stamps commemorating the Fair.

Much of the architecture flaunted strikingly ultramodern
lines, with garish, eye-catching colors and designs. Outstanding
were the national buildings and such structures as the Glass
Building with its shimmering tower, the Food Building with its
ornate façade, and the Hall of Fashion and the Home of Jewels
with their lavish exhibits.

The Trylon, seven hundred feet high, and the massive ball-
shaped Perisphere, were the landmarks of the World's Fair.
These two structures, which received more comment than any
other feature of the fair, furnished the theme for the commemorative stamp.

149

Washington Taking the Oath of Office

854 · 3¢ purple · 1939

WHEN GEORGE WASHINGTON wearily laid down the burden of commanding the American army in 1783, he looked forward longingly to a pleasant life of retirement at his beloved Mount Vernon. Yet six years later he was unanimously chosen the first President of the United States.

On his way to New York, then the country's capital, a bustling metropolis of thirty-five thousand, Washington was filled with misgivings about the difficult task ahead of him.

When he appeared on the balcony of Federal Hall in Wall Street on April 30, 1789, he was extremely pale and obviously trembling. Someone offered him a chair and he sat down gratefully. Then he rose, and Chancellor Robert R. Livingston administered the Presidential oath.

After the ceremony, the crowd cheered its idol as church bells tolled and guns boomed at the Battery. Then Washington entered the Senate chamber, and in a faint voice read his inaugural address from the paper in his shaking hands.

Yet Washington's admirers had made no mistake. Despite his misgivings, he guided the young nation through its early trials with the same integrity, firmness, and moderation he had shown in the Revolution.

Youngsters
Playing Baseball

855 · 3¢ purple · 1939

ACCORDING TO a widely-accepted theory, Abner Doubleday (1819-1893) invented the game of baseball at Cooperstown, New York, in 1839. Though the town has a Baseball Museum and Hall of Fame in his honor, painstaking students have proved that Doubleday had little or nothing to do with baseball. They point out that he never claimed to have invented baseball; the claim was made for him about fifteen years after his death.

Whatever its origin, baseball soon took a strong hold on the imagination of Americans. The earliest team game seems to have been played on June 19, 1845, between the Knickerbockers and the New York Nine. By 1866 there were already over two hundred clubs.

The Cincinnati Red Stockings were the first professional team. Apparently they outclassed their opposition by a wide margin; in 1869 they won sixty-four games in a row—a record never equaled.

The National League came into existence in 1876, the American League in 1901. The first World Series to determine national supremacy took place in 1903. As the outstanding event of the baseball season, the World Series arouses more interest than any other sports event of the year.

151

25th Anniversary of the Official Opening

856 · 3¢ purple · 1939

EARLY IN 1907, President Theodore Roosevelt appointed Colonel George Washington Goethals (1858-1928) chief engineer of the Panama Canal.

Two other engineers had already proved unequal to this formidable assignment (see stamp 398), which included digging the famous Culebra Cut through a mountain. Here it was necessary to empty out almost one hundred million cubic yards of dirt to form a gap eight miles long, three hundred feet deep, and seventy-three feet wide.

However, Goethal's superiors had great faith in him. "Whatever I gave him to do," said one man who knew him well, "I relieved my mind of it. I knew it would be done right." That was why Goethals received the Panama Canal assignment.

Goethals was more than a great engineer; he was a great leader of men. Realizing full well that men are even more important than machines, he gave standing orders that workmen were to be spoken to courteously at all times. Building the "Big Ditch" required the cooperation of thousands of men; therefore, said Goethals, "to successfully accomplish anything, it is necessary not only that you shall give it the best that is in you, but that you should obtain for it the best there is in those who are under your guidance."

Introduction of Printing in Colonial America

857 · 3¢ purple · 1939

IN 1639 Stephen Daye established the first printing press in Colonial America by bringing a press from England to Cambridge, Massachusetts. For a time the press remained in the home of Henry Dunster, first president of Harvard College. Later on, Daye set up the Cambridge Press, the earliest printing plant in the colonies.

Old-time presses were hand operated, and it took a powerful man to press down the lever. For many years, presses and even ink had to be imported from England. The first American-made presses did not appear until 1750; type was not cast in the colonies until 1768.

The most famous of all colonial printers was Benjamin Franklin—printer's devil, typesetter, newspaper editor, author, bookseller, librarian, and publisher. Franklin paid special attention to the quality of his ink, paper, and type metal, and was admired for the elegant appearance of his printed page. Even more important was Franklin's clear understanding of the valuable part played by newspapers in creating a national feeling in the colonies.

The chief feature of the commemorative stamp is a reproduction of Stephen Daye's press.

50th Anniversary of North Dakota, South Dakota, Montana, and Washington

858 · 3¢ purple · 1939

IN 1889 four new states entered the Union. Two of them were carved out of the Dakota Territory, which had been created in 1861. North Dakota, the thirty-ninth state, remains sparsely settled to this day, having only four towns with a population of more than ten thousand people.

South Dakota, the fortieth state, is also thinly populated. In 1876 it experienced a boisterous influx of fortune hunters when gold was discovered in the Black Hills. Farming and ranching possibilities were the attractions for later settlers.

Montana, the forty-first state, has immense resources of mineral wealth. Its capital, Helena, was originally called Last Chance Gulch because a group of prospectors made a rich gold strike there after having given up all hope. However, most Montana gold was well below the surface and could be extracted only by expensive machinery.

Washington, the forty-second state, had become a Territory in 1853. Its early history is described under stamp 1019. Railroad communication did not come to Washington until the 1880's, when Washington's population increased almost 400 per cent.

The commemorative stamp features an outline map, with the names and locations of the new capitals.

Washington Irving
(1783-1859)

859 • 1¢ green • 1940

WHILE STILL a young man, Washington Irving made his reputation as a leading American writer when he published his *A History of New York* in 1809 under the pseudonym of Diedrich Knickerbocker.

In this remarkably successful book, Irving poked gentle fun at the Dutch burghers of New Amsterdam and displayed a delightful sense of humor that endeared him to English as well as American readers. Irving became the first American writer to win acclaim in Europe, and for this reason Americans took a patriotic pride in his success.

In later years, Irving served with the American embassy at Madrid and was minister to Spain from 1842 to 1846. The Spanish scene appealed to him, and it was during this period that he wrote his biography of Columbus and retold the picturesque old Moorish legends in *The Alhambra*. He also wrote a five-volume biography of George Washington in addition to books about his travels in Europe and the Far West.

Though Irving's collected works fill many volumes, he is remembered today for *Rip Van Winkle* and *The Legend of Sleepy Hollow*, two stories that retain a lasting place in American literature.

James Fenimore Cooper
(1789-1851)

860 • 2¢ red • 1940

JAMES FENIMORE COOPER's childhood near Lake Otsego, in New York, was an exceptionally happy one. His boyhood adventures included meetings with woodsmen and trappers, and their tales of Indian and Revolutionary warfare held the impressionable boy spellbound.

Many years later, without any previous training as a writer, Cooper undertook, on his wife's dare, to write a novel. It was a failure, but his next one, *The Spy,* a story with a Revolutionary setting, was an international success.

Now launched on a notable career, Cooper wrote more than thirty novels. The most successful were the Leather-Stocking Tales, a series of five books including *The Deerslayer* and *The Last of the Mohicans.* For the central figure in these stories, Cooper chose Natty Bumppo, a magnificent fictional frontiersman who was thoroughly at home in the wilderness, far from towns and cities.

To Europeans chafed by class restraints and conventions, these books had an even stronger appeal than to Cooper's own countrymen. Though Cooper's vogue has passed, his Leather-Stocking series remains a superb symbol of the freedom of the frontier.

Ralph Waldo Emerson
(1803-1882)
861 · 3¢ purple · 1940

RALPH WALDO EMERSON, whose ancestors came to Concord, Massachusetts, in 1635, was descended from a long line of scholars and preachers who loved learning and despised riches. It is said that Emerson was forty-seven years old when he received his first check and he had to be shown how to endorse it. His ancestors would have approved such unworldliness.

For almost sixty years Emerson lived in the little town, turning it, by his distinguished presence, into the intellectual capital of America. Aided by a small legacy, he made a living from his lectures.

Though Emerson was an intimate of philosophers, he addressed his lectures to ordinary folk. He had a knack of expressing sublime thoughts in simple language; at the same time, his delightful turn of fancy and flair for the vivid phrase lighted up even the most familiar subject.

Though Emerson modestly described his lectures as "peddling my literary pack of notions," he was an inspiring speaker. His radiance and serenity impressed even scoffers, and his pithy wisdom had the saving grace of humor. Once, when a fanatic told him the world was coming to an end, Emerson replied, "I'm glad to hear it. Man will get along better without it."

Louisa May Alcott

(1832-1888)

862 • 5¢ blue • 1940

BRONSON ALCOTT, Louisa May Alcott's father, was rich in unworldly wisdom but poor in worldly goods. He liked to ponder philosophical problems, but the art of making a dollar was a complete mystery to him. His daughter described him as "a man up in a balloon, with his family and friends holding the ropes which confine him to earth, and trying to draw him down."

Though Louisa loved children, she never married because, while still a young girl, she had to shoulder the burden of supporting her family. She worked as a governess, a seamstress, even as a servant.

During the Civil War, Louisa was a nurse at the Union hospital in Georgetown, Virginia. Her vivid descriptions of wounded soldiers in a book called *Hospital Sketches* established her as a notable writer.

Louisa wrote her most famous book, *Little Women,* in response to her publisher's request for a "girls' story." She owed a great deal to the immediate members of her family for the material of the book, which she wrote in twelve weeks in a furious blaze of creative activity. The book made her famous overnight. Reprinted in countless editions, it still retains its popularity, and has twice served as the subject of successful films.

Samuel Langhorne Clemens
(1835-1910)

863 · 10¢ brown · 1940

DURING HIS days as a reporter in the wild mining towns of Nevada in the 1860's Sam Clemens changed his name to Mark Twain. This was a term used by Mississippi River pilots; it meant two fathoms—twelve feet—safe depth for a steamboat. His pen name was to become much better known than his real name.

Young Sam Clemens spent several years as a journeyman printer and then achieved the great ambition of his life, to become a pilot on a Mississippi steamboat. The next four years were exciting ones for him, described later in his nostalgic *Life on the Mississippi*.

Afterwards, Sam sought a different kind of excitement by trying his luck as a prospector in Nevada. Hard experience proved that he was not cut out to be a miner.

Soon, he became a reporter. His writing, factual or imaginative, had a humorous twist that enchanted his readers. He turned his talent for tall tales to good effect by lecturing to packed houses. Eventually he came East, where he wrote the books that brought him fame and wealth. *Tom Sawyer* and *Huckleberry Finn*, which grew out of his childhood experiences in a small town on the banks of a great river, are but two of the books for which Mark Twain is remembered today.

Henry Wadsworth Longfellow

(1807-1882)

864 · 1¢ green · 1940

AFTER HIS graduation from Bowdoin College, Henry Wadsworth Longfellow traveled widely in Europe, obtaining an extensive knowledge of French, Spanish, Italian, Portuguese, and German literature. Although these studies profoundly stimulated his poetic imagination, his career as a poet was very slow in getting under way. Described as "probably the most accomplished scholar in America," he devoted himself to teaching for twenty-five years.

When Longfellow at last turned to writing, he soon became America's best-loved poet. The simplest proof of his enduring popularity is the familiar ring of famous lines from such poems as *The Village Blacksmith, Paul Revere's Ride,* and *Evangeline.*

The Song of Hiawatha, perhaps the most popular of all of Longfellow's poems, has received the tribute of imitation and parody. Though it sounds like a translation of Indian speech, its repetitive, hypnotic quality stems from the meter of the *Kalevala,* the Finnish epic, deeply admired by Longfellow.

Translations of Longfellow's works in all the modern tongues made him known over the world—very appropriately, for his melodious lines ranged over many subjects and settings.

John Greenleaf Whittier
(1807-1892)

865 · 2¢ red · 1940

WHEN WE hear Whittier's name, we think of *The Barefoot Boy,* with its famous opening lines:

> Blessings on thee, little man,
> Barefoot boy, with cheek of tan!

Whittier is also remembered as the poet of the serene and simple life on the farm as he pictured it in his best-loved work, *Snowbound.*

But pleasant reminiscence is only one aspect of Whittier's poetry. As a "fighting Quaker," he wrote many poems of passionate protest against Negro slavery. For years he was one of the outstanding writers of the Abolitionist movement.

When Whittier was eighteen, he made slippers and sold them for eight cents a pair, earning enough to see him through two terms at Haverhill Academy. "He calculated so closely every item of expense that he knew before the beginning of the term he would have twenty-five cents to spare at its close, and he actually had."

From these humble beginnings, Whittier's wide reading stimulated his natural expressiveness until he developed into a poet second only to Longfellow in popularity.

James Russell Lowell

(1819-1891)

866 · 3¢ purple · 1940

JAMES RUSSELL LOWELL, one of America's most distinguished men of letters, was an outstanding figure of that glorious period of New England literature that produced the works of Longfellow, Emerson, Thoreau, Hawthorne, Whittier, and Holmes, as well as the histories of Motley and Prescott.

Lowell was trained for the law but turned to a literary career after the success of his first volume of poetry. He was still in his twenties when he wrote *The Biglow Papers,* a highly popular satire in Yankee dialect on some of the foibles of his day.

In 1856 Lowell was appointed professor of modern literature at Harvard, and a year later he became the first editor of *The Atlantic Monthly.* Lowell rounded out a notable career as minister to Spain and minister to England. Though in his youth he had enjoyed tweaking the British Lion's tail, he later helped to create friendlier relations between the United States and England.

Lowell had an extraordinary feeling for language. Though his Latin was as fluent as his English, he prided himself on his sensitive ear for Yankee speech. The best poetry, as he put it, came from "the tongue of the people in the mouth of the scholar."

Walt Whitman

(1819-1892)

867 · 5¢ blue · 1940

As A young man, Walt Whitman worked at a bewildering variety of jobs. But there were times when he wanted to "loafe and invite my soul."

In 1855 he published the first edition of *Leaves of Grass,* his major work. Though Ralph Waldo Emerson admired the poems, most people were shocked by what Whitman humorously called his "rude barbaric yawp."

When the Civil War broke out, Whitman devoted himself to tending the wounded. "He seemed to leave a benediction at every cot as he passed along." But the strain proved too much for him and resulted in permanent injury to his health.

The assassination of Abraham Lincoln, whom Whitman idolized, inspired him to write *O Captain! My Captain!* and *When Lilacs Last in the Dooryard Bloom'd,* two of the most haunting expressions of grief ever penned.

In 1873 Whitman had a paralytic stroke from which he never quite recovered. His admirers bought him a tiny house in Camden, New Jersey. Here "the good gray poet," mellow despite poor health and slowly ebbing strength, spent his last years surrounded by friends, the neighbors' children, and the unsold copies of his poems.

James Whitcomb Riley
(1849-1916)

868 • 10¢ brown • 1940

THE MAN who became famous and successful as the "Hoosier Poet" took a long time to discover what his lifework was to be. He tried his hand at selling Bibles, painting signs, and entertaining with banjo and guitar and mimicking.

When he was twenty-eight, Riley found a job as editor and reporter for a country paper. He wrote most of his items in verse and, in his own wry words, "in a few months strangled the little thing into a change of ownership."

Soon, Riley began publishing poetry in the Indianapolis *Journal.* His lectures became more and more popular, and his collections of poems, such as *The Old Swimmin' Hole,* were best-sellers. His public readings of his works were very successful, despite his talent for missing a train or getting on the wrong one.

Riley's poems, written in Hoosier dialect about the people of Indiana's farms and small towns, had elements of sentiment, drollery, and pathos that appealed to children as well as their elders. In an age of industrialization and far-reaching change, Riley's gentle and whimsical portrayal of bygone times and simple pleasures enabled millions of Americans to relive their childhood and youth.

Horace Mann

(1796-1859)

869 · 1¢ green · 1940

HORACE MANN, the "father of the American public-school system," had a poverty-stricken, unhappy childhood, harried by the harsh discipline of his teachers.

Nevertheless, he was a brilliant pupil. Later he became a successful lawyer. In 1837 he was elected to the Massachusetts legislature and was soon appointed secretary of the Massachusetts Educational Board.

School structures were desperately inadequate; teachers poorly paid and hopelessly untrained; the curriculum was stodgy, the discipline bleak. The school term was often only two months long, and fully one-third of the children had no schooling at all.

Mann was determined to improve conditions. He started the first American schools for training teachers; he educated public opinion by means of annual conventions and reports and by his publication of the *Common School Journal*. To study the best methods of teaching, he went to Europe.

Through Mann's efforts, teachers' salaries were substantially increased, new schools were built, teaching standards were improved. In all his work for education, Mann was animated by this thought: "Be ashamed to die until you have won some victory for humanity."

Mark Hopkins
(1802-1887)

870 · 2¢ red · 1940

SPEAKING OF his undergraduate days at Williams College, President Garfield once remarked that the ideal university consisted of a log with Mark Hopkins at one end and himself at the other end.

This homely figure of speech tells us something of Hopkins's simplicity and effectiveness as a teacher. In all the years that he was president of the college, from 1836 to 1872, he had no use for harsh discipline. He taught philosophy, ethics, and other courses for fifty-one years without ever insisting on compulsory attendance or taking the trouble to keep records of absences.

Hopkins felt that if he could not interest his students, they were under no obligation to attend. Actually, he ran little risk of being neglected; his classes were so absorbing that even dullards could not stay away. To Hopkins, book learning mattered less than independent thinking and the clash of diverse opinions.

The benign influence of Hopkins was one that students felt for the rest of their lives. That is why he is remembered as one of the outstanding American educators of the nineteenth century.

Charles William Eliot

(1834-1926)

871 · *3¢ purple* · *1940*

CHARLES W. ELIOT was the most original and influential American educator of his time.

During his term of office as president of Harvard University from 1869 to 1909, Eliot was a brilliant administrative success. The university's enrollment increased from a thousand to four thousand, the faculty roster from sixty to six hundred, and the endowment fund rose from approximately two and a half million to twenty million dollars. More graduate schools were established at Harvard, and their professional standards were raised considerably. Entrance requirements became stricter.

As an educational reformer Eliot was even more outstanding. His fundamental aim was to minimize discipline from outside sources and to help students develop self-reliance and a sense of responsibility. To achieve these ends, Eliot relied on the honor system, greatly widened the scope of elective courses, and even made chapel attendance optional instead of compulsory.

Eliot was equally solicitous for the welfare of his faculty; he introduced the sabbatical year and exchange professorships and fought hard for increased salaries and pensions. After his retirement from Harvard at the age of seventy-five, Eliot devoted his remaining years to the cause of world peace.

Frances Elizabeth Willard

(1839-1898)

872 • 5¢ blue • 1940

AFTER TEACHING school for several years, Frances Willard held administrative positions in a number of girls' schools. Although she did her work well, she felt dissatisfied with herself.

In 1874 she discovered her lifework when she joined the Woman's Christian Temperance Union. Until her death she continued to head this organization that gave her a cause in which she believed passionately and which absorbed all her energies. In every way she knew, she fought the evil of heavy drinking that had brought on the ruin of thousands of families.

Often she would go with other women to saloons, singing hymns and kneeling on the sawdust-covered floor to recite prayers and thus redeem hardened drinkers from their sinful ways. On her speaking tours for the Woman's Christian Temperance Union, she visited every state and territory in the Union. During a period of ten years she averaged a meeting a day.

Even those who disagreed with Frances Willard respected the deep sincerity that animated all her work for the cause of prohibition. In 1905 the state of Illinois placed her statue in the Capitol at Washington. She is the only woman who has been honored in this way.

Booker Taliaferro Washington
(1856-1915)

873 · 10¢ brown · 1940

BOOKER T. WASHINGTON, born a slave in Virginia, became one of America's leading educators.

In 1881, when Washington was only twenty-five, he was appointed principal of Tuskegee Institute, in Alabama. His arrival in Tuskegee was a keen disappointment when he found the school had no land, no buildings, no equipment. Nevertheless, he started school with thirty pupils in a run-down shanty and an abandoned Negro Methodist church.

Over the years, Washington's incredibly hard work for Tuskegee brought amazing results. The student body increased to two thousand, while the school gradually built up an endowment fund of almost two million dollars. Grounds were increased to two thousand acres, with upwards of a hundred buildings—most of them constructed by the students. One after another, schools of agriculture, business, education, home economics, nursing, music, dietetics, veterinary medicine, and aviation made their appearance.

Up From Slavery, Washington's beautifully written autobiography, gives an unforgettable description of his work for Tuskegee. To this day the Institute remains one of the towering achievements of American educational activity.

169

John James Audubon
(1785?-1851)

874 • 1¢ green • 1940

AFTER SPENDING his childhood and early youth in France, John James Audubon came to the United States. For many years he wandered along the Florida coasts, in Maine and New Brunswick, through the Great Lakes country, and up and down the Mississippi valley. In all these regions he spent happy hours observing and sketching birds and other creatures of the wild. Vivid yet exact, his writings as well as his chalk drawings and water colors reflect his enthusiasm and affection for the abundant wildlife that has disappeared since his day.

Audubon devoted much of his life to the preparation of *Birds of America,* a collection of his magnificent pictures. To publish this work, he spent twelve years securing subscriptions at one thousand dollars apiece and raising money by selling his paintings. For some of these paintings he received as little as five dollars.

Prepared with much loving toil at a cost of more than a hundred thousand dollars, *Birds of America* finally appeared in 1838. It proved an immediate success, but it is saddening to think that Audubon, who loved the outdoors more than anything else, had to spend years far from "the forest primeval" to raise the funds for his publishing venture.

Crawford Williamson Long
(1817-1878)

875 · 2¢ red · 1940

BY A cruel paradox, the work of the surgeon and the dentist was a curse as well as a blessing to the human race for centuries. Nowadays, we accept anesthesia as a matter of course; we find it difficult to realize that up to the middle of the nineteenth century unfortunate patients suffered excruciating agonies.

Though feasible anesthetics had been proposed as early as 1799, the suggestions were ignored. At last, in 1842, Crawford W. Long, an obscure but capable physician of Jefferson, Georgia, hit on the idea of using ether during an operation. He was quite successful in sparing his patient any pain.

In later operations, Dr. Long continued to use ether with success—without bothering to publish his findings until 1849. Meanwhile, Dr. William Morton of Boston convincingly demonstrated the value of ether at the Massachusetts General Hospital in 1844.

For years, a bitter controversy raged as to which of these two men deserved credit for the discovery of anesthesia. Their claims have since been reconciled in this way: Dr. Long is acknowledged to have pioneered in the *use* of ether, while Dr. Morton is remembered as the first man to demonstrate to the medical profession the effectiveness of ether as a pain-killer.

Luther Burbank

(1849-1926)

876 · 3¢ purple · 1940

MILLIONS OF people all over the world have benefited by Luther Burbank's amazing successes in breeding over two hundred improved kinds of plants. Burbank did astonishing things with trees, fruits, vegetables, and flowers. By crossbreeding different varieties, he combined the good features of each and eliminated their unsatisfactory qualities.

From early boyhood Burbank enjoyed working with plants. When he was twenty-one he bought a farm and became a truck gardener. About this time he read a book by Charles Darwin which inspired his lifework of improving plant varieties.

Outstanding among Burbank's early achievements was the Burbank potato—larger, sturdier, and more nourishing than any previously known. Today, the crop of this one vegetable is valued at millions of dollars. And in the case of the plum, Burbank transformed it from a small sour fruit with a rather large pit to the delicious fruit that we enjoy today.

Burbank gave twenty years of patient and persistent effort to perfecting the spineless cactus. Such devotion was typical of his long, useful career. But usefulness was not always his goal. He helped make the world around us more beautiful through his work with roses, petunias, and other lovely flowers.

Walter Reed
(1851-1902)

877 · 5¢ blue · 1940

YELLOW FEVER used to take a fearful toll: during severe epidemics, as many as eighty out of a hundred stricken with the dread disease would not survive. In the Spanish-American War, more American soldiers were killed by "yellow jack" than by enemy bullets.

Once the war was over, American rehabilitation work in Cuba met a stubborn obstacle: Havana was one of the worst spots subject to yellow fever. In 1900, United States authorities decided to fight the disease through a Yellow Fever Commission headed by Dr. Walter Reed, a major in the Medical Corps.

Several attempts to control the fever proved futile. At last, Reed acted on the belief of Dr. Carlos Finlay, a noted Cuban doctor, that the virus of yellow fever was transmitted by mosquitoes. To test Finlay's theory, Reed had to infect heroic volunteers with the dangerous disease.

Reed's daring experiments finally established that the fever is transmitted by the female *Aëdes* mosquito. By destroying the breeding places of this insect, the Army Medical Corps freed Cuba from the grip of yellow fever for the first time in centuries. Reed did not live to see work started on the Panama Canal, but his researches made it possible to construct the "Big Ditch."

Jane Addams
(1860-1935)

878 · 10¢ brown · 1940

JANE ADDAMS, called the "best-loved woman in the world," opened the first American settlement house in 1889 in one of Chicago's worst slum areas. The building was surrounded by a livery stable, a junk yard, a saloon, a funeral parlor—and of course many run-down tenements.

For weeks, no neighbor ventured inside Hull House. The people were shy, suspicious, fearful. Very slowly and patiently, Jane Addams wore down their distrust by making friends with their children and helping them with their housework.

Cleaning up the neighborhood streets was the first of her many crusades. At one spot where she swept and dug, she removed eighteen inches of rubbish before striking pavement.

To help her neighbors of thirty-six nationalities, Jane Addams started a nursery, a gymnasium, a doctors' and nurses' visiting service, a coal-buying cooperative, a public library, free concerts, art and music classes—and many other services.

In time, Jane Addams turned to the international scene, though she never forgot her immediate neighbors and friends. In 1931 she received the Nobel Peace Prize. Her work lived on after her, for Hull House has been the model for many other settlement houses.

Stephen Collins Foster
(1826-1864)

879 · 1¢ green · 1940

STEPHEN FOSTER, who wrote some of America's most popular songs, is the most tragic figure in the history of American music. Completely lacking any business sense, Foster gave away his best songs or realized next to nothing on them. Though he lived in poverty, he made fortunes for other men.

Foster knew little about classical music, but was inspired by Negro music from early childhood: the spirituals he heard in Negro churches, the chanteys sung by Negro roustabouts on the Pittsburgh wharves, the comic songs that contributed to the popularity of minstrel shows. Most of the many songs he composed in his short life were in Negro dialect.

Oh! Susanna, one of Foster's earliest successes, became the theme song of the forty-niners as they braved hunger, thirst, Indians, wild beasts, and other perils in their often futile quest for riches. The publisher made thousands from the song, while Foster was paid off in free copies. This was the story of many of his successes.

As time went on, he was unable to support his wife and child. Thirty-eight cents was the sum total of his worldly goods when he died, yet the melodies he created out of his unhappiness have been enjoyed by countless people.

John Philip Sousa

(1854-1932)

880 · 2¢ red · 1940

JOHN PHILIP SOUSA'S musical gifts were so outstanding that when he was thirteen he was conducting his own band. It was at this time that he joined the United States Marine Band as an apprentice player.

Sousa became the conductor of the Marine Band before he was thirty. By constant rehearsals, careful arrangements of suitable music, and the magnetic force of his attractive personality, Sousa built up the band into a world-famous organization. After twelve years with the Marine Corps, he retired to form his own band.

Sousa was an outstanding showman and had a gift for making friends quickly. Personal contacts with his appreciative audiences meant so much to him that he could never reconcile himself to the age of "canned music."

For many years Sousa toured the United States and Europe, giving pleasure to millions of people with his brilliant arrangements of his own marches. He composed over a hundred of these; the best known are *Semper Fidelis, The Washington Post,* and *The Stars and Stripes Forever.* Such marches—joyous and bursting with energy—earned Sousa the title of the "March King."

Victor Herbert

(1859-1924)

881 · 3¢ purple · 1940

VICTOR HERBERT was born in Ireland, brought up in England, given his musical education in Germany, and acclaimed as a success in the United States.

Herbert was long known as a fine cello player, but years passed before he started to compose music—on the suggestion of an acquaintance. Throughout his career there were to be other slow starts followed by remarkable swiftness in mastering whatever new task he set himself.

Herbert came to the United States at the age of twenty-seven when his beautiful wife was hired to sing at the Metropolitan Opera. For years Herbert devoted himself to performing serious music. Not until he was thirty-five did he begin writing the tuneful operettas which made him America's favorite composer: *The Wizard of the Nile, Babes in Toyland, Naughty Marietta, Mlle. Modiste,* and many others.

Herbert was a stout, genial man, fond of good food and comfortable living. Despite his easygoing ways, he was a hard worker; there was a period when he composed four operettas at one time, working at four desks in one room. Yet, harried as Herbert may have been at times, his music remained fresh and melodious as ever.

177

Edward Alexander MacDowell

(1861-1908)

882 · 5¢ blue · 1940

WHEN EDWARD MACDOWELL was fifteen years old, he entered the Paris Conservatory of Music to develop his gifts as a pianist and composer.

Before this handsome and brilliant young American was twenty, he had composed a concerto abounding in pianistic fireworks. Though painfully shy, young MacDowell was persuaded to bring the composition to Franz Liszt. Liszt, then a very old man, heard MacDowell play, and rewarded him with generous praise for his promising composition and outstanding performance.

MacDowell returned to his native land in his middle twenties, admired and deeply respected for his European reputation as one of the leading pianists of the age. He accepted the post of Professor of Music at Columbia University, a rare honor for such a young man.

After MacDowell's death, his widow turned their Peterboro, New Hampshire, home into a retreat where outstanding American artists, writers, and composers have done some of their best work. Edward MacDowell will always be honored as the first American musical artist to achieve recognition in the Old World.

Ethelbert Nevin

(1862-1901)

883 · 10¢ brown · 1940

THOUGH ETHELBERT NEVIN was already writing songs during his college days, he got off to a very slow start as a serious music student. The boy's father opposed a musical career for his son, and young Nevin had to wait until he was twenty to study the piano in earnest.

Forced to devote much of his time to dull drilling that should have been disposed of in childhood, Nevin often gave way to discouragement and boredom. Nevertheless, the pleasant times he enjoyed in Europe brought him back to his work with renewed zeal.

Nevin's career paralleled that of MacDowell to some extent, for Nevin completed his European musical studies with distinction and then returned to his native land to become a successful composer. One listener described their piano styles in this way: "MacDowell plays more like the devil; Nevin plays like a poet."

The Rosary, which Nevin wrote as a gift for his mother, has sold more copies than any other song ever written. His *Narcissus* was played so often that Nevin disgustedly called it "that nasty little *Narcissus.*" *Little Boy Blue* and *Mighty Lak' a Rose* are among the other tuneful Nevin melodies that will probably never lose their fascination for Americans.

179

Gilbert Charles Stuart

(1755-1828)

884 • 1¢ green • 1940

ON THE eve of the American Revolution, Gilbert Stuart left his native America for England. He remained there from 1775 to 1793, building up a reputation as one of the finest portrait painters of his day.

Stuart was well paid but he was deplorably extravagant. Once, when he was imprisoned for debt, he painted enough portraits to pay for his release. He was admired for his wit, and distinguished people sought him out for the charm of his conversation. Yet eventually he decided to leave England in order to paint the portrait of the greatest American of his day.

In 1793 Stuart returned to the United States to paint George Washington's portrait. Actually, Stuart did several portraits of our first President, and they are well represented in stamp issues. Stuart portraits of Washington appear on two stamps of the Washington Bicentennial issue (see stamps 707 and 715).

The most famous portrait of all was used on the 10¢ stamp of the first United States issue in 1847 and has since been used repeatedly; see stamps 947 and 982 for two examples. This is the portrait of which Mark Twain said, "If George Washington should rise from the dead, and should not resemble the Stuart portrait, he would be denounced as an impostor!"

James Abbott McNeill Whistler

(1834-1903)

885 · 2¢ red · 1940

WHISTLER WENT to Paris at the age of twenty-one to study art. He never saw his native land again, living in London for the rest of his life.

Whistler's unconventional art owed much to Japanese influence. His favorite subject, to which he returned repeatedly, was the Thames at night. Partly because he loved to mystify people, he called his pictures nocturnes, symphonies, and arrangements. He gave one of these provocative titles to his most famous painting, the portrait of his mother (see stamp 737).

On another occasion Whistler did a painting of two little girls which he called *Symphony in White, No. III,* although there was no white in it. In this way he achieved notoriety and irritated the critics.

Whistler devoted almost as much time to controversy as he did to painting, using arguments that were often witty and sometimes cruel. He was impudent, cynical, and fond of shocking people; insults, quarrels, and lawsuits were his special delight.

Eventually, Whistler recorded his favorite insults in a book he called *The Gentle Art of Making Enemies.* It was a subject on which he wrote with authority.

Augustus Saint-Gaudens
(1848-1907)

886 · 3¢ purple · 1940

AUGUSTUS SAINT-GAUDENS, the most noted American sculptor of his day, was born in Dublin and brought to this country as an infant. He had a French father and an Irish mother.

Saint-Gaudens obtained his early art training by attending Cooper Institute and the National Academy of Design at night, while working by day as a cameo cutter. In 1867, reversing the usual process of immigrants coming to the New World, the young man went to Europe as a steerage passenger.

The Renaissance masterpieces of Italy made a deep impression on him and opened up new vistas. Yet instead of using classical themes, he began a *Hiawatha*. After several years of poverty, hard study, and harder work in Paris and Rome, he gradually achieved recognition. His Lincoln statue at Lincoln Park, Chicago, was copied for the Lincoln Memorial Stamp of 1909 (stamp 367).

Aside from his work as a sculptor, Saint-Gaudens also excelled in medallion work. At the request of his friend Theodore Roosevelt, he designed the gold pieces issued in 1907 and still considered the most handsome examples of American coinage. One variety of the gold pieces is valued, in its uncirculated state, at three thousand dollars.

Daniel Chester French

(1850-1931)

887 • 5¢ blue • 1940

DANIEL CHESTER FRENCH gained fame while still quite young with his alert, determined, and vigorous-looking *Minuteman,* completed in 1874 for the centennial of the Battles of Lexington and Concord. The statue appears on one of the stamps in the Lexington-Concord Sesquicentennial issue of 1926 (stamp 619). The Minuteman has been working in the field, and his left hand still rests on the plow.

The masterpiece of French's old age was his Lincoln Memorial statue, dedicated at Washington, D. C., in 1922. The sculptor provided a pedestal eleven feet high for the monumental seated figure, which is nineteen feet high.

The statue, made of twenty-eight blocks of Georgia marble, is housed in the Lincoln Memorial Building, a structure of Colorado marble in the form of a classic Greek temple. The Gettysburg Address is inscribed on the north wall. Around the walls are forty-eight columns symbolizing the Union that Lincoln gave his life to preserve.

One end of the Memorial Building is open, as if the brooding President were gazing out at the Capitol and the Washington Monument. The impressive setting does full justice to the sublime figure with its rugged and careworn yet benign expression.

Frederic Remington

(1861-1909)

888 · 10¢ brown · 1940

FREDERIC REMINGTON was the last great chronicler of the Old West in pictures. "I paint for boys," he said, "boys from seven to seventy." He was a keen observer, portraying Indians, pioneers, trappers, cowboys, prospectors, gamblers, and bandits with a vivid, almost brutal documentation.

Remington had very little formal art training. During his comparatively short career he produced close to three thousand paintings and drawings. He turned to sculpture without any previous training, and his first effort in this field, *The Bronco Buster,* became his most popular one.

His favorite subjects were horses and Indians. He liked to depict violent action, and he stripped it of false glamor; the lurking danger of death lends a somber quality to many of his paintings. (Engravings from his work appear in stamps 289 and 291.)

Remington, a native of New York, made many trips to the West, spurred on by a poignant feeling that he was studying and recording a world that was disappearing forever. Owen Wister recognized this documentary aspect of Remington's work when he said of him, "He is not merely an artist, he is a national treasure."

184

Eli Whitney

(1765-1825)

889 · 1¢ green · 1940

BEFORE ELI WHITNEY invented his cotton gin—short for engine —cotton production was severely hampered by the difficulty of separating the seed from the fiber. It took a slave a whole day to remove the seeds from a single pound of cotton.

Whitney's simple but effective device made it possible to process as much cotton in one day as had previously required three months. As a result, production increased steadily: 140,000 pounds in 1791, 225,000,000 pounds in 1825. At the same time, Negro slavery became more widespread.

Whitney also pioneered in manufacturing with standardized, interchangeable parts. In 1798 he built a musket factory in New Haven and undertook to fill a government order for ten thousand muskets in two years. In those days this was a fantastically brief time limit, as all articles were made one at a time at a snail's pace.

First Whitney made a single musket—the very best. Then he prepared patterns for each part, so that his employees could turn out virtually identical—and therefore interchangeable—parts. The various standard parts were then fitted together. Whitney's success in this work made him one of the most important forerunners of the modern technique of mass production.

Samuel F. B. Morse

(1791-1872)

890 · 2¢ red · 1940

As A portrait painter Samuel Morse was so successful that at one time he painted a hundred and fifty canvases in a few weeks. In 1832 he became interested in the idea of using electricity to send messages.

Unfortunately, his painting had lost its vogue, and he lacked the money for experimental equipment. However, an appointment as Professor of the Literature of the Arts of Design at New York University tided him over his early difficulties. But more setbacks were in store for him.

Helped by his friend Alfred Vail, Morse worked out a practical signal code of long and short taps with a telegraph key which sent the sound along a wire. In 1837 Morse demonstrated his invention before Congress, but the lawmakers were not impressed.

Two more attempts to interest Congress also failed. Finally, when Morse had almost given up the last shred of hope, he was voted an appropriation of thirty thousand dollars to build a forty-mile electromagnetic telegraph line from Washington to Baltimore. On May 24, 1844, Morse sent the historic message, "What hath God wrought?" ushering in a new age in the history of communication.

186

Cyrus Hall McCormick
(1809-1884)

891 · 3¢ purple · 1940

FOR THOUSANDS of years after man learned to grow crops he continued to harvest grain by slow, cumbersome, back-breaking toil. The sickle was an improvement on the scythe; yet it still took a whole day of one man's work to harvest a single acre.

As the acreage devoted to growing wheat in the United States rose into the millions, it became vital to harvest the wheat crop before it rotted in the fields. The solution appeared in 1831, when Cyrus McCormick, barely out of his teens, invented a horse-drawn mechanical reaper which enormously speeded up harvesting.

Three years later, young McCormick patented his invention and set about marketing it. Unlike most inventors, he was a shrewd businessman. Since farmers were either skeptical or unable to buy a reaper outright, he adopted the then daring plan of selling his machine on installment payments. After ten years of marketing his reaper, McCormick was selling four thousand machines annually.

The resulting widespread use of the reaper started the trend in mechanizing agriculture. This has made it possible to feed an ever growing population, and at the same time it has freed productive skills from a lifetime of laborious drudgery.

Elias Howe

(1819-1867)

892 · 5¢ blue · 1940

ELIAS HOWE died a relatively young man, worn out by the stormy ups and downs of his efforts to have the first successful sewing machine accepted by the people of his time. The initial idea came to him, so the story goes, one evening while he was watching his wife sewing: why not invent a machine that would do the work of her fingers?—fifty times faster.

Though Howe and his wife were on the verge of starvation, he kept working on his invention. The reactions to his clever device were anything but encouraging. Some people laughed at him, others paid him the compliment of stealing his ideas. Still others hated him.

Harried as he was by trouble of all kinds, Howe struggled courageously for his rights. So well did he fight back that by the time he was thirty-five, his invention was bringing him a yearly income of two hundred thousand dollars.

Soon, Howe became one of the first American millionaires. Remembering his own hardships, he contributed generously, but without fanfare, to many charities. Unlike the careers of other inventors who were cheated out of the fruit of their labors, Howe's life is more remarkable than the rags-to-riches stories of Horatio Alger.

Alexander Graham Bell

(1847-1922)

893 · 10¢ brown · 1940

ALEXANDER GRAHAM BELL was born in Scotland and came to Canada for his health. While working as a speech teacher in Boston, he began experimenting with the transmission of speech by electricity.

Bell's first workable telephone model was made up of two disks connected by an electrified wire, with each disk reproducing sound vibrations from the other end. On March 10, 1876, the first message was sent along a wire two hundred feet long. Even in its rudimentary stage, the telephone was a sensational success when shown at the Philadelphia Centennial Exhibition of 1876.

In October of the same year a two-mile wire was strung between Boston and Cambridge. Long-distance lines reached out further and further until coast-to-coast telephoning became a reality in 1915. By 1881 a million messages were being sent daily; forty years later the daily figure had risen to more than thirty million.

The complex instrument that we use today took a long time to evolve from Bell's original model. Parallel with this development, the telephone has come to play an ever more important part in our daily lives.

80th Anniversary

894 · 3¢ brown · 1940

"WANTED—young, skinny, wiry fellows, not over eighteen. Must be expert riders, willing to risk death daily. Orphans preferred." This advertisement conveys the daring spirit of the Pony Express riders, who braved hunger and fatigue and exposure, Indians and outlaws, mountains and deserts, blizzards and flooded roads and snow avalanches to deliver mail over two thousand miles of almost uninhabited territory.

The freight-forwarding firm of Russell, Majors, and Waddell conceived the idea of the Pony Express for carrying mail between St. Joseph, Missouri, and Sacramento, California. Eighty expert horsemen were to carry the mail in ten days, changing mounts every fifteen miles or so at express stations.

The Pony Express started on April 3, 1860, and lasted for nineteen months. With the extension of telegraph lines to the West Coast in 1861, there was no further need for the adventurous riders who had created one of the unforgettable epics of the settlement of the West. Typical was the feat of "Buffalo Bill" Cody, then fourteen years old, who on one occasion rode 322 miles without resting.

A noteworthy feature of the commemorative stamp is the contrasting of a buffalo skull with a sheaf of wheat to symbolize the changes that took place between 1860 and 1940.

50th Anniversary

895 · 3¢ purple · 1940

In 1890 the United States took the initiative in forming the Pan-American Union in order to create stronger ties with the countries of South and Central America.

Until 1933, however, these countries remained distrustful of what they called the Colossus of the North. After 1933, the administration of President Roosevelt, by means of its Good Neighbor Policy, brought about a much friendlier attitude.

As for the commemorative stamp, the designer had the extremely interesting idea of representing North, Central, and South America by three female figures inspired by ancient Greek mythology. These are the Three Graces, daughters of Zeus and Eurynome, and their names are: Euphrosyne (Joy), Thalia (Bloom), and Aglaia (Brilliance).

The figures, as they appear on the stamp, are copied from the famous allegorical painting *Springtime* by Sandro Botticelli (1447-1510). The lettering on the stamp is also of interest, being copied from fourteenth-century English script.

Botticelli (meaning Little Barrel) was born Alessandro di Mariano Filipepi, a native of Florence, the city that contributed most to the Renaissance. *Springtime* is typical of the gentle, dreamy melancholy that is found in most of his works.

191

50th Anniversary

896 · 3¢ purple · 1940

To THE best of our knowledge, no white man entered the Idaho country until 1805, the year of the Lewis and Clark expedition.

Fur traders in the employ of the Northwest Company founded the first Idaho trading post in 1809. Soon, other companies entered the field. Fort Hall, later an important way station on the Oregon Trail, was built in 1834. Fort Boise, the future territorial and state capital, was built the same year. In 1843 Captain Frémont and Kit Carson explored part of Idaho while searching for the best migration routes to the West.

After being part of the Oregon Territory for years, Idaho came under the jurisdiction of Washington Territory in 1859. The next year a group of Mormons founded Franklin, the first permanent white settlement in Idaho.

During the years 1860-1863, gold and silver deposits were discovered in several localities. Mining towns sprang up overnight and the increase in population led to the organizing of Idaho Territory in 1863. Later on, when the precious metals petered out, the prospectors departed, leaving ghost towns in their wake.

The stamp commemorating Idaho's admission to the Union as the forty-third state is dominated by a picture of the State Capitol.

50th Anniversary

897 · 3¢ purple · 1940

IT IS thought that French explorers visited Wyoming as early as 1740, but Lewis and Clark (1805) were the first white men definitely known to have entered the region. Soon other daring spirits came to Wyoming.

Fort Laramie, the first settlement and one of the most famous frontier posts, was built in 1834. Fur traders and trappers who journeyed to Wyoming laid out the routes that later became part of the Oregon Trail. Some of the most difficult stretches of the famous trail wound through the mountains of Wyoming.

For years a part of the Oregon Territory, Wyoming was organized as an independent territory in 1868. The following year women were given the right to vote—Wyoming Territory was the first governmental unit in the United States, perhaps in the world, to extend this right. In 1870 the territory pioneered again in giving women the right to sit on juries.

The enmity between cattlemen and sheep herders and the struggle of ranchers with cattle rustlers brought on a state of open warfare that lasted until law and order were finally established in Wyoming. In 1890 Wyoming entered the Union as the forty-fourth state. It is known as the Equal Rights state because its constitution was the first to grant female suffrage.

Coronado
and His Captains

898 · 3¢ purple · 1940

THE SPANIARDS who came to the New World braved every risk
and credited every old wives' tale in their avid search for gold.
They were particularly attracted by the legend of the Seven
Cities of Cíbola with their hoards of gold and silver and precious
stones.

To the Viceroy of Mexico it seemed a pity that all this
treasure should go begging for lack of conquistadors to carry it
off. In 1540 he sent Francisco Vásquez de Coronado to find the
fabled cities of gold.

On reaching New Mexico, Coronado's expedition turned
up nothing more exciting than seven humdrum cities of the
cliff-dwelling Zuñi Indians. Coronado thereupon divided up
his forces, and in the next two years his men wandered over a
third of the present-day United States. Without any maps to
guide them, the Spaniards penetrated as far east as Kansas, as
far north as Nebraska, as far west as California. They saw such
wonders as the Great Plains and the Grand Canyon and
"hunchbacked kine" (buffaloes), but no gold.

In 1542 Coronado and his men straggled wearily back to
Mexico City, richer in experience if not in gold. Coronado was
stripped of his rank, a sad reward for his courageous and competent leadership.

Statue of Liberty

899 · 1¢ green · 1940

In EIGHT fateful weeks, beginning on April 9, 1940, Germany's irresistible army and air force crushed Denmark, Norway, Luxembourg, the Netherlands, Belgium, and France into submission.

In June, as the British prepared desperately for imminent invasion of their island, Prime Minister Churchill appealed to the United States for military supplies. Before the end of the month, the first shipment arrived in Britain. The supplies included five hundred thousand rifles, eighty thousand machine guns, nine hundred 75-millimeter field guns, and one hundred and thirty thousand rounds of ammunition.

Early in September the United States gave fifty over-age destroyers to Great Britain to fight the submarine menace. In return the United States acquired ninety-nine-year leases of naval and air bases on British possessions in the New World.

The swift collapse in Europe created consternation among Americans and led to a greatly intensified military program in the United States. On May 16 Congress appropriated two and a half billion dollars to expand the armed forces and to meet President Roosevelt's announced production goal of fifty thousand airplanes a year. A month later Congress authorized the sale of munitions to other American republics.

Antiaircraft Gun

900 · 2¢ red · 1940

Other vital measures followed rapidly. On July 20 a bill providing for a two-ocean navy became law; on August 18 the United States and Canada set up a Joint Defense Board; and on September 16 Congress passed the Selective Training and Service Act.

During this time of crisis, an issue of three stamps appeared to call attention to the national emergency. The Statue of Liberty appears on the 1¢ stamp, and an uplifted torch is shown on the 3¢ stamp, stressing the defense of free institutions. On the 2¢ stamp, dedicated to the armed forces, there is a picture of a 90-millimeter antiaircraft gun. These stamps superseded the regular postal issues until well into World War II.

Uplifted Torch

901 · 3¢ purple · 1940

"Emancipation" Statue in Lincoln Park, Washington, D.C.

902 · 3¢ purple · 1940

ABRAHAM LINCOLN was nineteen years old when he got his first real glimpse of slavery and saw Negroes being sold on the auction block at New Orleans. Thirty years later, Lincoln's hard-hitting attacks on slavery in his debates with Stephen A. Douglas really won him the Presidency in 1860.

Lincoln's Emancipation Proclamation, which took effect on January 1, 1863, during one of the grimmest periods of the Civil War, freed over three million slaves. The proclamation thrilled lovers of freedom everywhere; yet it was strictly a war-time measure and did not affect the slaves in Kentucky, Missouri, and other loyal border states. Similarly, the proclamation did not apply to the slaves in reconquered areas in Tennessee, Virginia, and Louisiana.

After his re-election in 1864, Lincoln moved vigorously to assure the unconditional freedom of all slaves in the United States. He strongly urged the passage of the thirteenth amendment to the Constitution, which forbade slavery throughout the United States. The amendment became law in January, 1865, and was later strengthened by the fourteenth and fifteenth amendments.

197

State Capitol

903 · 3¢ purple · 1941

ALTHOUGH VERMONT was not one of the original thirteen colonies, her Green Mountain Boys scored two of the most important American successes in the Revolution by their victories at Ticonderoga and Bennington. (See stamp 643 for the story of the Bennington battle.)

In 1776 Ethan Allen led the Green Mountain Boys in the seizure of Fort Ticonderoga, the most valuable fortress in North America. As Allen told the story, he demanded the surrender of the stronghold "in the name of the great Jehovah and the Continental Congress." A later writer slyly pointed out that Allen "held a commission from neither source."

When the Continental Congress brushed aside Vermont's claims to statehood in 1777, the sturdy Vermonters proclaimed an independent republic which remained in existence until 1791. In that year Vermont ratified the new United States Constitution and was admitted to the Union as the fourteenth state. Vermont, by the way, was the first state to grant universal male suffrage.

The commemorative stamp features Vermont's State Capitol at Montpelier. At the right we see a shield with thirteen stars for the original states. A larger star represents the fourteenth state—Vermont.

Daniel Boone
and
Three Companions

904 • 3¢ purple • 1942

DANIEL BOONE (1735-1820), the most famous American frontiersman, was always in search of greener pastures; a wisp of smoke from a cabin several miles away was a warning that it was time to be moving on.

Boone had little schooling, as we know from the famous inscription on a tree: "D. Boone kilt a bar hear." But he was a past master when it came to reading the language of the forest; he was also a crack shot, and resourceful enough to live through many a narrow escape from the Indians.

Men like Boone were not impressed by George III's proclamation of 1763 forbidding settlement across the Alleghenies. Nor were they held back by the hostility of the Indians who wanted no white men on the "dark and bloody ground" of Kentucky.

By cutting the Wilderness Road through the forest in 1775, Boone made it possible for many pioneers to settle in Kentucky. Once the settlements had been started, they largely owed their preservation to Boone's courage and foresight. In 1792 Kentucky was admitted to the Union as the fifteenth state—the first state from the West.

The commemorative stamp fittingly honors Boone by picturing him and three companions as they gaze across the Kentucky River at the future site of Frankfort.

American Eagle

905 · 3¢ purple · 1942

THIS STAMP, issued on July 4 to symbolize America's will to victory, appeared at a time when the Axis military might in World War II was at its highest point.

In the Pacific and in Asia, Japan had conquered the Philippines, the Dutch East Indies, Hong Kong, Malaya, Thailand, and Burma. In Africa, in Russia, and on the Atlantic the outlook for successful resistance to the Axis powers was dubious. German submarines were a formidable threat to Allied shipping. The Luftwaffe was battering England with thousands of bombs. France had been knocked out of the war in a few weeks.

Nevertheless, the tide was about to turn. In May and June American naval and air units had inflicted smashing blows on the Japanese in the Coral Sea and at Midway. The bitterly fought island-hopping campaigns were about to start in the Pacific; the American invasion of North Africa was in the offing; and in other sectors the Axis forces were to be slowly forced back.

The Win the War stamp was issued to replace the 3¢ National Defense stamp of 1940 (stamp 901). The central design shows an American eagle with wings outstretched in the form of a V— "V for victory." The eagle is encircled by thirteen stars representing the original thirteen states.

Abraham Lincoln
(1809-1865)

Sun Yat-sen
(1866-1925)

906 · 5¢ blue · 1942

AFTER YEARS of feeble misrule by the Manchu dynasty, China became a republic in 1912 through the revolutionary activities of Sun Yat-sen and other leaders. Though the republic started out in an atmosphere of optimism, it was soon hopelessly torn by dissension.

There were many reasons for China's plight, chief among them the vastness of the country, its poor communications, its phenomenal technical backwardness, the poverty and illiteracy of its people. Bandits ranged the countryside and warlords set up their ephemeral regimes. Meanwhile, Japan and Russia were poised for large territorial seizures—Japan in Manchuria and Russia in Mongolia.

The timing of the Japanese was crafty. In 1915, during World War I, they presented twenty-one highhanded demands assuring widespread penetration into Chinese affairs; in 1931, during the world-wide economic depression, they invaded Manchuria on a flimsy pretext; and in 1937, during a European crisis, they began an undeclared war on China.

An outline map of China, flanked by portraits of Abraham Lincoln and Sun Yat-sen, appears on a commemorative stamp issued on the fifth anniversary of Chinese resistance to the Japanese invasion of 1937.

Palm Branch and Swords

907 · 2¢ red · 1943

IN 1941 President Roosevelt coined the term United Nations to describe the countries opposed to the Axis forces. In August of that year the Atlantic Charter tentatively supplied a set of principles for the United Nations.

President Roosevelt and Prime Minister Churchill declared in the charter that "their countries hope to see established a peace which will afford to all nations the means of dwelling in safety." The final clause of the charter looked forward to the abandonment of force and the disarming of any nation that might threaten aggression. Twenty-six countries signed this document and so took the first step in forming the United Nations.

This organization was planned to be the successor to the old League of Nations, which had proved a failure for a number of reasons. One of them was the absence of the United States from the League. Many people felt that the participation of the United States in the United Nations would assure its success.

The United Nations stamp is impressive in its simplicity. It pictures an upright palm branch standing out from a triangular pattern of swords held aloft. This stamp, issued on Lincoln's Birthday, replaced the 2¢ National Defense stamp of 1940 (stamp 900).

Liberty Holding Torch of Freedom and Enlightenment

908 · 1¢ green · 1943

IN HIS message to Congress on January 6, 1941, President Roosevelt unfolded his momentous Lend-Lease plan to aid the victims of German and Japanese aggression. During the course of this message the President outlined "the four essential human freedoms" that he wanted to see prevailing all over the world: freedom of speech and expression; freedom of worship; freedom from want; freedom from fear.

This short and simple summary of American aims, which immediately became known as the Four Freedoms, took a powerful hold on the imagination of people all over the world.

Soon Congress enacted the main recommendations of the presidential message by passing the Lend-Lease Act. This law enabled the United States to provide food, supplies, and services for nations whose war effort was vital to American welfare.

In August, 1941, President Roosevelt and Prime Minister Churchill held their Atlantic Conference on a warship off the Newfoundland coast. At the end of their talks they issued the Atlantic Charter, in which they set forth in concrete detail their program for making the Four Freedoms a reality.

The Four Freedoms stamp shows Liberty holding the Torch of Freedom and Enlightenment. The stamp was issued to replace the 1¢ National Defense stamp of 1940 (stamp 899).

Poland

909 · 1943
5¢ white and red

In 1943 and 1944 the United States issued a series of stamps as a tribute to the thirteen countries invaded and enslaved by the Axis forces.

With the exception of Austria and Denmark, these countries formed governments in exile to continue the struggle as best they could. All of them, with the exception of Austria, had heroic resistance movements that fought back against the invaders by such methods as sabotage, strikes, slowdowns, espionage, illegal newspapers, aiding Allied airmen to escape to freedom.

A number of these countries contributed valuable personnel to the armed forces of the United Nations and to vital scientific research. The vast merchant shipping resources of Norway and the Netherlands helped to meet the critical need for vessels.

Meanwhile the Germans systematically murdered millions of the inhabitants of the overrun countries of Europe and deported millions more to Germany for slave labor. The fate of these unfortunate countries was grim in many other respects as well.

Korea was the first to be overrun, long before World War II. After specifically guaranteeing Korean independence in 1905, Japan seized the country in 1910 and made it part of the Japanese Empire in 1919.

Czechoslovakia

910 · 1943
5¢ red, white, and blue

The Japanese industrialized Korea, built up a railroad network, and fostered the growth of trade. But all this was for their own benefit; they deliberately reduced the Koreans' standard of living and tried hard to stamp out any trace of national spirit.

After the Japanese surrender in 1945, United States and Russian forces occupied Korea, with the thirty-eighth parallel of latitude serving as the dividing line.

All the other overrun countries were in Europe. Their sad chronicle began on March 12, 1938, when German troops marched into Austria; it was formally annexed the following day. In April, 1945, American and Russian armies drove the Germans out and the country was divided into American, Rus-

Norway

911 · 1943
5¢ red, white, and blue

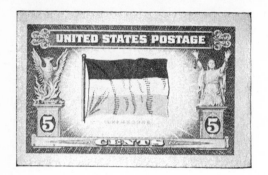

Luxembourg

912 · 1943
5¢ red, white, and blue

sian, British, and French zones. The city of Vienna likewise came under four-power control.

The Munich pact of September, 1938, allowed Germany to seize the Sudeten areas of Czechoslovakia but guaranteed the independence of the rest of the country. In March, 1939, Germany violated the pact and took over the rest of the country. President Benes fled and organized a government in exile.

Czech resistance during World War II brought on brutal retaliation, notably the Lidice massacre of 1942. American and Russian armies disposed of the German forces in Czechoslovakia in 1945.

In April, 1939, Italy invaded Albania and incorporated it into the Italian Empire. When Italy surrendered in 1943, her troops left Albania and the Germans took their place. In 1944 Albanian partisans, headed by a Communist named Enver Hoxha, chased the Germans out.

Poland was the most brutally martyred of all the overrun countries. When the Germans demanded Danzig in 1939, the Poles refused to give in. Thereupon, Germany signed a pact with Russia and invaded Poland—the opening hostilities of World War II. The German conquest of Poland took only a short time, after which the country was divided up between

Netherlands

913 · 1943
5¢ red, white, and blue

Germany and Russia. Once again, as in the eighteenth century, Poland had been partitioned.

When the Germans invaded Russia in 1941, they took over all of Poland and established their chief murder camps there. In 1945 the Russians hurled back the German armies, and this sorely tried country fell into Soviet hands.

Germany followed up its nonaggression pact with Denmark by seizing the country early in 1940. To avoid pointless bloodshed, Christian X asked the Danes to offer no military resistance. The King then announced that he considered himself a prisoner and refused to cooperate with the Germans. The Danish underground fought hard against the invaders, scuttling ships, blowing up trains, and hampering production in many ways. The Germans left Denmark in 1945.

In Norway the unprovoked German invasion of April, 1940, scored an easy triumph. King Haakon and his cabinet escaped to London, where they set up a government in exile. Meanwhile, Vidkun Quisling founded a collaborationist Norwegian regime.

The extensive Norwegian merchant marine, fourth largest in the world, played a valuable role for the Allies. The Norwegian underground was unusually daring and resourceful.

Belgium

914 · 1943
5¢ black, yellow, and red

Outstanding among feats of the European resistance heroes was the carefully planned destruction of the Nazi heavy water plant at Vemork, Norway, which dashed German hopes of winning the atomic-weapons race. The Germans had to declare martial law in 1941; they remained in Norway until the end of the war.

The Germans occupied Luxembourg early in 1940. Grand Duchess Charlotte escaped with her cabinet and set up a government in exile in Montreal. Part of the famous Battle of the Bulge spilled over into Luxembourg, and as a result of that struggle the Germans were driven out of the country in 1945.

In May, 1940, the Germans pounced on Belgium without any warning. Eighteen days later Leopold III surrendered without

France

915 · 1943
5¢ blue, white, and red

Greece

916 · 1943
5¢ blue and white

consulting his cabinet—a premature capitulation that nearly resulted in the destruction of the British and French armies.

By way of punishing the Belgians for their resistance activities, the Germans deported hundreds of thousands of them to slave labor in Germany. In September, 1944, an Allied invasion supported by Belgian resistance forces drove the Germans out of Belgium.

The unprovoked German invasion of the Netherlands in May, 1940, featured the "object-lesson" bombing of Rotterdam, the appearance of paratroopers as if by magic, and the well-coordinated activities of Dutch fifth columnists. The Dutch surrendered in five days, but Queen Wilhelmina and her ministers escaped to London and set up a government in exile.

Germany punished Dutch resistance activities with characteristically brutal measures. The lack of food in 1944-1945 forced the Dutch to feed their children tulip bulbs to keep them alive. Before retreating in face of the Allied invasion of September, 1944, the Germans opened the dikes and ruined large tracts of laboriously reclaimed land. Despite German boasts that the havoc was beyond repair, the Dutch soon restored their ruined cities and their precious farm land.

Yugoslavia

917 · 1943
5¢ blue, white, and red

Only a few weeks after the invasion of France, the hastily formed Vichy government of Marshal Pétain signed Germany's surrender terms on June 22, 1940. No less than a million and a half French prisoners of war were deported to Germany. After the Germans divided France into an occupied zone and a free zone under the Vichy regime, Pétain substituted the slogan, "Family, Labor, Fatherland," for the old motto of the Republic, "Liberty, Equality, Fraternity."

Meanwhile, the Free French rallied under General Charles de Gaulle and gave new hope to the Frenchmen who had been dazed by the catastrophe of their country's sudden collapse. After the American invasion of North Africa in November, 1942, the Germans prepared for the prospective invasion of France by occupying the whole country. The French resistance movement changed its name to FFI (French Forces of the Interior) and engaged in many underground activities.

After the Normandy landings of June 6, 1944, the days of the Germans in France were numbered. The FFI gave valuable aid to the American and British troops, and Paris was liberated on August 20, 1944.

By that time the Germans were streaming out of Greece,

Albania

918 · 1943
5¢ red and black

which had originally been invaded by the Italians on October 28, 1940. After seizing Albania, Italy had acquired a common border with Greece. Following the usual Axis pattern, Italy had given Greece many assurances of friendship before the invasion.

Though the Greeks were poorly equipped, they drove the invaders back into Albania. In 1941 England sent troops and equipment to Greece. At this point, Germany took a hand and after smashing through Yugoslavia, German troops invaded Greece, captured Athens, forced the evacuation of British and Anzac troops, and captured the important Mediterranean island of Crete. Eventually, the Germans could not maintain their

Austria

919 · 1943
5¢ red, white, and red

bryanmc(oy

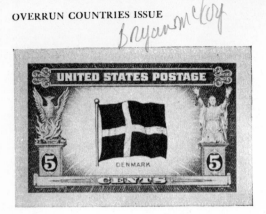

Denmark

920 · 1943
5¢ red and white

hold on Greece and left the devastated country in 1944. The German occupation forces were needed on the home front.

Partly to get through to Greece and partly to control the Balkans before embarking on the great Russian adventure, the Nazis invaded Yugoslavia in 1941. Their easy victory proved deceptive, for the Yugoslav partisans harried them endlessly. In October, 1944, partisan forces supported by a Russian army drove the Germans out.

Soon after its appearance, the Overrun Countries set became the most popular of all the commemorative stamps. This was due to a combination of two irresistible factors: the attractive design, and the sentiment responsible for the issue.

Korea

921 · 1944
5¢ white, blue, and red

75th Anniversary

922 · 3¢ purple · 1944

THE BUILDING of the first transcontinental railroad started toward the end of the Civil War. Recognizing the problems confronting the builders, Congress gave them generous land grants in addition to loans of $16,000 per mile of prairie construction and $48,000 per mile through mountainous country.

The Union Pacific worked west from Omaha, Nebraska, while the Central Pacific, starting east from Sacramento, had a maddeningly difficult task through the Sierra Nevada Mountains. Indian attacks, labor shortages, and the delays of shipping supplies around Cape Horn all added to the difficulties.

General Grenville M. Dodge was in charge of construction. The Indians called him "Long Eye" because he could see so far ahead with his surveyor's glass. They were infuriated because the noisy and smoky locomotives scared off buffalo.

The last stage, before the two sets of workers met at Promontory Point in Utah, turned into an exciting race to see which side could make the most mileage and thereby obtain the largest amount of government loans. On May 10, 1869, the two roads met, with the Union Pacific having completed 1038 miles and the Central Pacific 638 miles. At last the United States was linked from coast to coast.

125th Anniversary of First Steam-Propelled Voyage Across the Atlantic

923 · 3¢ purple · 1944

THIS STAMP carries a picture of the *Savannah,* a full-rigged vessel with paddle wheels, and the inscription: "First steamship to cross the Atlantic." The ship left Savannah on May 22, 1819, and arrived at Liverpool twenty-nine days later. This was only twelve years after the successful trial trip of Robert Fulton's *Clermont* (see stamp 372).

An ocean crossing made wholly by steam was really out of the question in 1819. The machinery was still untrustworthy, the flimsy paddle wheels could not stand the buffeting of ocean waves, and it was impossible to store enough wood for fuel.

What, then, is the explanation of the *Savannah's* record? It is this: the vessel used sail for four-fifths of the trip, relying on steam for less than a hundred hours during the opening and concluding phases of the voyage. The day of sail-less steam-propelled ships was still far off!

The first crossing of the Atlantic by a vessel relying exclusively on steam did not come until 1838. In that year two British ships, the *Sirius* and the *Great Western,* made the westward crossing. The *Sirius* took fifteen days, the *Great Western* eighteen days. In 1840 Samuel Cunard obtained a contract from the British government for making regular voyages to carry passengers, mail, and freight. By 1870 steam had largely replaced sail.

214

Telegraph Pole and Wires

924 · 3¢ purple · 1944

IT TOOK almost a year after Samuel Morse's historic telegraph message in 1844 (see stamp 890) to make his invention suitable for general use. During the first four days that the instrument was available to the public, the total receipts amounted to one cent—the fee for a single coded message.

After a few years, however, the time-saving value of the telegraph was generally recognized. Accordingly, Cyrus W. Field, an enterprising young New York businessman, wondered whether it was possible to link the New World and the Old by means of a telegraph cable beneath the Atlantic Ocean.

Field asked Michael Faraday, the noted British scientist, how long it would take for sound to pass through a wire two thousand miles long. "About one second," Faraday replied.

Heartened by this information, Field interested a number of wealthy men in financing his project. It was fortunate that he had the right kind of temperament for this enterprise.

Between 1857 and 1866 Field sent out ships seven times to lay a cable, at a cost of millions of dollars to himself and his backers. After six heartbreaking failures, the seventh attempt proved successful. This first oceanic cable was followed by many others, which enormously increased the usefulness of Morse's invention.

Map of Corregidor

925 · 3¢ purple · 1944

SHORTLY AFTER the Japanese attacked Pearl Harbor on December 7, 1941, they began their conquest of the Philippines. Outnumbered and unprepared, the defenders could not hope for reinforcements.

The last strongholds of the heroic delaying action of American and Filipino troops were on Bataan and Corregidor. The narrow entrance to Manila Bay is commanded from the north by the Bataan Peninsula on southwest Luzon, and from the south by the small rocky island of Corregidor. The island was so heavily fortified that it was nicknamed the "Gibraltar of the Pacific."

The defending force of forty-five thousand Filipinos and ten thousand Americans, attacked by two hundred thousand Japanese, was driven onto the Bataan Peninsula. Despite severe shortages of ammunition, equipment, and food, the defenders fought on for ninety-eight days—until April 9, 1942.

Just before the capitulation, some resourceful men succeeded in escaping to Corregidor. Despite a series of terrific bombardments, the island fortress managed to hold out until May 6. Though the Corregidor resistance was hopeless, it was of inestimable value in giving the United States time to build up its counterattack in the Pacific areas.

50th Anniversary

926 · 3¢ purple · 1944

THE INVENTION of the motion-picture camera and the earliest showing of motion pictures are two subjects about which there is a great deal of disagreement.

In the 1880's inventors in several countries were working on a motion-picture camera. This camera takes a series of images on film so rapidly that the long procession of "stills" gives us the illusion of continuous motion. Each "movement" blends into the previous one and the next one. A five-minute picture needs more than five thousand individual photos.

Thomas Edison, one of the pioneers in this field, concentrated on the kinetoscope, a tiny peep show viewed through an eyepiece. Strategically marketed in penny arcades, Edison's "films" delighted people by their vivid displays of motion—dancing, acrobatics, rushing trains, violent waves, and the like. In 1889 William Friese-Greene, an Englishman, invented the first motion-picture camera that projected images on a large screen.

The commemorative stamp shows a group of American soldiers looking at a motion picture on a tropical island in the Pacific during World War II. The exotic setting conveys graphically the world-wide triumph of motion pictures after their modest beginning in the 1890's.

State Seal

927 · 3¢ purple · 1945

JUAN PONCE DE LEÓN, the Spanish governor of Puerto Rico, is believed to have been the first white man to land in Florida. He arrived in 1513 in search of gold and a fountain of youth, but found neither.

Thereafter Spanish colonization lagged until 1565, when the Spaniards founded St. Augustine. After the English settled Carolina and Georgia, there were constant quarrels between the English and the Spaniards. In 1763 an international treaty gave Florida to the English, and in 1783 another treaty returned Florida to the Spaniards.

After the United States came into existence, Florida's boundaries were fiercely disputed. In 1819 the Spanish government prudently decided to sell Florida to the United States for five million dollars. Soon thereafter East and West Florida were united into Florida Territory.

Andrew Jackson became the first territorial governor of Florida in 1821. The building of roads brought many settlers, and large cotton plantations appeared in the northern part of the territory. In 1845 Florida entered the Union as a slave state.

The State Seal appears in the center of the commemorative stamp, with the gates of St. Augustine on the left and the State Capitol on the right.

"Toward
United Nations"

928 · 5¢ blue · 1945

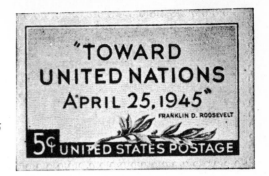

FROM 1942 on, the countries fighting against the Axis powers began to feel more and more strongly the need for some international organization to succeed the old League of Nations.

The new group was to be called the United Nations and was first to be made up of countries that had declared war on the Axis powers. By February, 1945, the structure of the United Nations Organization had been fairly well determined.

The first conference was scheduled to take place on April 25. Thirteen days before came the tragic news of the sudden death of President Roosevelt, the chief architect of the United Nations Organization.

Despite the President's death, the conference opened as scheduled. United States Secretary of State Edward R. Stettinius presented the United Nations Charter, made up of a preamble and one hundred and eleven articles. Later conferences held in 1945 voted for the establishment of the United Nations headquarters in the United States. The first meeting of the General Assembly opened in London on January 10, 1946.

The United Nations commemorative stamp is extremely simple in design. President Roosevelt's last official act, half an hour before his fatal seizure, was to order the first copies of this stamp.

Hyde Park

930 · 1¢ green · 1945

WHEN FRANKLIN DELANO ROOSEVELT was elected President in 1932, twelve million workers were unemployed in the United States. Prices of farm products had sunk to the lowest levels ever known. The national income had decreased from eighty billion dollars in 1929 to forty billion in 1932. Thousands of factories were idle, five thousand banks had closed their doors, bankruptcies were reaching a thousand a month. Worst of all, perhaps, was the pervasive mood of baffled despair.

To combat the crisis, President Roosevelt presented his New Deal program. While many of the New Deal measures have been harshly criticized, it is interesting to see how many have stood the test of time.

A comprehensive public works program built badly needed bridges, roads, public buildings, schools, and other facilities. Unsightly slums were torn down and replaced by comfortable, inexpensive housing.

The Federal Deposit Insurance Corporation (FDIC) put the nation's bank deposits on a sound basis. The Home Owners' Loan Corporation (HOLC) saved thousands of home owners from foreclosure. The Farm Credit and Farm Security Administrations helped large numbers of farmers to hold on to their farms. The Securities and Exchange Commission (SEC)

"Little
White House"

931 · 2¢ red · 1945

ended some of the worst abuses of the stock market. The Civilian Conservation Corps and other agencies applied Theodore Roosevelt's conservation theories on a much wider scale.

The Tennessee Valley Authority (TVA) was one of the outstanding achievements of the New Deal. By preventing erosion, controlling floods, and supplying hydroelectric power, the authority brought prosperity and well-being to large numbers of people. Grand Coulee and other vast reclamation projects economically combined the same functions, and in addition increased the nation's farm land.

The Social Security Acts of 1935 provided Federal benefits for the unemployed, the aged, and the disabled for the first time. These benefits, bitterly attacked when the legislation was first proposed, have been enlarged and extended since 1935.

With the coming of World War II, the scope of the problems facing the President increased a thousandfold. It is interesting to know that stamp collecting was his favorite means of relaxing. "I owe my life to my hobbies," he once remarked, "especially stamp collecting."

No matter where the President's travels took him or how busy he was, he always managed to devote at least half an hour a day to his stamps. As a rule he was unable to get to his albums

White House

932 · 3¢ purple · 1945

until just before bedtime, but invariably he found such a session relaxing and refreshing.

His interest in stamp collecting began in early childhood and never waned. Stamps of all kinds—not merely rarities or specialties—fascinated him. Generally he paid no more than ten dollars for a stamp, and his collection was not in the same class with those of King George V of England and other famous collectors. In a lifetime of collecting, President Roosevelt assembled 150 albums containing two hundred and fifty thousand stamps, as well as about a million ungraded and unsorted stamps.

Part of the President's collection came from gifts of admirers from all over the world. When his collection was sold after his death, it realized about two hundred thousand dollars.

President Roosevelt took the keenest interest in the two hundred and twenty-five stamps issued during his administrations. He personally approved the sketches and proofs for all new issues. Occasionally he pointed out mistakes, and in several cases he prepared the original rough design.

President Roosevelt's love for stamps lends a special interest to the stamps which were issued in his memory. On the 1¢ stamp we see his home at Hyde Park, the large, old-fashioned, rambling house where he spent his happiest days. In his will the

Four Freedoms

933 • 5¢ blue • 1946

President bequeathed Hyde Park to the nation. His home remains exactly as it was in his lifetime. Millions of Americans have visited the grave of the President, who lies buried in a nearby rose garden.

The 3¢ stamp pictures the "Little White House" at Warm Springs, Georgia. When Franklin Roosevelt was stricken with infantile paralysis in 1921 at the age of thirty-seven, he refused to give up hope. Bathing at Warm Springs helped him, and eventually he was able to move about with the aid of braces, a cane, and someone to lean on. In order to help other unfortunates afflicted with polio, he established the Warm Springs Foundation in 1927. He liked to visit Warm Springs, and bought a home nearby which later became known as the "Little White House." It was here that the President died suddenly on April 12, 1945, a few weeks before Germany's surrender.

The 5¢ stamp succinctly sums up the Four Freedoms which in the President's view gave meaning to his strategy in the global conflict of World War II.

These stamps were by no means the only ones issued to honor President Roosevelt's memory. So many foreign countries added their postal tributes that Roosevelt stamps have become a favorite collector's specialty.

Marine Corps: Iwo Jima

929 • 3¢ green • 1945

THE MARINE CORPS bore the brunt of the Pacific island-hopping campaign, which took brilliant planning, masterly organization, patient training. Fierce Japanese resistance took a heavy toll of the invaders.

In February, 1945, the Marines were ready to storm Iwo Jima, less than seven hundred miles from Tokyo. On this island, with its area of eight square miles, the Japanese had entrenched a defense force of twenty-three thousand men, under orders to resist to the death.

The Japanese exhausted their ingenuity in fortifying Mount Suribachi, an extinct volcano, with thousands of pillboxes and blockhouses. After cutting and tunneling through the mountain, they crowded it with machine guns, cannon, rocket weapons, and mortars.

Preceded by warships and bombers, sixty thousand marines attacked Iwo Jima. One out of every twelve was killed, one out of every four, wounded. After four days of the most furious kind of fighting, a party of Marines succeeded in scaling Mount Suribachi. At the summit they raised the Stars and Stripes, and Joe Rosenthal of the Associated Press took the thrilling photo which is reproduced on the commemorative stamp.

Army: Liberation of Paris

934 · 3¢ khaki · 1945

THE UNITED STATES ARMY did most of its fighting in World War II in North Africa and Europe. At the time of Pearl Harbor the Army numbered a million and a half men; by the time of Germany's surrender this figure had risen to over eight million.

In the Pacific fighting, the outstanding achievements of the Army were the recovery of New Guinea and the Philippines from the well-entrenched Japanese forces.

The American assault on North Africa, the prelude to invasion of Europe, came in November, 1942. After beating down the resistance of the desert-hardened Nazis, the Americans and British were ready to invade Sicily, across the Mediterranean.

The Axis defenders were dazed by the swift mechanized thrusts against Sicily. Starting on July 10, 1943, the campaign was over by August 17. A month later the Allied forces invaded Italy.

One more invasion was needed to assure victory—the long-awaited, carefully planned invasion of the Normandy beaches. After their landing on June 6, 1944, the American forces broke through with unexpected speed and liberated Paris as early as August 20. The commemorative stamp, showing American troops marching under the Arc de Triomphe, is based on a photograph taken on that joyous day.

Navy:
Group of Sailors

935 • *3¢ blue* • *1945*

THE TASK that confronted the American Navy after the disaster at Pearl Harbor is one that staggers the imagination. While the Navy distinguished itself in several theaters of war, its work in the Pacific was outstanding.

The airplane carriers dominated the struggle with the Japanese. In May, 1942, American carrier-based planes blasted Japanese hopes of invading Australia by inflicting heavy losses in the Battle of the Coral Sea.

The four-day Battle of Midway in June, 1942, the greatest combat ever fought at sea, was actually the turning point of the Pacific war. It was a duel of airplane carriers, fought at long range. The Japanese lost four carriers as well as smaller ships, and two hundred and seventy-five planes. American losses consisted of one carrier, one destroyer, and about a hundred planes.

In the Atlantic the Navy concentrated on convoy duty and fighting submarines. The U-boats inflicted heavy losses on Allied shipping before destroyers and planes succeeded in fending them off with radar, rockets, and depth charges.

Such costly struggles had to be backed up by a magnificent production effort. By the war's end the Navy had over eleven hundred major fighting ships and almost two hundred and fifty submarines—the greatest armada ever assembled.

Coast Guard: Landing Craft

936 · 3¢ green · 1945

IN 1790 Congress authorized the formation of the Coast Guard, under the name of Revenue-Marine, to prevent smuggling. Since that time the Coast Guard has taken on many other duties, serving under the Treasury in peacetime and the Navy in wartime.

During World War II Coast Guard cutters did valuable convoy work on the shipping lanes to Greenland. Coast Guard personnel devised beach-landing techniques and training methods for all our water-borne invasions of World War II. During the Normandy invasion the Coast Guard rescued fifteen hundred men.

In the course of its patrol of thousands of miles of American coastline, the Coast Guard captured several would-be saboteurs landed from German submarines. After North Atlantic weather reports were discontinued, the Coast Guard supplied the necessary information to Allied vessels and planes. In addition, the Coast Guard supervised all shipping of explosives and other dangerous cargoes. The wartime woman's reserve of the Coast Guard was known as the SPARS.

These were some of the ways in which the Coast Guard rendered distinguished service in World War II and justified its motto of *semper paratus* (always ready).

Merchant Marine: Liberty Ship

939 · 3¢ green · 1946

THOUGH MERCHANT seamen were not in the armed forces, they risked their lives to make victory possible. The American Merchant Marine carried four-fifths of all the supplies used by the United Nations—food, gasoline, tanks, trucks, ammunition, weapons, hospital supplies. Axis torpedoes and bombs sank over six hundred merchant vessels and took more than six thousand lives.

American technical skill had to meet this challenge: could American shipyards turn out cargo vessels faster than the Germans could sink them? To solve this problem, design was largely standardized and concentrated on the rather slow Liberty ship of ten thousand tons. Eighty shipyards employing almost a million workers produced six thousand ships. By the end of the war, the United States had the largest merchant fleet in history.

Three hundred thousand seamen manned the cargo ships. Sometimes the vessels unloaded their precious cargoes under enemy fire. Though they were only lightly armed, a few succeeded in striking back at their tormentors by shooting down enemy planes or sinking submarines.

The commemorative stamp pictures one of the famous Liberty ships unloading cargo.

Alfred Emanuel Smith

(1873-1944)

937 • 3¢ purple • 1945

THE MAN whom Franklin Delano Roosevelt called "the happy warrior" was born on New York's lower East Side. Al Smith used to say jokingly that Fulton Fish Market was his alma mater. He started working there when he was fourteen years old.

When Smith was elected to the state assembly in 1903 he was mystified by the tortuous language of legislation. To make up for his lack of education, he pored over the statutes until he acquired an unequaled grasp of New York law.

The tragic Triangle Shirtwaist Company fire, in which one hundred and fifty women and young girls perished, gave Smith a lasting interest in reform legislation. From then on he led the fight for progressive laws.

Al Smith gained such popularity that he was elected governor four times. With magnificent disregard for patronage claims, he consolidated one hundred and sixty-five state departments into eighteen. He devoted himself to child welfare, workmen's compensation, highways, parks, schools, housing, hospitals, and other worth-while causes.

Smith's bid for the presidency in 1928 aroused rancorous arguments that assured his defeat. Yet he could still look back with pride on his terms as governor, with their unexcelled record of distinguished service.

Stars and Stripes
and
Lone Star Flag

938 · 3¢ blue · 1945

ALTHOUGH TEXAS became a republic in 1836 (see stamp 776), it did not adopt the Lone Star flag until 1839. Even the heroic defenders of the Alamo used a Mexican banner. The Lone Star flag consisted of a single large star on a blue field flanked by a broad white horizontal stripe and a broad red horizontal stripe.

By 1845 the United States was expanding westward so rapidly that the annexation of Texas was in order. Texas became the twenty-eighth state on December 29, 1845, and a few months later Mexico and the United States were at war. The decisive defeat of Mexico ended any further Mexican claim to Texan territory.

The man who played the most important part in the early history of Texas was Sam Houston, a brawny, fearless, tempestuous giant of a man. After commanding the victorious Texan army he was successively president of Texas, United States senator from Texas, and governor of the state. Because Houston opposed secession at the time of the Civil War, he was deposed from the governorship and died in poverty two years later.

The Texas statehood stamp is one of the most striking commemorative stamps ever issued. The design features the Stars and Stripes and the Lone Star flag, with a single ray shining from the twenty-eighth star to the single star on the Texan flag.

230

"Honoring Those Who Have Served"

940 · 3¢ purple · 1946

MEMBERS OF the armed forces in World War II were mustered out on a point system. This method took into account the number of months served, with extra credit for overseas service. Combat decorations, such as the Silver Star, provided additional credits. Commissioned officers had to earn a higher number of points than enlisted men before they could be released from service.

In 1944, when the fighting was at its height, Congress passed the Servicemen's Readjustment Act, or GI Bill of Rights, as it came to be called. The purpose of this law was to provide some help to veterans as a partial return to them for the time spent in military service.

One of the main provisions of the law made it possible for veterans to receive subsistence allowances while completing their educational or professional training. Another important feature was the extending of loans on favorable terms for starting a business or buying a home. The enlightened treatment of the veterans not only eased return to civilian life but also had a very stimulating effect on the national economy.

The commemorative stamp reproduces the Honorable Discharge Emblem, together with five stars in memory of the war dead from the five services.

Andrew Jackson
(1767-1845)
John Sevier
(1745-1815)

941 • 3¢ purple • 1946

ABOUT 1750 adventurous folk in the Carolinas began to make their way into the Tennessee country. Despite the ever present Indian menace and other hardships of frontier life the pioneers prospered. In 1785 these self-reliant people set up an independent republic called Franklin or Frankland, which became the State of Tennessee in 1796.

The commemorative stamp reminds us that Tennessee is known as the Volunteer State. This nickname dates from 1847, when Governor Brown called for twenty-eight hundred volunteers to fight in the Mexican War. No less than thirty thousand Tennesseans answered his call.

The stamp also pictures John Sevier and Andrew Jackson, the two outstanding men of Tennessee's stirring early history. They started as friends but ended as bitter rivals.

Sevier, an early settler in Tennessee, became the idol of the frontiersmen as one of the leaders in the Battle of King's Mountain (1780). In 1785 he was elected governor of Franklin, and later he was Tennessee's first governor.

Andrew Jackson grew to manhood in the hurly-burly of Tennessee's hard frontier life. In 1829 he was elected President of the United States—the first man from the frontier to achieve that honor.

State Flag
over Outline Map

942 · 3¢ blue · 1946

IOWA, one of the states carved out of the fifteen-million-dollar Louisiana Purchase, produces crops valued at two billion dollars annually. Land of the finest quality is technically known as "grade one." Iowa has one-fourth of all such soil in the United States. Of every hundred acres in the Hawkeye State, ninety-six are devoted to farming.

Figures such as these explain how Iowa is able to raise one-fifth of the country's corn and produce an equal percentage of its hogs. Nevertheless, Iowa was sparsely settled in early times (stamp 838); from 1821 to 1834 it did not even have civil government. However, the introduction of steamboat travel on the Missouri River and the defeat of the Indians in the Black Hawk War spurred on the settlement of Iowa.

In the 1830's many pioneers were drawn to Iowa by attractive reports of its rich farm land. From a figure of ten thousand the population rose to a hundred thousand in 1846, when Iowa entered the Union as the twenty-ninth state. During the great railroad-building decade of the 1850's, Iowa's population doubled.

On the commemorative stamp there appears an outline map of Iowa with the state flag superimposed. Stalks of corn, Iowa's most famous product, fill both side panels.

233

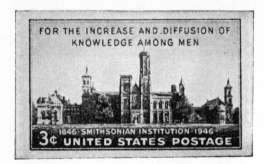

Smithsonian Institution

943 · 3¢ maroon · 1946

THE SMITHSONIAN INSTITUTION was founded in the nation's capital in 1846 through the generosity of James Smithson, a wealthy Englishman who bequeathed half a million dollars to the people of the United States "for the increase and diffusion of knowledge among men." Since then, the Smithsonian has received millions of dollars in private gifts, but its main income is from annual appropriations by Congress.

Many people visit the Smithsonian to see the Wright brothers' Kittyhawk plane or Lindbergh's *Spirit of St. Louis.* Also notable are the Smithsonian's zoological collections embracing twenty-seven million specimens. The two and a half million botanical specimens fill a room ten thousand feet square. The museum's impressive collection of minerals and gems is said to be the largest of its type in the world.

Some of the Smithsonian highlights are housed in separate buildings. The National Numismatic Collection and the National Philatelic Collection are among the finest of their kind. The National Gallery of Art contains one of the choicest collections in the world.

So huge are the number and extent of the Smithsonian exhibits that a visitor spending eight hours daily on them would need a century and a half to see them all.

Entry into
Santa Fe

944 · 3¢ maroon · 1946

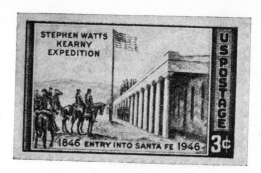

AFTER SERVING in the War of 1812, Stephen Watts Kearny (1794-1848) was stationed at frontier outposts for many years. Because he was an exceptionally experienced and competent officer, he was placed in charge of the Army of the West at the outbreak of the Mexican War in 1846.

Setting out from Fort Leavenworth with a force of about sixteen hundred mounted Missouri volunteers, Kearny had instructions to capture Santa Fe—by peaceful means if possible.

Kearny's expedition completed a trek of eight hundred miles along the Santa Fe Trail, plagued by the blazing sun, rattlesnakes, and buffalo gnats. The polluted drinking water was "so bad that one who drank it would have to shut both eyes and hold his breath until the nauseating dose was swallowed."

Kearny took Santa Fe without any opposition and established an American provisional government over the New Mexico region. The commemorative stamp shows the entry of Kearny's forces into Santa Fe as the American flag is raised over the Mexican governor's palace.

Later, Kearny brought his forces to California. The defeat of the Mexicans had left a confused situation there, but Kearny re-established order when he became the military governor. His death in 1848 cut short a distinguished career.

Thomas Alva Edison

(1847-1931)

945 · 3¢ purple · 1947

THOMAS EDISON'S early successful inventions were generally valuable improvements on already existing devices. While he was still in his twenties he received forty thousand dollars for his improved stock-ticker machine. His work on the telegraph resulted in a machine that sent four messages simultaneously over a single wire.

Edison's invention of the talking machine was inspired by his improvements on Alexander Graham Bell's telephone. The device Edison invented worked with wax cylinders, and we know it today as the dictaphone or Ediphone. (The phonograph or gramophone, using flat plastic disks, was a later invention by a German named Berliner.)

It is said that Edison made fifty working models at a cost of two million dollars before he was satisfied with his talking machine. His work on his most famous invention, the incandescent lamp (see stamp 654), tried his patience even more severely.

Edison was by far the most prolific inventor of all time. At one time he worked on forty-five ideas simultaneously. He had over a thousand inventions to his credit, with close to three thousand patents.

Joseph Pulitzer
(1847-1911)

946 · 3¢ purple · 1947

JOSEPH PULITZER, the amazingly dynamic man who revolutionized American newspaper publishing, was born in Hungary. He came to the United States at the age of seventeen, during the Civil War, and immediately enlisted in the Northern Army.

After the war Pulitzer wandered over the country, working at odd jobs. He studied law intensively and in a few years he was admitted to the bar. Deeply engrossed in reform politics and in the newspaper business as well, he founded the St. Louis *Post-Dispatch* in 1878. It is still an outstanding newspaper.

A little later Pulitzer purchased the New York *World* and turned it into one of the most interesting papers of the day. Always a crusader for worth-while causes, he sometimes resorted to cheap sensationalism to build up circulation. Pulitzer had always had poor eyesight and eventually he went blind. With the aid of three secretaries he was able to keep in touch with events and continue managing his newspapers.

Pulitzer, a generous and intelligent philanthropist, donated two million dollars to found the Columbia University School of Journalism as well as the funds for the Pulitzer Prizes and Scholarships. In making these admirable bequests he was true to his finest ideals.

237

George Washington
(1732-1799)
Benjamin Franklin
(1706-1790)

947 • 3¢ blue • 1947

THE UNITED STATES postal system owes much to the organizing genius of Benjamin Franklin. In 1753, before he became Deputy Postmaster General of the colonies, the mails were slow, inefficient, costly, and unreliable. Franklin realized that improving the system would bring the scattered colonial centers into closer contact. As a patriotic Philadelphian, he hoped to make that city the hub of the postal system.

As soon as Franklin received his appointment, he gave all his shrewdness and energy to the much needed reforms. He put mail transportation on a twenty-four-hour basis, improved old routes and mapped new ones, and required postmasters to mail out all newspapers—not merely their own.

For eight years Franklin not only received no pay for his work; he actually contributed money of his own! Finally, he recovered all his expenses and sent on a handsome profit to the British Treasury—the first profit ever shown on the operation of the colonial mail service.

The portraits on the commemorative stamp are copied from the first United States postage stamps, issued in 1847. A Pony Express rider, an old-time steam locomotive, a modern Diesel engine, a steamship, and a four-motored plane make up a colorful pageant of communication methods.

"The Doctor"
by Sir Luke Fildes

949 · 3¢ maroon · 1947

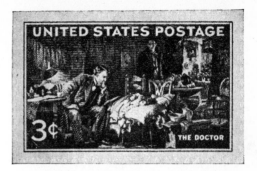

SINCE 1847, the year in which the American Medical Association was founded, the practice of medicine has made enormous progress.

Louis Pasteur's discovery of the role of bacteria in causing disease opened up a wide field for fruitful research. Later investigators studied the cause of each disease and sought methods of preventing or curing the ailment.

The establishment of public health agencies and the really large-scale building of hospitals date from the middle of the nineteenth century. The magnificent work of Florence Nightingale and Henri Dunant (see stamp 1016) revolutionized the treatment of wounded and sick soldiers.

It was also about this time that anesthesia began to be used consistently. The steady improvement in surgical techniques has saved many lives.

In the twentieth century discoveries have come with bewildering frequency. Perhaps most notable of all have been the discovery of the value of vitamins and the development of the antibiotics.

The commemorative stamp is copied from one of the world's most famous paintings. It portrays more eloquently than any word could, a doctor's concern for his patient.

"This Is the Place"

950 · 3¢ purple · 1947

THE WORD Mormon is derived from the English word *more* and the Egyptian word *mon* ("good"). Mormonism started when an angel of the Lord allegedly visited Joseph Smith in a dream and told him of a new Bible—*The Book of Mormon*—inscribed in Egyptian hieroglyphics on plates of gold.

Because of their unorthodox beliefs, the Mormons were driven from their homes in Ohio, Missouri, and Illinois. At last, Brigham Young (1801-1877), their leader, decided that his people could find safety only in the wilderness. They had no other choice, unless they renounced their beliefs.

In 1846 the Mormons, twenty thousand strong, set out on a seventeen-month trek from Illinois to Utah. The hardships they endured dwarf all other accounts of pioneer travel. A granite shaft at the mouth of Emigration Canyon, in the Wasatch Mountains of Utah, marks the site where Brigham Young uttered the famous words, "This is the place!" The extraordinary beauty of this setting repaid all the sufferings of the Mormon pioneers.

Working hard and trading profitably, the Mormons built up prosperous communities. Toward the end of his long life Brigham Young said proudly, "I have made no man poor, but I have made thousands rich."

150th Anniversary of Launching

951 · 3¢ green · 1947

THE UNITED STATES frigate *Constitution*, affectionately nick-named Old Ironsides, was the luckiest and most popular ship in the United States Navy.

Launched in 1797 and equipped with forty-four guns, the *Constitution* played an important role in the blockade and bombardment of the Barbary Coast. Its days of glory really arrived in the War of 1812, with stirring victories over the *Guerrière* and the *Java* and thrilling escapes from powerful British squadrons.

Though Americans had been wildly enthusiastic over the *Constitution*'s victories and escapes, in 1830 the Navy Department decided to scrap the vessel rather than foot the bill for repairing the costly ravages of time. It was then that Oliver Wendell Holmes saved Old Ironsides with his rousing poem that begins:

> Ay, tear her tattered ensign down!
> Long has it waved on high . . .

The commemorative stamp shows sixteen stars representing the sixteen states in the Union at the time the *Constitution* was launched. At each side of the stamp is one of the formidable twenty-four-pounders that humbled the British frigates.

Heron and Outline Map of Florida

952 · 3¢ green · 1947

EXTREMELY HEAVY rainfall produced the Everglades, that unique region in Florida that is part swamp, part shallow lake, filled with tiny islands covered with tangled subtropical growths. Here are found many wild creatures that exist nowhere else in the United States.

Everglades National Park, about a hundred miles long and fifty wide, is one of the few unspoiled wildernesses left in the United States. During the nineteenth century its wildlife was exposed to large-scale butchery. Game laws passed about 1900 saved the wildlife from utter destruction, and the establishment of the national park has made this protection even more effective.

The Everglades birds breed in profusion, and a single rookery contains thousands of them. They include the extremely beautiful wood ibis and heron, the anhinga with its snakelike head, the greedy cormorant, the once near-extinct snowy egret, the roseate spoonbill, and the tall, graceful, "Technicolored" flamingo that eats with its head upside down.

The commemorative stamp shows a heron silhouetted against an outline map of Florida, indicating the Everglade region.

George Washington Carver
(1864?-1943)

953 · 3¢ purple · 1948

To PUT together his first laboratory at Tuskegee Institute, George Washington Carver took his handful of students on trips to rubbish piles where they picked up scraps of wire, tin cans, bottles, and other junk.

In this homely laboratory, where he used discarded perfume bottles for test tubes, Carver revolutionized the farming economy of the South.

To popularize the sweet potato and soybean as well as the peanut, Carver developed hundreds of amazing new products from them. In the case of the peanut, he "simply" broke it down into its components—water, fats, oils, gums, resins, sugars, starches, pectoses, pentoses, legumen, lysin, anima, and amino acid. By almost magical rearrangements he turned them into dyes, paper, shaving cream, cheese, linoleum, ink, paints, and hundreds of other seemingly unrelated products.

Carver's convincing experiments proved to the farmers of the South that rotation of crops brought them profitable returns while it renewed the exhausted soil. Unworldly as Carver was, he brought millions of dollars to the new South without accepting any payment for his discoveries. To this kindly, deeply religious man, his scientific abilities were a gift from God.

Sutter's Mill

954 · 3¢ purple · 1948

JOHANN AUGUSTUS SUTTER became the richest man in California by virtue of a land grant from the Mexican government. On January 24, 1848, he suffered a misfortune that eventually turned him into a pauper: gold was discovered on his land.

Soon, miners were swarming all over Sutter's property and ruining it. Defective land titles left him helpless when he tried to fight back. Nearby San Francisco, which had fifteen thousand people in 1848, mushroomed into a ramshackle city of nearly a hundred thousand by 1850.

The forty-niners, people from every walk of life, stormed into the California diggings in prairie schooners; by ship and mule-back via the Isthmus of Panama; even by the long, tedious voyage around Cape Horn. The prices of food and equipment skyrocketed. At first prospectors swirled shallow river water in pans, but this was too slow and laborious. Later they used sluice boxes to wash away the gravel.

Five hundred vessels, most of them deserted, were moored in San Francisco Bay. Flour sold for four hundred dollars a barrel; a rowboat, for five hundred. In the first eight years five hundred million dollars worth of gold was mined. Not until the gold rush fever abated did Californians realize that their state offered treasures more enduring than its gold supply.

Winthrop Sargent

(1753-1820)

955 · 3¢ maroon · 1948

CLAIMED AND settled in turn by the French, British, Spanish, and Americans, Mississippi had a turbulent early history. For years after the American Revolution, the claims to this region were cloudy but clamorous.

In 1795, the United States, by means of a treaty with Spain, got a clear title to the area which now comprises Mississippi and Alabama. All that was lacking was the southern coastal strip on the Gulf of Mexico, which at that time was part of West Florida and still a Spanish possession.

Three years later the United States government set up the Mississippi Territory, with Winthrop Sargent as the first territorial governor. During his administration Sargent found himself trapped in the factional struggles of the old French families, the equally aristocratic British Loyalist group, and the aggressively democratic American frontiersmen.

The western part of the territory entered the Union as the State of Mississippi in 1817. The eastern part was then organized as Alabama Territory, and became a state in 1819.

The commemorative stamp intentionally carries a curious mistake. When the State Department originally prepared the territorial seal, someone misspelled the name of the new territory, making it "Missisippi"; the stamp reproduces this mistake.

"Interfaith
in Action"

956 · 3¢ black · 1948

ONE NIGHT in January, 1943, the *Dorchester,* a wheezy five-thousand-ton freighter converted into a troopship, left a Massachusetts port of embarkation and headed for a bleak outpost in Greenland.

The German submarine menace was at its height. The American Navy was so overextended by convoy duty that only Coast Guard vessels were available to guard convoys to Greenland.

As the *Dorchester* was plodding slowly through the iceberg-infested waters near Greenland, a perfectly aimed German torpedo smashed into the vessel's engine room. In less than a minute the furious jet of steam and oil killed a hundred men.

As the stricken ship began to list, scenes of wild, hysterical terror broke out on the crowded deck. The captain, officers, medical men, and four chaplains did their best to calm the men and get them over the side in orderly fashion.

Toward the end, the heroic chaplains gave away their life jackets to soldiers who needed them. Then all four—George Fox and Clark Poling, Protestant ministers; John Patrick Washington, a Catholic priest; and Alexander Goode, a rabbi—linked arm in arm, stayed on the vessel as it sank beneath the waves. "Greater love hath no man than this, that a man lay down his life for his friends."

State Capitol and Outline Map of Wisconsin

957 · 3¢ purple · 1948

AFTER JEAN NICOLET's early visit to Wisconsin in 1634 (see stamp 739), French explorers and traders journeyed to that distant region from time to time. Wisconsin was French territory for almost a century before it finally passed into British hands in 1763.

In 1783, after the end of the Revolutionary War, Wisconsin was ceded to the United States as part of the Northwest Territory. However, Wisconsin was so far away from the original states that it was a part of America only on the maps. American military and diplomatic strength was inadequate to drive out the British, who continued to remain in control until after the War of 1812.

Up to the early years of the nineteenth century, emigration to Wisconsin was scanty and the region remained a paradise for fur traders. Wisconsin's land boom began in the late 1820's and after that settlement was rapid indeed.

In the 1830's large numbers of land-hungry European farmers started to arrive in Wisconsin. They sent rhapsodical descriptions of the rich soil to their friends and relatives, and this led to new waves of immigration.

The commemorative stamp contains an outline map of Wisconsin and a picture of the State Capitol.

247

Pioneer Heading
Westward with
Covered Wagon

958 · 5¢ blue · 1948

NORWEGIAN EMIGRATION to the United States, though substantial, was completely overshadowed by that of the Swedes. No less than a million Swedes came to this country in the nineteenth century.

This is a phenomenal figure, for Sweden had a nineteenth-century population of only some six million. But economic opportunities in Sweden were scarce and taxes were burdensome. Famine created many emigrants in the 1860's. America had still another attraction. The absence of class distinctions in the New World was a welcome change from Europe.

The Swedes who settled on the western plains made an important contribution to the development of the Middle West. Accustomed to hard work from early childhood, they loved farming and willingly braved cold, drought, and disease. They made a point of saving their money to buy the best machinery, and formed cooperatives for purchasing and marketing.

The commemorative stamp shows a Swedish pioneer traveling west with his covered wagon. The twelve stars represent the states of the Midwest where the Swedes settled: Ohio, Indiana, Illinois, Michigan, Wisconsin, Minnesota, Iowa, Missouri, Kansas, Nebraska, and North and South Dakota.

248

Lucretia Mott
(1793-1880)
Elizabeth Cady Stanton
(1815-1902)
Carrie Chapman Catt
(1859-1947)

959 · 3¢ purple · 1948

As FAR as voting in national elections was concerned, American women remained second-class citizens until the passage of the nineteenth amendment in 1920.

At the beginning of the nineteenth century, women had many legal disadvantages. Since then, there have been far-reaching changes. We owe most of them to four great Americans—Susan B. Anthony (see stamp 784) and the three women pictured on this commemorative stamp.

Lucretia Mott, who became a Quaker minister at the age of twenty-five, was an attractive woman and a brilliant speaker. She pioneered in the fight for women's rights.

Elizabeth Cady Stanton, drawn into the feminist cause by Lucretia Mott, called the first Woman's Rights Convention in 1848. Her bold resolution for the right to vote infuriated men and even scandalized women.

Carrie Chapman Catt was the disciple who brought the struggle for voting rights to a successful conclusion. In her day, organized effort replaced brilliant but scattered activity. She was a superb planner, an efficient fund-raiser, a tireless lobbyist. Neither scathing ridicule nor personal tragedy kept these brave and gifted women from carrying on their historic mission.

Outline Map of
the Five Boroughs

C 38 · 5¢ red · 1948

FOR MANY years the city of New York was only a part of Manhattan Island. In fact, until well into the nineteenth century, a substantial part of the island remained woods and farm land. As late as 1855, Twenty-third Street was "too far uptown."

Under the continual pressures of immigration and booming business, the city pushed its way north. In 1873 it officially passed the bounds of Manhattan when an act of the state legislature extended the city limits north of the Harlem River. Such expansion possibilities were vitally necessary as Manhattan became more and more crowded with unhealthy slum neighborhoods toward the turn of the century.

By 1890 there was a clear need for consolidating New York with adjoining counties in order to form a more efficient municipal government. In 1894 the legislature provided for a "Greater New York" made up of Manhattan, Brooklyn, Queens County, Staten Island, and the Bronx (then in Westchester County).

After the voters in these areas approved the proposal, Greater New York came into existence on January 1, 1898. The commemorative stamp, issued fifty years later, shows an outline map of the five boroughs. A ring encloses the map to symbolize the golden anniversary of Greater New York.

William Allen White

(1868-1946)

960 · 3¢ purple · 1948

LIKE WILL ROGERS, William Allen White became world-famous precisely because he insisted on remaining a small-town American. Second to none as a newspaper editor, White preferred to identify himself with the little Kansas town of Emporia.

White wrote with just as much zest about a church social or a barn fire as he did about the weightiest events on the international scene. Yet, for all his placid good nature, he could lash out with stinging words at cruelty and injustice.

Starting in the newspaper business as a printer's devil, White went on to become a reporter and an editorial writer. In 1895 he augmented his capital of $1.25 with a loan of $3,000 to buy the Emporia *Gazette,* which he turned into one of the best-known newspapers in the United States.

White's editorials were outstanding for their forthright style. In 1896 his editorial "What's Wrong With Kansas?" acquainted the whole country with this brilliant country editor who wrote with humor as well as shrewdness, maintaining a balanced combination of the liberal and conservative outlooks.

Open-mindedness always remained White's ideal. "For facts change, and with changing facts come changing conclusions. Consistency is a paste jewel that only cheap men cherish."

Niagara Railway
Suspension Bridge

961 · 3¢ blue · 1948

THE BOUNDARY line between American and Canadian territory is the longest demilitarized border in the world. Canada and the United States share a border 3987 miles long, while the boundary between Alaska and Canada is 1538 miles long.

The commemorative stamp, which shows a view of the Niagara Railway Suspension Bridge at Niagara Falls, celebrates "a century of friendship" from 1848 to 1948. While the friendship undoubtedly exists, it has been marred by disagreements from time to time.

The most glaring instance of bad feeling arose during the Civil War. In October, 1864, twenty-two Confederate soldiers, dressed as civilians, left Canada and entered the banks of St. Albans, Vermont, at gunpoint. They concluded their bold raid by escaping to Canada. In the dispute that followed, Canada maintained that the raid had been a legitimate act of warfare. Nevertheless, the Canadian Parliament made a fifty-thousand-dollar grant to the Vermont banks as an act of good will.

Congress ended the reciprocity treaty between the two countries, and for a while armed guards faced each other across the border. Since that time, however, the United States and Canada have formed many close ties of friendship and business and have been allies in two world wars.

Francis Scott Key

(1779-1843)

962 · 3¢ red · 1948

FRANCIS SCOTT KEY wrote *The Star-Spangled Banner* during the War of 1812 at one of the most crucial moments of American history. The defeat of Napoleon in Europe had given the British an opportunity to concentrate their military and naval might against the outnumbered forces of the United States.

In August, 1814, a powerful British invasion force landed on the shores of Chesapeake Bay and set fire to the White House. Later, the British fleet began a heavy bombardment of Baltimore. Key, a native of that city, stayed awake the whole night of September 13-14 to learn whether Fort McHenry could hold out against the withering fire directed on it by the British fleet.

In an agony of impatience Key waited for "the dawn's early light" to see if "our flag was still there." Overjoyed to see the Stars and Stripes still flying over the American fort, Key wrote *The Star-Spangled Banner*. The poem immediately achieved such popularity that it became, informally, the national anthem. Curiously enough, Congress did not adopt *The Star-Spangled Banner* officially until 1931.

The commemorative stamp displays Key's portrait flanked by an American flag of our own day and one of 1814. At the left you can see the home of the Key family; on the right, Fort McHenry.

253

"Saluting Young America"

963 · 3¢ blue · 1948

THIS STAMP is one of several that have been issued in honor of young Americans. Other commemorative stamps pay tribute to the Boy Scouts (stamp 995), the 4-H Clubs (stamp 1005), and the Future Farmers of America (stamp 1024). Another commemorative stamp (stamp 974) is devoted to the memory of Juliette Gordon Low, the founder of the Girl Scouts.

These organizations, and others like them, have more and more come to be appreciated for their role in providing healthful and enjoyable activity for millions of young Americans. This has been especially important in view of the unrest that inevitably followed in the wake of World War II.

Juvenile delinquency has come to be recognized as one of the most troubling problems of American life. Slums, gangs, and poor family relations have contributed their share to this problem. Most people realize that the threat of severe punishment is not effective. State and municipal agencies rely on psychiatric guidance, recreational programs, and vocational training to help children and adolescents who are in difficulties.

The Salute to Youth stamp was issued to call attention to Youth Month, sponsored by the Theatre Owners of America in cooperation with the National Conference for Prevention and Control of Juvenile Delinquency.

John McLoughlin
(1784-1857)

Jason Lee
(1803-1845)

964 · 3¢ brown · 1948

FOR YEARS there was bitter rivalry between British and American fur traders in the Oregon country. John McLoughlin, a Canadian, was in charge of the Hudson's Bay Company's highly profitable Columbia district from 1824 to 1846. From his headquarters at Fort Vancouver he shipped about $125,000 worth of furs every year to England.

McLoughlin is remembered gratefully because, despite the merciless competition, he treated American missionaries and settlers with great kindness. If not for his generous treatment of the Oregon pioneers, many of them would have starved to death or else failed to establish permanent settlements. Eventually he became an American citizen.

Jason Lee was one of the first Methodist ministers to found missions for the Indians of the Oregon country. Later on, the first settlements naturally grouped themselves around Lee's missions and he became influential in attracting new settlers to Oregon.

Lee went East twice to bring out more missionaries to Oregon and to obtain government aid for the new settlers. He died during the second trip while still a comparatively young man.

Both these men are honored on the stamp issued to commemorate the formation of the Oregon Territory in 1848.

Harlan Fiske Stone
(1872-1946)

965 · 3¢ purple · 1948

IN 1924 the Department of Justice stood discredited by the Teapot Dome scandals. On taking office, President Coolidge sought an attorney general whose integrity, learning, and ability would restore public confidence. He found such a man in Harlan Fiske Stone, who had been dean of the Columbia Law School since 1910.

A year later the President appointed his new attorney general to the Supreme Court. Though Stone was conservative by temperament, his approach to cases before the high tribunal came as a great surprise. Instead of siding with the deeply conservative majority, Stone almost invariably joined in the brilliant dissenting opinions of Justices Holmes and Brandeis, and later on of Justices Brandeis and Cardozo.

When New Deal measures came before the court, Stone consistently voted for them. While he did not always approve of them, he felt that he should try to rule out his own likes and dislikes in weighing the constitutionality of a law. He was greatly respected for his statesmanlike attitude.

In 1941 Stone became chief justice and served in that capacity until his death in 1946. His moderation and self-discipline set a good example in a time of unequaled stress and upheaval.

Dedication of the Observatory

966 · 3¢ blue · 1948

THE GIGANTIC Hale telescope on Mount Palomar, the largest instrument of its kind, took twenty years to plan and build at a cost of $6,500,000. It is operated jointly by the California Institute of Technology and the Carnegie Institution.

The reflector of the telescope weighs 19 tons. Resting on a 500-ton mounting, it has a diameter of 200 inches and magnifies objects 600,000 times. It took eleven years to grind the lens until it was ready to be used.

The steel dome of the observatory weighs 1000 tons and is supported by massive concrete walls. The dome rotates on 32 four-wheeled trucks so delicately constructed that they cause no vibration in the telescope. Despite the huge size of the telescope, its rotation is controlled by push button and synchronized with the rotation of the earth and the apparent motion of the stars.

The telescope, dedicated in 1948, reaches out millions of light-years to photograph stars, some of which are no brighter than a candle "seen" from a distance of 40,000 miles. Used together with camera and spectroscope, this superb instrument tells astronomers the size, mass, density, and velocity of tremendous numbers of stars.

Clara Barton

(1821-1912)

967 · 3¢ red · 1948

WHEN CLARA BARTON saw the soldiers marching off to battle at the outbreak of the Civil War, she was filled with pity. At first she raised money for supplies to the wounded. But that was not enough.

In 1862 she became a nurse on the battlefield, risking her life repeatedly in such bloody battles as those at Antietam and Fredericksburg. After the war was over, she went to Switzerland to regain her strength. When she learned of the existence of the International Red Cross (see stamp 1016), she began a long struggle to bring the United States into the organization. After years of repeated rebuffs from government officials, she founded the American Red Cross in 1881.

About this time she wrote tartly to President Arthur: "If the United States is fortunate and diligent enough, perhaps it will make the thirty-second in the list of humanity and civilization. If not, it will remain where it is, among the barbarians and the heathen." Strong language this, to the President of the United States.

Taking Clara Barton at her brusque word, the President signed the Geneva Convention in 1882 and Congress ratified it unanimously the same year. Even in advanced old age Clara Barton continued to help sufferers wherever disaster struck.

Light Brahma Rooster

968 · 3¢ brown · 1948

THE POULTRY industry, with its estimated 1950 income of three billion dollars, is "big business." In that year Americans consumed an average of four hundred eggs each. The poultry industry has made more progress in the last hundred years than in the previous three thousand years.

In Colonial times game birds were so plentiful that there was little point in raising chickens for their meat. As towns and cities grew, eggs steadily became a more important item of the American diet. By the middle of the nineteenth century poultry raising was ready to enter its golden age. The invention of the steel plow and the reaper had released the labor of many farmers for other tasks.

The next step was experimental breeding of the birds that lay the most eggs and supply the most meat of the best quality. First, a number of Asiatic breeds were imported. The most popular, originating in China, were the Brahmas and Cochins. Eventually, American poultrymen developed breeds outstanding for eggs and meat; the best known are the Rhode Island Red, Plymouth Rock, and Wyandotte.

The commemorative stamp, issued for the centenary of the poultry industry, pictures a Light Brahma, the oldest specialized breed used in this country.

259

Star on Palm Leaf

969 • 3¢ gold • 1948

THE GOLD STAR MOTHERS CLUB is an organization made up of mothers whose sons have died in the line of duty while serving in the armed forces.

At the beginning of 1954, there were approximately thirty thousand members distributed over six hundred chapters. The Gold Star Mothers devote themselves to the entertainment of hospitalized veterans, for they feel they can best forget their own sorrow by helping others who have suffered from the ravages of war.

Despite the unparalleled destruction of the two World Wars, the Civil War still remains the costliest, in terms of human lives lost, in which the United States has taken part. In World War I United States forces lost about 125,000 men. In World War II the losses were far more severe, amounting to about 400,000.

In the Civil War, Union losses alone amounted to about 360,000. Confederate losses, based on incomplete figures, are estimated at 135,000.

The Gold Star Mothers stamp, featuring a star superimposed on a palm leaf, is one of the most striking in the whole commemorative series.

"Guardian of the Pioneer"

970 · 3¢ purple · 1948

FORT KEARNY, one of the most famous frontier outposts of the West, was named for General Stephen Watts Kearny (see stamp 944). It was originally built in 1846 on the banks of the Missouri River in Nebraska to protect the westward advance of the pioneers.

Soon, it became evident that the site was a poor one, far removed from the main emigration routes. In 1848 Fort Kearny was moved west two hundred miles to the Platte River. Here it became an important post on the Oregon Trail and on the California Gold Rush route. Many thousands of forty-niners stopped at Fort Kearny on their way to California.

The Fort Kearny garrison gave emigrants much-needed protection against marauding Indians, while the post served as a convenient place to rest, make repairs, obtain food, water, and supplies, and form wagon trains. In addition to block houses and a lookout station, the post had a sawmill, stables, and a blacksmith shop.

Later on, Fort Kearny became a valuable base for the Pony Express and the Overland Stagecoach route, as well as for the extension of the telegraph and the building of the first transcontinental railroad. Fort Kearny was abandoned in the 1870's after it had outlived its usefulness.

Peter Stuyvesant

(1592-1672)

971 · 3¢ red · 1948

THE HONOR of organizing the first volunteer firemen's brigade in America belongs to Peter Stuyvesant, the last governor of New Netherland (see stamp 1027).

The Dutch built their homes, with their distinctively gabled fronts, completely of wood. Worse yet, many of the houses had thatched roofs. Keenly aware of the danger of a devastating fire, Stuyvesant forbade the use of wooden chimneys or thatched roofs. After setting up a system of fire wardens to inspect homes for hazards, Stuyvesant required the burghers to keep on hand a leather bucket of water; after sundown they had to leave three buckets on the doorstep.

Since fires often blazed out of control, Stuyvesant and the town council set up a fire fighting organization in 1648. It had eight members, who took turns patrolling the streets at night.

To sound the alarm, they shook wooden rattles and shouted, "Throw out your buckets!" to the accompaniment of tolling bells. Roused from their sleep, the citizens dressed sketchily and ran out to take their place in the bucket brigades. As each bucket held about three gallons of water, trying to put out a blaze was often a hopeless job.

The commemorative stamp features a picture of Stuyvesant flanked by old and modern fire engines.

Outline Map of Oklahoma and Seals of the Five Civilized Tribes

972 · 3¢ brown · 1948

IN THE 1830's the Cherokees, Chickasaws, Choctaws, Muscogees (Creeks), and Seminoles were forcibly uprooted from their homes in the South and Southeast and driven away to land set aside for them in the Indian Territory—now part of Oklahoma. Of these Five Civilized Indian Tribes, as they came to be known, the Cherokees stand out as having had the most advanced culture among all the American Indians.

In 1821 a Cherokee named Sequoyah devised a Cherokee alphabet of eighty-five letters. Two years later the Cherokees adopted a constitution closely patterned on that of the United States. In 1828 they founded their own newspaper. It was printed in Cherokee and English.

The Cherokees lost their homes and farms in 1838 when United States soldiers rounded them up and forced them onto the "Trail of Tears"—a twelve hundred mile trek to the Indian Territory. A third of them died on the way.

The Five Civilized Indian Tribes lived peaceably, worked hard and prospered, and founded democratic governments and schools and churches. Many married white people. In 1906 the tribes were granted United States citizenship, and in the following year Oklahoma Territory and the Indian Territory were combined into the new state of Oklahoma.

263

50th Anniversary

973 · 3¢ maroon · 1948

AT THE outbreak of the Spanish-American War, Theodore Roosevelt was Assistant Secretary of the Navy. But a desk job, no matter how important, did not satisfy colorful, energetic "Teddy" Roosevelt.

Roosevelt's patriotism and love of adventure led him to organize the First Regiment of United States Cavalry Volunteers—the "Rough Riders." This picturesque group, made up of cowboys, ranchers, Indians, hunters, football stars, and polo players, contributed their own horses and weapons.

The victorious advance of the Rough Riders to the top of heavily fortified San Juan Hill has become an American legend. "On the open hillside there was no protection; shot and shell from the batteries roared. Then came the order, 'Forward! Charge!' Lieutenant-Colonel Roosevelt led, waving his sword. In the open, men went up the hill. Death seemed certain. Up, up they went with colored troops alongside of them, not a man flinching."

The Rough Riders took the hill, and the dramatic story made Teddy Roosevelt a national hero overnight. The spirit of that gallant charge is conveyed on the commemorative stamp by the equestrian statue of Captain William Owen ("Bucky") O'Neill, who was killed in the assault.

Juliette Gordon Low

(1860-1927)

974 · 3¢ green · 1948

JULIETTE GORDON LOW, who was born in Savannah, went to England to live after her marriage in 1886. Years later, when her husband died, she sought some activity to banish her acute loneliness.

She found the solution in 1909 when she met Lord Baden-Powell, the founder of the Boy Scout movement, and his sister, who had formed a similar organization for girls, called the Girl Guides. Realizing how useful such a group could be in her native land, Mrs. Low returned to the United States to form an organization for young girls.

In 1912 Mrs. Low founded the Girl Scouts of America. The following year she set up a small national office in Washington, D. C. Despite the handicap of being quite deaf, Mrs. Low did practically all the work of the office for three years and paid all the bills. Her pioneering efforts helped to build an organization that in 1950 had two million members.

Mrs. Low is gratefully remembered by the Girl Scout movement, and Girl Scout Week is observed every year to include her birthday, October 29. Another way in which the Girl Scouts have honored their founder is by establishing the Juliette Low World Fellowship Fund, which sponsors friendly contacts among Girl Scouts and Girl Guides all over the world.

Will Rogers

(1879-1935)

975 · 3¢ purple · 1948

WILL ROGERS, who was born on a ranch in the old Indian Territory, was very proud of his part-Cherokee ancestry. The death of his mother when he was ten years old left him a lonely, restless child. He never quite settled down even when he became successful.

Will left school to become a cowboy; later he joined a circus troupe and was billed as "the champion trick roughrider and lasso thrower in the world." Soon, he became an outstanding artist on the stage.

Will's friendly drawl appealed to audiences so strongly that his rope-twirling became a minor part of his act. People relished his shrewd observations, which were less innocent than they sounded, yet free from malice.

Though Will had never thought of himself as a writer, his brief pungent bits in *The New York Times* made many Americans chuckle over an otherwise dismal array of news items. His death in an airplane crash in Alaska in 1935 stunned his millions of admirers and well-wishers.

The two sayings Will Rogers is best remembered for are, "Well, all I know is what I read in the papers," and, "I never met a man I didn't like. I am proud of it."

Rocket Ascending over Fort Bliss

976 · 3¢ brown · 1948

IN 1848 the United States Army founded the Post of El Paso in the arid, cactus-grown country near the Mexican border. Six years later the post was renamed Fort Bliss, after General Zachary Taylor's chief adjutant.

Fort Bliss became the Army's most important cavalry center, and the First Cavalry Division, organized here, had such famous officers as Robert E. Lee and George Custer. When Jefferson Davis was Secretary of War in the cabinet of Franklin Pierce, he imported Arabian camels for use in the desert. Unfortunately, the animals did not flourish away from home. (In prehistoric times, though, camels roamed over North America.)

In the 1890's Fort Bliss was a valuable base of supplies in the Indian wars in the Southwest. Today, though the age of cavalry is long past, Fort Bliss is more important than ever. At the White Sands Proving Ground, the Army, Navy, and Air Force are carrying on a combined research project involving intensive study of supersonic planes, antiaircraft fire, radar-guided missiles, and radio-controlled targets.

The commemorative stamp shows a rocket ascending over Fort Bliss. A mountain scene appears on the left, a mission on the right.

267

Moina Michael
(1870-1944)

977 · 3¢ red · 1948

EARLY IN World War I the poppy, which grows in great profusion in France and Flanders, became the soldiers' favorite flower. The poppy was used more often than any other flower to decorate the graves of the war dead.

Colonel John McCrae wrote the most popular verses of the war in the lines beginning:

> In Flanders fields the poppies blow
> Between the crosses, row on row. . . .

Thus, even before the end of the war, the appropriateness of the poppy as a memorial flower was well established. To Moina Michael, a member of the YMCA Overseas Headquarters in New York, belongs the honor of starting the custom of wearing poppies in remembrance of the dead. On November 9, 1918, Miss Michael, a native of Athens, Georgia, presented poppies to the men attending the twenty-fifth conference of the YMCA.

In 1920, as the direct result of Miss Michael's efforts, the American Legion adopted the poppy as its national memorial flower. The following year the Legion and its Women's Auxiliary started the program of selling artificial poppies to raise funds for aiding wounded veterans. This program is soundly based on the view that helping the living sufferers is the best memorial to the dead.

85th Anniversary

978 · 3¢ blue · 1948

THREE DAYS of desperate fighting left more than ten thousand dead strewn on the once peaceful fields and hillsides of Gettysburg.

Five months later the new cemetery at Gettysburg was dedicated. The chief speaker at the ceremony was Edward Everett, the most polished orator of the day. Almost as an afterthought, the President of the United States was invited to give a brief address.

Everett spoke for two solid hours, severely testing the staying powers of the audience. Then the weary President had the task of explaining why it was important to preserve the Union. Though burdened with the worries and horrors of the war crisis, Lincoln had prepared his message with a great deal of care. Unfortunately his words were lost on most of the audience.

Few of the lonely man's listeners could appreciate the lofty views of this gaunt, awkward speaker who had a heavily lined face and deeply melancholy eyes and a nasal, high-pitched voice.

One newspaper wrote that Lincoln's words were "dishwatery," another that his performance was "ludicrous." Only after his death did the Gettysburg Address come to be generally recognized for what we now know it to be: the noblest utterance ever made on the spirit of American government.

"Sound Mind, Sound Body"

979 · 3¢ red · 1948

THE FAILURE of the German Revolution of 1848 forced many freedom-loving Germans to leave their native land. Large numbers of them came to the United States, settling on farms in the Midwest or concentrating in such cities as Cincinnati and St. Louis. Though they retained the customs of their homeland, they enjoyed their new-found freedom and took an active part in politics.

Carl Schurz, Franz Sigel, and Friedrich Hecker, the outstanding men in this group of new Americans, all became strong antislavery fighters and fervent admirers of Abraham Lincoln. They led brigades in the Northern Army during the Civil War.

Friedrich Hecker also revived on American soil one of the favorite leisure-time activities of his homeland. He organized the American Turners *(Turnvereine)*, a national federation of clubs devoted to gymnastics and wholesome recreation. Hecker looked to the organization to "advance the health, happiness, prosperity, and progress of mankind."

The national emblem of the Turners, shown on the commemorative stamp, features a reproduction of an ancient Greek statue (see stamp 719) and the motto: "Sound mind, sound body."

Joel Chandler Harris
(1848-1908)

980 · 3¢ purple · 1948

DURING HIS Georgia childhood, Joel Chandler Harris was deeply interested in Negro folklore and the shadings of Negro dialect. In later years he put his expert knowledge to good use.

While working as a printer's devil for a country newspaper, Harris managed to insert material of his own into its columns from time to time. In his early twenties he acquired a local reputation as a newspaper humorist.

From 1876 to 1900 Harris worked for the Atlanta *Constitution,* writing editorials, feature articles, book reviews, and even fiction. One day he was asked to write some humorous sketches in Negro dialect, and the result was a story that made him famous.

Out of his childhood memories of plantation days Harris created the dignified and wise Uncle Remus; from the myths of the Cherokee Indians he took the droll figure of Brer Rabbit, who always managed to foil the sinister Brer Fox.

"The Wonderful Tar-Baby Story" was followed by other Uncle Remus stories almost equally good. Though Harris wrote about a single locality and used a highly specialized dialect, his work was popular all over the United States, and in England as well.

271

Minnesota Pioneer

981 · 3¢ green · 1949

WE DO not know who the first white men were to reach Minnesota. Pierre Radisson, who was instrumental in founding the Hudson's Bay Company, arrived in the Minnesota region in 1660. France claimed the area in 1671, and in 1680 Father Louis Hennepin discovered the Falls of St. Anthony. This was the logical site for a flour milling industry and the future source of the prosperity of Minneapolis, a city founded many years later.

For almost a hundred years French explorers, traders, and missionaries traveled in Minnesota. In 1783 eastern Minnesota became part of the Northwest Territory (stamp 795). The Louisiana Purchase brought western Minnesota under the Stars and Stripes.

The first rush of settlers into Minnesota did not get under way until the 1830's. The great logging boom started near the end of the decade, when the first commercial sawmill was built in Minnesota. By 1849 the population had grown enough for Minnesota to be organized into a territory.

The Indians were not fully defeated until the 1860's. Minnesota's riches of timber, wheat, and iron attracted many immigrants. Extension of the railroads brought new prosperity.

The commemorative stamp shows a Minnesota pioneer moving westward with his Red River oxcart.

George Washington
(1732-1799)
Robert E. Lee
(1807-1870)

982 · 3¢ blue · 1949

THOUGH ROBERT E. LEE was a Southerner, he was opposed to slavery and to secession. Yet when he was privately offered command of the Union Army in 1861, he was filled with anguish. How could he make war on his family, his friends, his fellow Virginians? He resigned his commission in the United States Army and with a heavy heart joined the Southern cause.

Lee was a master strategist. Against the superior numbers, equipment, and resources of the North he could oppose only his superior generalship. It was enough to break such Union commanders as McClellan, Pope, Burnside, and Hooker; but the day of reckoning was bound to come. And in defeat Lee could still say, "There is a true glory and a true honor, the glory of duty done."

Though Lee's citizenship was never restored after the war, he worked tirelessly for reconciliation between the North and the South. "I have led the young men of the South in battle; I have seen many of them die on the field; I shall devote my remaining energies to training young men to do their duty in life."

True to his resolve, Lee became president of Washington College at Lexington, Virginia, where he took a fatherly interest in every student and instructor. After his death, the college was renamed Washington and Lee University, in his honor.

Puerto Rican Farmer

983 · 3¢ green · 1949

IN 1947 Congress authorized the first gubernatorial election in Puerto Rico. Luis Muñoz Marin, the statesmanlike leader of the Popular Democratic party, won the 1948 election and was inaugurated on January 2, 1948.

Another Congressional measure gave Puerto Ricans the right to prepare their own constitution. This new basic law, which went into effect in 1952, turned Puerto Rico into a commonwealth voluntarily associated with the United States. Governor Muñoz Marin, a firm believer in cooperation with the United States, was re-elected.

Under the new constitution, Puerto Ricans remain American citizens, but they cannot vote in United States elections and have no voting representative in Congress. On the other hand, they do not pay United States income taxes and are free to sever their tie with the United States. In addition, Puerto Rico receives about seventeen million dollars in annual Federal grants for hospital and housing programs as well as highways and welfare aid.

On the commemorative stamp we see a Puerto Rican farmer holding a cogwheel in one hand and a ballot box in the other. The cogwheel represents the modern industrialization program ("Operation Bootstrap") for raising living standards.

Seal of Alexandria

C 40 · 6¢ red · 1949

THE VIRGINIA town of Alexandria, near the nation's capital, has a pervasive Colonial charm that attracts many visitors. Mount Vernon is also near by, and there are many mementos of George Washington in Alexandria.

There is Christ Church, where Washington was a vestryman and where his pew still carries his name plate. The Friendship Fire Company had a wagon donated by Washington; he was a member of the Masonic Lodge and kept his account in an Alexandria bank.

On the commemorative stamp the seal of Alexandria is flanked by a picture of Gadsby's Tavern, where Washington spent much of his time, and of the Carlyle House, where Braddock (see stamp 688) planned his expedition.

Alexandria was incorporated in 1749 and named for John Alexander, a settler of the 1680's. George Washington, a lad of seventeen in 1749, helped to survey the streets.

Alexandria prospered steadily as its tobacco shipments increased, enabling its affluent merchants to build the elegant eighteenth-century brick houses that give the town its distinctive charm. But time does not stand still, even in Alexandria, which now has an airport, a naval torpedo station, and modern industrial plants.

Seventeenth-Century Map

984 · 3¢ blue · 1949

In 1649 a number of Puritans left Virginia to escape religious persecution and settled in Maryland on Chesapeake Bay. They called their colony Providence. Despite quarrels with the governor of Maryland, the new settlement flourished and soon became known as Anne Arundel's Town, named for the wife of the second Lord Baltimore.

When the town became Maryland's capital in 1694, its name was changed to Annapolis, in honor of Anne of England. As the leading tobacco port of Maryland, Annapolis became the chief center of Chesapeake shipping.

In the decades just before the Revolution, prosperous planters built the handsome Georgian residences that still attract appreciative visitors to Annapolis. These houses were luxuriously furnished from England and surrounded by lovely gardens of English flowers. After the beginning of the nineteenth century Annapolis lost its pre-eminence to Baltimore as the leading shipping center of Maryland.

The commemorative stamp is rich in interesting detail. The main feature is an antique map showing the location of the original settlement. On this are superimposed reproductions of a compass rose and Lord Baltimore's seal, as well as a seventeenth-century vessel and a boatload of colonists coming ashore.

276

Civil War Veteran

985 · 3¢ red · 1949

DURING THE Civil War, the North put about two million fighting men in the field. The early reliance on volunteers proved a failure, and in 1863 Congress had to pass a draft law. There was bitter resentment over a provision which allowed any man to buy himself out of military service by paying three hundred dollars. In New York the terrible draft riots raged for more than a week, taking a toll of over a thousand lives. Another cause of the war-weariness in the North was the high death rate in the Union Army.

After the war the veterans of the Union Army formed the Grand Army of the Republic. The organization first observed Memorial Day, the traditional day of honoring the Civil War dead in the North, in 1868. At its peak the GAR had 490,000 members, and in 1901 there were still 350,000 survivors.

But by 1949 their number had dwindled to a pitiful seventeen, and that year's "encampment" was the last reunion of the Grand Army of the Republic. The commemorative stamp pictures a weary, white-haired old man side by side with a lightly etched portrait of the same man as a young, buoyant Civil War soldier. In the top left corner almost all the sand in an hourglass has sifted to the lower half, indicating that time has nearly run out for the veterans.

Edgar Allan Poe

(1809-1849)

986 • 3¢ purple • 1949

EDGAR ALLAN POE is admired in this country, and even more in France, as one of our most imaginative writers. Yet his short life was wretched in the extreme. Orphaned at the age of three, he was brought up by foster parents who opposed his becoming a writer. Gambling and hack work, drink, debt, and disgrace tell the story of the rest of his life.

In "The Gold Bug," "The Purloined Letter," and "The Murders in the Rue Morgue" Poe created the detective story and inspired hundreds of imitators. If he did not create the horror story and the story of suspense, he certainly pointed the way for later writers.

Poe's verse had an eerie, almost hypnotic quality. He was less interested in communicating a meaning than in creating a mood by the sound of his words. This is apparent in "The Raven" and "The Bells," where he achieves powerful effects with trifling subjects. This is the aspect of Poe's work which had the most lasting effect on French literature.

The Poe commemorative stamp, like the poets' stamps in the Famous Americans series, carries a reproduction of Pegasus, the winged horse that served the ancient Greeks as the symbol of poetic imagination.

278

Post Office Building in Washington, D.C.

C 42 · 10¢ purple · 1949

BEFORE THE founding of the Universal Postal Union in 1874, the handling of international mail abounded in absurd contradictions. Each country had an extra charge for transit mail—mail passing through that country from another country and destined for a third country. Another difficulty was that the charges varied according to the routes; a letter from the United States to Australia might cost anywhere from five cents to more than a dollar, depending on the route used.

The variety of units of weight—ounces, grams, or "loths"—added to the confusion. Multiplicity of handling systems made for irritating delay. Postage wars, in which one country tried to get the better of another were all too frequent.

The Austro-German Postal Union, organized in 1850 with Austria, Prussia, and all the smaller German states as members, pioneered in the establishment of uniform rates and handling. Though the result was highly satisfactory, the old methods continued in force in other parts of the world.

An international conference on postal problems, suggested by the United States in 1862, was skillfully sabotaged by enemies of change. But the need for an orderly international postal system became more and more acute. On the initiative

279

Globe Encircled by Doves

C 43 · 15¢ blue · 1949

of Heinrich Stephan, Germany's chief postmaster, another conference took place in Berne, Switzerland, in 1874. This meeting was a success.

The twenty-two countries represented at this meeting signed a treaty bringing the Universal Postal Union into existence. The greatly reduced rate for foreign mail was made uniform, and transit mail was to be sent free across national boundaries. All provisions were to be equally binding on all members.

The Universal Postal Union has proved highly successful, and has gained many new members since its founding. An international staff handles its affairs at Berne, and congresses meet at five-year intervals to solve current problems. The handling of airmail presents difficulties, for the passage of airplanes across international boundaries has military implications.

The United States might have had airmail as early as 1912 if Congress had made an appropriation for experimental airmail service, as requested by the Post Office Department that year. Finally, six years later, trial airmail delivery started between Washington, D. C., and New York.

Coast-to-coast airmail in the United States began in 1920— but on a daylight basis and with relay changes of pilots and planes. By the following year, however, the first nonstop trans-

Four-Motored
Plane Flying over
the Pacific

C 44 · 25¢ red · 1949

continental airmail delivery was made successfully. The trip took twenty-seven hours and relied on revolving beacons to make night flying safer. Since that time, planes, instruments, and flying techniques have undergone tremendous improvement.

The successful operation of the Universal Postal Union and the use of the airplane as a postal carrier climax thousands of years of effort to develop a postal system. These efforts depended originally on runners and then on horseback riders. Stagecoaches came into use much later, and still later the railroads made postal service really efficient.

Twenty-four hundred years ago Herodotus wrote about the mounted Persian messengers of King Cyrus: "Neither snow, nor rain, nor gloom of night stays these couriers from the swift completion of their appointed rounds." Today these words are even more apt.

The three airmail stamps of this commemorative issue make use of graceful airplane motifs. The 10¢ stamp carries a picture of the Post Office Building in Washington, D. C. At the left is a twin-motor plane superimposed on part of the Universal Postal Union monument in Berne, Switzerland. The 15¢ stamp shows a globe encircled by doves bearing messages, while the 25¢ stamp features a four-motor plane flying over the Pacific Ocean.

Wilbur Wright
(1867-1912)

Orville Wright
(1871-1948)

C 45 · 6¢ red · 1949

OF ALL the many people who were experimenting with powered flight at the turn of the century, the Wright brothers were the only ones who had no formal scientific training. In fact, neither one was even a high-school graduate.

In a sense, their lack of book learning was an asset. They were untroubled by inherited dogmas; they could always take a fresh view of problems and methods that were years or even centuries old. When scientific data proved incorrect, they experimented patiently and naturally to assemble correct information.

But if the brothers lacked scientific training, they possessed scientific aptitudes. They were intensely alert and curious; their powers of observation were quite out of the ordinary; they were mechanically minded to an exceptional degree.

Above all, the Wright brothers had an enormous store of patience. They never shirked repeating a test or calculation hundreds of times until it yielded the result they were looking for. How they finally achieved success is described on page 317.

Like most inventors, the Wright brothers were ahead of their time; they met with little encouragement on the part of government officials. The military use of airplanes developed rather slowly, while their adoption as mail carriers was, surprisingly enough, even more tardy.

75th Anniversary

987 · 3¢ green · 1950

BEFORE THE passage of the National Banking Act of 1863, state-chartered banks often issued wildcat currency in boom times and then failed in panics. The result was ruin for their unlucky depositors and the holders of the worthless money.

At the outbreak of the Civil War, the Federal government was compelled to issue the inflationary greenbacks. The National Banking Act stabilized the national finances in addition to dealing with the state banks.

The new law of 1863 drove these banks out of existence and provided for national banks in their place. These national banks were allowed to issue currency only when it was backed by United States bonds. The passage of the Federal Reserve Act in 1913 was a further strengthening of the banking system.

The American Bankers Association was founded in 1875 "to promote the general welfare and usefulness of banks." In 1952 almost every bank and almost all the banking resources of the country were represented in the organization.

The main design on the commemorative stamp is in the form of the top half of a coin. Each item on the coin stands for some field in which banking plays a useful role. Included are a home (daily life); a farm (agriculture); a train (transportation); and a factory skyline (industry).

Samuel Gompers

(1850-1924)

988 · 3¢ purple · 1950

SAMUEL GOMPERS, who earned the title of "Labor Statesman of the World," was born in London and came to the United States in 1863. While still a child in England he became interested in labor organization when he saw silk weavers, displaced by labor-saving machinery, parading with banners that read, "We are starving."

Gompers started work as a cigar maker in 1865, and while he continued to work at this trade for many years, he also became active in union affairs. Having received little schooling, he filled in the gaps in his education by reading widely.

From the time of the organization of the American Federation of Labor in 1881 until his death in 1924, Gompers was continuously president of the Federation with the exception of one term (in 1895). Starting with an organization of a few thousand, Gompers built up the Federation until it had three million members.

Content to work for higher wages and shorter hours, Gompers was interested only in forming craft unions for skilled workers. As a cautious, tenacious man who favored middle-of-the-road policies, Gompers would have agreed with the man who said, "Politics is the art of the possible."

Statue of Freedom

989 · 3¢ blue · 1950

WASHINGTON, D.C., has often been called
the most beautiful capital in the world.
Actually, Washington was the third—not
the first—capital of the United States.
From 1785 to 1790 New York was the capital; then the seat of
government shifted to Philadelphia; and finally, in 1800, Washington became the capital.

Washington was the first modern capital to be designed in
detail instead of being allowed to grow haphazardly. The Capitol, housing the Senators and Representatives, was placed on
a high hill, with streets radiating from it like wheel spokes.
Pierre Charles L'Enfant, who planned Washington, looked
ahead to a time when the marshes and mud would have
disappeared.

The designs for the Presidential residence and the Capitol
were determined through prize contests. James Hoban was the
successful architect for the executive mansion, and the cornerstone was laid in 1792.

George Washington never lived in the White House, as the
President's home came to be called at a very early date. John
Adams, his successor, was the first President to occupy the White

White House

990 · 3¢ green · 1950

House. When he arrived in 1800, the building was far from finished. The streets were full of ruts and puddles; pigs and other barnyard animals wandered near by; the approaches were cluttered with workmen's shanties, lumber, and rubbish.

During the War of 1812, the White House was burned by the British. It was rebuilt and enlarged. The process of renovation has never stopped, and as recently as 1948 the White House underwent thorough reconstruction.

In that year President Truman noticed structural defects and called for a study of the building. It was found that ceilings were sagging, floors were in danger of falling through, stairways were on the point of crumbling. During the resulting repairs, which kept the Trumans out of the White House until 1952, the building was restored as nearly as possible to its previous appearance. It was strengthened structurally, however, by a new foundation of concrete piers.

The Supreme Court had no home of its own until 1935. Before then it held its sessions in a room of the Capitol.

The Supreme Court building is in the form of a Greek temple. The outer walls, of Georgia and Vermont marble, are decorated with reliefs. The interior, of Alabama marble, has large, handsome statues flanking the impressive marble stairway.

Supreme Court Building

991 · 3¢ purple · 1950

A broad corridor leads to the Supreme Court chamber. The contrasting Italian marble of the walls and the Spanish marble of the columns combine with the bronze gates and the rich mahogany furniture to create a worthy setting for the highest court of the land. A feature which creates wonderment is the apparent lack of support for two marble spiral stairways. This airy effect was obtained by wedging the inner ends of the steps deep into the wall.

William Thornton submitted the prizewinning plan for the Capitol in 1792, and the cornerstone was laid in 1793. Congress had its first meeting in the Senate chamber in 1800; the Representatives' chamber was not completed until 1807.

After its burning in 1814, the Capitol was not fully repaired until 1827. However, the admission of new states and the steady growth of population soon called for larger legislative chambers.

The new wings were completed in 1857, but the new dome took more time. This dome, made of cast iron, and weighing four thousand tons, was designed by Thomas U. Walter. The base is encircled by thirty-six columns representing the states in existence in 1857.

At the top of the dome, three hundred feet above the ground, a circle of thirteen windows is surmounted by the famous statue

Capitol

992 · 3¢ purple · 1950

of Freedom, represented by a robed woman who wears a helmet of eagle feathers. After being raised in place in December, 1863, during the critical days of the Civil War, this statue became one of the best-known landmarks of the capital. The work of Thomas Crawford, the statue is well known to stamp collectors, as it has more than once been a favorite subject for the regular postal issues.

The majestic portico of the Capitol leads up to the magnificent bronze doors on which the story of Columbus appears (see stamp 235). Inside is the rotunda or reception hall, with a stairway of three hundred and sixty-five steps leading to the dome.

The south wing contains the Representatives' chamber, the largest legislative hall in the world. The Senate chamber is in the north wing. In all, the Capitol contains four hundred and thirty rooms. Near by are the Senate Office building and the House Office building, with committee rooms, and offices for each legislator.

The set of four commemorative stamps, picturing the statue of Freedom, the Supreme Court building, the White House, and the Capitol, was issued for the sesquicentennial anniversary of the National Capital.

"Casey" Jones
(1864-1900)

993 · 3¢ maroon · 1950

JOHN LUTHER ("CASEY") JONES, a strapping six-foot-four giant of a man, was the Illinois Central Railroad's best-known locomotive engineer. He was famous for his daring and skill and his six-chime whistle that started with a crescendo and faded out in a whisper.

In 1900 Casey was assigned the crack Cannonball Express which traveled between Chicago and New Orleans. Erroneously informed, on the night of April 30, that the track was clear all the way, Casey let out the throttle to make up for lost time.

A freight train which should have been switched to a siding had been left on the main track. Ordering his fireman to jump to safety, Casey stayed at his post to slow down the train. It smashed through three freight cars. The crash killed Casey, but all the passengers were safe.

Wallace Saunders, a colored friend who was deeply grieved by the tragedy, composed a ballad about the wreck. Though Saunders was illiterate, his simple song had a heartfelt sincerity that gave it lasting popularity.

The commemorative stamp, issued fifty years after the wreck, pictures Casey Jones on a locomotive wheel. At the left is a locomotive of the turn of the century; at the right we see a modern Diesel.

Vista of Westport Landing and Kansas City

994 · 3¢ purple · 1950

AFTER FLOWING south for hundreds of miles, the Missouri River turns sharply east. This big bend is a natural site for a settlement, and today the twin cities of Kansas City, Kansas, and Kansas City, Missouri, are located on the south bank of the river.

In 1821 François Chouteau founded a trading post here. Another settlement, Westport Landing, grew up close by and served as a convenient outfitting place for pioneers and traders headed for the West. Both the Oregon and Santa Fe trails passed through Westport.

For a time, Independence, ten miles eastward, got much of this outfitting trade; but after a flood swept away the wharves of Independence, Westport Landing became the "gateway to the West."

In 1838 Westport Landing changed its name to the Town of Kansas, changing it again in 1853 to Kansas City. Because of its admirable location, the city became a great lumber and grain market, a meat-packing center second only to Chicago, and one of the most important transportation terminals of the United States.

The commemorative stamp gives us a vista of the old-time Westport Landing and the skyline of modern Kansas City.

40th Anniversary

995 · 3¢ brown · 1950

IN 1908 Lord Baden-Powell founded the Boy Scouts in England to develop self-reliance and resourcefulness among boys. He based his program on a study of existing organizations—including two American ones, the Sons of Daniel Boone (founded by Daniel Carter Beard) and the Woodcraft Indians (founded by Ernest Thompson Seton).

W. D. Boyce, a Chicago publisher, soon brought the Boy Scout idea to this country. The Boy Scouts of America was incorporated in 1910 and received a charter from Congress in 1916. By 1952 the Boy Scouts had close to three million members.

Scouting has spread to more than fifty other countries all over the world. Friendly relations among the Scouts of these countries foster international good will.

There are three age levels for Boy Scout membership. Cub Scouts (eight to ten years old) learn hobbies and skills and study safety rules. Boy Scouts (eleven to thirteen years) concentrate on camping, outdoor skills, lifesaving techniques, and community projects. Explorers (fourteen years and older) are qualified for the advanced stages of these activities; they also benefit by vocational training.

The commemorative stamp pictures a Cub Scout, a Boy Scout, and an Explorer.

William Henry Harrison

(1773-1841)

996 · 3¢ blue · 1950

AFTER OHIO became a territory in 1800, the rest of the Old Northwest Territory (see stamp 837) was renamed the Indiana Territory. William Henry Harrison, who became the governor of the Indiana Territory, soon found that dealing with the Indians was his most pressing problem.

Between 1760 and 1809 the Indians of the Northwest Territory region surrendered nearly fifty million acres to the land-hungry whites. To halt further inroads, the statesmanlike Shawnee chief Tecumseh (1768?-1813) formed an Indian confederacy extending all the way from the Great Lakes to the Gulf of Mexico.

Governor Harrison met this opposition in 1811 by crushing the Indian allies at Tippecanoe. Thirty years later, Harrison was elected President on the catchy slogan of "Tippecanoe and Tyler too!"

Indiana assumed its present boundaries in 1809 and was admitted to the Union in 1816. Settlement was so brisk that in the next fifteen years its population jumped from sixty-five thousand to three hundred and fifty thousand. New roads and canals helped bring settlers to Indiana's lush farm land. After the Civil War, Indiana played an important part in the industrial development of the Midwest.

California Pioneers

997 · 3¢ yellow · 1950

IN 1845 California had a population of fifteen hundred Mexicans and a thousand Americans. After several minor revolts and the expulsion of the last Mexican governor, the situation became extremely confused.

Commodore John D. Sloat, commander of the Pacific Squadron, feared that British naval forces might take advantage of the chaos to seize Upper California. In 1846 Sloat occupied Monterey, the capital.

Later that year, Californians set up the Bear-Flag republic, which lasted three days until American naval forces took over and raised the Stars and Stripes. The negotiations of 1848, after the Mexican War, officially ceded California to the United States. After gold was discovered near Sutter's fort (page 244), the population increased so rapidly that California was admitted to the Union in 1850.

At the left of the commemorative stamp we see a prospector panning gold; at the right a pioneer and his wife advance ahead of their ox-drawn covered wagon. Further to the right, oil derricks are faintly outlined. In the left panel citrus fruits are shown above a reproduction of the *Oregon,* the vessel which brought the news of Congressional enactment of California's statehood.

293

FINAL REUNION · UNITED CONFEDERATE VETERANS

UCV

3 CENTS

UNITED STATES POSTAGE

Civil War Veteran

998 · 3¢ gray · 1951

To APPRECIATE the long and stubborn struggle waged by the Confederacy during the Civil War, we must take account of the fact that the South was hopelessly outnumbered in population, resources, and fighting men. In all, the South mustered about a million fighting men—about half the number in the Northern forces. Both sides suffered severe losses in combat, and even heavier losses from inadequate medical and sanitary services.

After the war the soldiers of the South formed the United Confederate Veterans. Like their Northern counterparts, these veterans had an annual reunion and paid tribute every year to the Civil War dead. These observances took place on three different days—April 26, May 10, and June 3 (the birthday of Jefferson Davis).

The commemorative stamp was issued for the last reunion of the United Confederate Veterans. Like the Grand Army of the Republic stamp (page 277), this one pictures a soldier in his youth and in his old age.

The hourglass is again used to convey the idea that time is running out for the veterans. It was a happy thought to picture the same individual on both stamps, thus alluding to the reconciliation of North and South after the costliest conflict in American history.

First Permanent Settlement

999 · 3¢ green · 1951

NEVADA WAS part of the territory ceded by Mexico to the United States in 1848 after the Mexican War. The first permanent settlement was at Reese's Landing (later called Genoa) in 1851.

The Comstock Lode, the richest silver strike ever made, was discovered on public lands in 1857; soon, fierce squabbles raged over ownership claims. Nearby Genoa, which has a population of two hundred nowadays, was so flourishing that forty-four thousand tons of freight passed through the town in a year's time.

The Federal government established Nevada Territory in 1861, and benefited to the extent of minting forty-three million dollars' worth of Nevada gold and silver during the Civil War. This helped to relieve the critical wartime inflation. Later on a United States mint was established at Carson City in Nevada.

In 1864 Nevada was admitted to the Union somewhat prematurely because an additional free state was needed to ratify the thirteenth amendment (see stamp 902). In order to be able to vote for Lincoln in the election of 1864, Nevada telegraphed the whole text of its new constitution to Washington at a cost of $3,416.74.

The commemorative stamp pictures the small log fort which was the first permanent settlement in Nevada.

Views of Detroit

1000 · 3¢ blue · 1951

DETROIT GETS its name from the French *détroit,* meaning "strait." In exploring the waterways leading to the West, the French found a strategic location for a post on the Detroit River which in effect is a narrow strait linking Lake St. Clair with Lake Erie.

In 1701 Governor Frontenac of Canada sent Antoine de la Mothe Cadillac to build a fort on the west bank of the river. Cadillac named this outpost Fort Pontchartrain du Detroit. Thriving from the start, it soon became the center of French power in the West.

All French territory on the continent passed into English hands in 1763. Detroit's cached furs at that time were valued at half a million dollars. Almost until the end of the century Detroit remained the British headquarters for fomenting Indian raids on American settlers.

Though Detroit was part of the Northwest Territory, ceded to the United States in 1783, the British were unwilling to part with this valuable post. Not until 1796 did they finally yield it to the Americans.

The commemorative stamp pictures Detroit as it was in Cadillac's time, while in the upper part of the stamp we see the skyline of modern Detroit.

State Capitol

1001 · 3¢ blue · 1951

COLORADO, the most mountainous state in the Union, was pieced together in three parts from the Louisiana Purchase, the annexation of Texas, and the cession of land by Mexico after the Mexican War.

A year after the panic of 1857 had brought hard times to farmers and workingmen, gold was discovered near Pikes Peak in Colorado. One hundred thousand "Argonauts," as they called themselves, set out in hopes of a bonanza.

Mining towns sprang up in profusion, but despite the breezy slogan of "Pikes Peak or bust," many Argonauts never reached their goal. However, the mining boom brought in so many new settlers that Colorado became a territory in 1861 and a state in 1876. Short-lived gold booms were followed by equally short-lived silver booms. Central City, with its incongruous opera house, was the most famous of the resulting ghost towns.

The State Capitol dominates the commemorative stamp. At the right is the State Seal and a cowpuncher. At the left we see a columbine, Colorado's state flower, and the Mount of the Holy Cross. This mountain, which rises to a height of fourteen thousand feet, is remarkable for two long snow-filled ravines which form a Latin cross two thousand feet long and eight hundred feet wide.

75th Anniversary

1002 · 1951
3¢ maroon

THIS REMARKABLY compact stamp succeeds in giving us a vivid idea of what modern chemistry has achieved and what methods it uses. In the center is the diamond-shaped emblem of the American Chemical Society. At the top of the emblem we see a phoenix, representing the chemist's transformation of matter. At the bottom is a Liebig bulb, named for Justus von Liebig, considered by some the greatest analytical chemist of the nineteenth century.

At the left is an alembic (a vessel for distilling, purifying, testing, or transforming liquids); a hydrometer (a sealed cylinder for testing the specific gravity of liquids); and an ionization indicator (an instrument for checking electrical phenomena).

"The horizon of the chemical century" appears on the right, displaying the towers of a catalytic cracking plant, where petroleum is broken down by heat and pressure; a fractionating unit, which does the same job by distillation or crystallization; and a butadiene reactor, used in making artificial rubber.

Thus, the stamp helps to explain the proud and well-justified boast of the American Chemical Society: "There is nothing the public uses today which is not better than it was twenty-five years ago because of the contributions of the chemist and the chemical engineer."

298

175th Anniversary

1003 · 1951
3¢ purple

LESS THAN two months after the Declaration of Independence was proclaimed, Washington fought the British for the first time. It came dangerously close to being the last time. The occasion was the Battle of Brooklyn, better known as the Battle of Long Island. It was badly planned, and badly fought by the raw American troops.

Unwilling to relinquish either Manhattan or Long Island to the invading British, Washington split his army into two parts. This left the defenders greatly outnumbered.

Only a sudden rain saved the American army from destruction. The roads turned into mud, the British waited for better weather—and Washington formed a plan. He sent out a call for every boat that could be found. On the night of August 29, 1776, he had the best oarsmen in the world, the Marblehead fishermen, and he had a thick fog.

All night the small craft ferried American troops across the East River to Manhattan. Washington himself left on the last boat as dawn was breaking.

The Americans had suffered a disastrous defeat, but it was still possible to fight on. Even in defeat, Washington gained in stature; after the masterly river escape he was always known to the British as the "old fox."

Betsy Ross

1004 · 3¢ red · 1952

THE THIRTEEN colonies had several unofficial flags before the Declaration of Independence. Many of the flags had a canton—a square or rectangular division—in the upper left corner.

The first official American banner was the Grand Union Flag. It made its first public appearance on January 2, 1776, when General Washington was reviewing his troops at Cambridge. There were thirteen horizontal stripes, alternately red and white, with a blue canton.

On June 14, 1777, the Continental Congress adopted an official American flag with "thirteen stripes, alternate white and red," and "thirteen white stars on a blue field." Arranging the stars in a circle proved to be the most attractive pattern.

This is the flag that time-honored legend credits to Betsy Ross. Yet we are far from certain that she had anything to do with the flag. Evidence on the point is conflicting.

In any event, we definitely know that this was not the first American flag. It was preceded not only by the Grand Union flag, but also by other banners, such as the Taunton flag, the Continental flag, and the Gadsden flag. The Taunton flag (1774) carried the words "Liberty and Union." The Continental flag (1775) carried a picture of a pine tree. The Gadsden flag (1775) showed a coiled snake, with the words "Don't tread on me."

"To Make the Best Better"

1005 · 3¢ green · 1952

THE 4-H CLUBS, sponsored by the United States Department of Agriculture and the state agricultural colleges, make up one of the largest youth organizations in the world.

There were 2,000,000 4-H members in the United States in 1951, with 87,000 clubs and 150,000 adult and junior leaders. At that time the members were cultivating 400,000 acres with a gross value (including livestock) of $50,000,000.

The 4-H Clubs, which date from the turn of the century, are open to boys and girls who live on farms or in towns with a population of less than 2500. The 4-H emblem is a green four-leaf clover with a white H on each leaf. New members take the following pledge:

> My Head to clearer thinking,
> My Heart to greater loyalty,
> My Hands to larger service, and
> My Health to better living, for
> My Club, my Community, and my Country.

The 4-H Clubs give their young members many opportunities for fun and sociability. The clubs also teach useful and profitable skills by offering expert guidance in the most advanced methods of farming, gardening, canning, and raising stock.

125th Anniversary

1006 · 3¢ blue · 1952

ON FEBRUARY 28, 1827, Maryland's legislature chartered the Baltimore and Ohio Railroad, with a view to recovering some of the trade lost to New York through the building of the Erie Canal. Construction of the road, aided by a five hundred thousand dollar contribution from the state, started on July 4, 1829.

The first experimental run took place on December 22, 1829, with a horse-drawn stagecoach. Though "the good Lord never intended people to travel at the terrific rate of thirteen miles an hour," the road had its first paying passengers a month later.

On May 24, 1830, the Baltimore and Ohio became the first American railroad to operate for public use. "Tom Thumb," the first American-built steam locomotive, carried twenty-three passengers at eighteen miles an hour on its initial run in August, 1830.

By 1846 the road's annual gross receipts had reached six hundred and fifty thousand dollars, and by 1857 it extended as far as St. Louis. During the Civil War, the Baltimore and Ohio was invaluable to the North, and Southern raiders did their best to keep it out of operation.

Against the background of the charter, the commemorative stamp features the original horse-drawn stagecoach, "Tom Thumb," and a modern Diesel.

50th Anniversary

1007 · 3¢ blue · 1952

IN 1895 the United States had four registered motor vehicles. By 1902 the figure had risen to twenty-three thousand. Even at this early stage, many of the problems involved in the use of motor cars had already appeared.

The American Automobile Association was formed in 1902 to help solve these problems. Since then, it has served not only motorists but the community as a whole.

Through the efforts of the AAA, three hundred thousand responsible boys and girls safeguard eight million school children at street crossings. Good roads were the organization's first concern in 1902, and it has done much to make our magnificent highways possible.

The AAA has fought hard for uniform and efficient safety methods and has sponsored much legislation to remove traffic hazards and prevent accidents. The magnitude of its task is indicated by the fact that in 1950 there were fifty million registered motor vehicles.

The commemorative stamp shows a school safety-patrol youngster preventing two children from crossing an intersection at a dangerous moment. At the right, an automobile of 1902 vintage is flanked by a modern car. The emblem of the AAA appears at the top right.

Torch Representing
Freedom and Peace

1008 · 3¢ purple · 1952

ON APRIL 4, 1949, the North Atlantic Treaty was signed by the United States, Canada, Great Britain, France, the Netherlands, Belgium, Italy, Norway, Denmark, Iceland, and Portugal. The treaty created an alliance for mutual defense among the signatories, on the principle that an attack on any one of them would be considered an attack on all.

In August of that year the North Atlantic Treaty Organization, popularly called NATO, came into existence. The North Atlantic Council approved the establishment of a united Western European army under Supreme Headquarters, Allied Powers, Europe (SHAPE). General Dwight D. Eisenhower became the first Supreme Allied Commander. Later on, when General Eisenhower gave up this post, he was succeeded by Generals Matthew Ridgway and Alfred Gruenther.

In September, 1951, the Council admitted Greece and Turkey to membership in NATO. On April 2, 1952, Supreme Headquarters opened its command and communications center in the outskirts of Paris. Its four hundred Allied officers are responsible for guarding four thousand miles of frontier.

The commemorative stamp features a torch which represents freedom and peace. The torch is upheld by hands symbolizing the cooperative spirit and strength of the NATO nations.

50th Anniversary
of the Federal
Reclamation Act

1009 · 3¢ green · 1952

THE GRAND COULEE DAM is the keystone of the Columbia Basin Project, built by the Bureau of Reclamation at a cost of $772,000,000. Grand Coulee is the largest dam—in fact the largest concrete structure—in the world. It contains more than twice the amount of concrete needed for a two-lane highway from the Atlantic to the Pacific, and is three times the size of the Great Pyramid of Egypt.

Situated about 90 miles northwest of Spokane, the dam has a reservoir of 151 square miles that raises the river level enough to irrigate one million acres of formerly arid land. The base of the dam is 500 feet thick and 3000 feet long; at the top it is only 30 feet thick but 4173 feet long. Grand Coulee towers 550 feet into the sky, the equivalent of a 46-story skyscraper.

In keeping with its stupendous size, Grand Coulee has the greatest power plant and pumping plant in the world. In time Grand Coulee is expected to recover three-quarters of its cost from the sale of current to the industrial plants of the Northwest which owe their existence to the mighty dam.

The commemorative stamp was issued in 1952 to mark the fiftieth anniversary of the passage of the Federal Reclamation Act of 1902. This exceedingly valuable legislation is a lasting monument to the efforts of President Theodore Roosevelt.

175th Anniversary of Lafayette's Arrival

1010 · 3¢ blue · 1952

MARIE JOSEPH PAUL ROCH YVES GILBERT MOTIER, MARQUIS DE LAFAYETTE (1757-1834) belonged to one of the most aristocratic families in France. Yet, from the day he heard of the American Revolution, "my heart was enrolled in it." John Quincy Adams called him the "knight-errant of the American Revolution."

Young, ardent, and adventurous, Lafayette was a major-general in the American army before he was twenty. His dashing example made it fashionable for French noblemen to fight for farmers and tradesmen and tipped the aristocracy toward a French-American alliance.

Forbidden to leave France, Lafayette fled secretly and arrived in America in July, 1777. He eagerly sought a combat role and spent a large sum of his own money on the American cause. Early in 1779 he sailed back to France to speed French aid to America. A year later he returned with the heartening news that a formidable French fleet was on its way to the New World, together with a large army well supplied with equipment and money.

Lafayette's portrait dominates the commemorative stamp. On the left is an American flag and a Revolutionary cannon; on the right, a French flag and a miniature reproduction of *La Victoire,* the vessel that brought Lafayette to America.

25th Anniversary

1011 · 3¢ green · 1952

THE MOUNT RUSHMORE NATIONAL ME-
MORIAL, carved out of the granite cliffs
of the Black Hills in South Dakota, is
one of the world's majestic monuments.

The memorial is four hundred and sixty-five feet high, and
the huge, powerfully carved faces of George Washington,
Thomas Jefferson, Theodore Roosevelt, and Abraham Lincoln
can be seen miles away. Each face is sixty feet high.

Gutzon Borglum (1871-1941), born of Danish parentage in
Idaho, designed the memorial. To execute his heroic conception, Borglum employed fifty men who worked on it for five and
a half years. They blasted the statues out of the rock, using
models scaled one inch to the foot. Borglum did not live to see
the completion of his work, which was supervised by his son,
Lincoln Borglum.

All of Borglum's sculpture reflects the rugged simplicity of
the frontier where he was born and grew up. His outstanding
works include a memorial for the Gettysburg battlefield and two
Lincoln masterpieces. But Borglum was proudest of all of the
Mount Rushmore National Memorial. He called it his "shrine
of democracy" and exulted in the thought that it would remain
visible for two million years.

George Washington Bridge and Nineteenth-Century Bridge

1012 · 3¢ blue · 1952

THIS STAMP vividly illustrates the advance in civil engineering techniques by contrasting a typical nineteenth-century bridge with the George Washington Bridge.

In the nineteenth century, wooden bridges were the rule for short spans. They were generally covered to protect them against bad weather, and some remained in use for as much as sixty-five years. The one pictured on the stamp crossed Octorara Creek, in Pennsylvania. It was built in 1855 and had an over-all length of sixty-one feet. As late as 1930 there were still almost five hundred of these old-fashioned bridges in use.

In modern times the use of steel has allowed bridge builders to experiment with a variety of styles, such as the center-swing, panel-truss, cantilever, vertical-lift, and suspension types. All are notable for sturdy construction qualities.

The George Washington Bridge, built across the Hudson River and completed in 1931, is one of the triumphs of modern engineering. The bridge, with a total length of forty-seven hundred feet, carries eight lanes of traffic and is suspended on two giant cables each of which is three feet in diameter.

Bridge building is only one facet of the civil engineer's wizardry, which is also applied to such projects as highways, tunnels, airports, harbors, dams, canals, railroads, and irrigation systems.

Women in Uniforms of the Armed Services

1013 · 3¢ blue · 1952

DURING WORLD WAR II about three hundred thousand women served in the armed forces, thus releasing a large number of men for combat duty. In the Navy, Marine Corps, and Coast Guard women acted as storekeepers, radio operators, ship's cooks, pharmacist's mates, and aviation instructors. In the Army, women served as clerks, secretaries, weather observers, jeep drivers, and hospital aides, and performed a great many other duties.

The Women's Army Corps (WAC) eventually reached a wartime strength of one hundred and fifty thousand and served in every war theater. The highest rank was colonel, reserved for the director of the corps.

Women in the Navy were known as WAVES (Women Accepted for Voluntary Emergency Service). Their wartime strength was eighty-six thousand and they served in the continental United States and Hawaii. About a thousand WASPS (Women's Air Force Service Pilots) were trained during the war to deliver and break in new planes.

On the commemorative stamp issued to honor the women in the armed forces we see four women who are wearing the distinctive uniforms of their service: Marines, Army, Navy, and Air Corps.

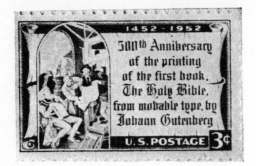

500th Anniversary

1014 · 3¢ purple · 1952

PRINTING WAS known in China and Korea long before it appeared in the Western World. Before the age of printing, books were extremely rare. Lettered and illustrated by hand on parchment or vellum, these books required many hours of patient and loving toil to produce. Few people were able to read; only church dignitaries and rich men had libraries.

The Gutenberg Bible was the first sizable book—certainly the first Bible—ever printed. The dates assigned for the printing of this Bible range all the way from 1452 to 1456.

Today some forty-five copies of this Bible are known. Of the three on vellum, the Library of Congress copy is appraised at one million dollars. The text, known as the Vulgate, is in Latin, and was completed by St. Jerome in 385 A.D.

Despite the legend on the commemorative stamp, we have very little dependable information about Johann Gutenberg (1397?-1468) and the invention of printing. There is no general agreement on the year of Gutenberg's birth. We are not even certain that he discovered the principle of movable type, or that he assembled the first press, or that he printed the Gutenberg Bible! Even the incident pictured on the commemorative stamp —the presentation of a proof to the Elector of Mainz—is a detail that cannot be verified.

Newspaperboy on His Route

1015 · 3¢ purple · 1952

THE FIRST newspaper in America was published in 1690 by Benjamin Harris. It was called *Publick Occurrences Both Foreign and Domestick* and lasted exactly one issue; it was confiscated by royal officials.

At the time of the Revolution, there were thirty-five newspapers in the colonies. During the nineteenth century, the number of American newspapers rose into the thousands, aided by a number of favorable factors.

The introduction of free public education created millions of potential readers. The invention of the telegraph and the laying of the Atlantic cable greatly speeded the gathering of news. Constant improvements in printing machinery made possible the modern newspaper as we know it today. Although the number of newspaper readers has increased enormously, the heavy expenses entailed in newspaper publishing have greatly reduced the number of newspapers in recent years.

Despite its elaborate structure and costly financing, the newspaper industry is unique in relying for a good deal of its distribution on children of elementary-school age. The commemorative stamp, issued as a tribute to the newspaperboys of America, pictures a typical newspaperboy against the background of a residential community.

Illuminated Globe and Red Cross

1016 · 1952
3¢ blue and red

WE OWE the founding of the International Red Cross to the self-sacrifice and tenacity of Jean Henri Dunant (1828-1910), who was awarded the first Nobel Peace Prize while living in a poorhouse.

In 1859, Dunant, a prosperous Swiss banker, learned the meaning of war from the Battle of Solferino, between French and Austrian troops. Ten hours of furious slaughter left forty thousand casualties on the blood-soaked battlefield—with no medical care provided by either side.

From then on, Dunant appealed unceasingly to the conscience of the world. It was due to his efforts that the Geneva Convention was signed in 1864, bringing the International Red Cross into existence.

Giving away most of his money and neglecting his business to further the cause that meant so much to him, Dunant soon went bankrupt. Ignored by the world, he spent the second half of his long life in obscurity and direst poverty.

When belated recognition came to Dunant with the award of the Nobel Peace Prize in 1901, his reaction was typical: he donated the money to charitable agencies. The last words of Dunant's will were, "I am a disciple of Christ as in the first century, and nothing more."

National Guardsman

1017 · 3¢ blue · 1953

THE NATIONAL GUARD is older than the United States, for it originated as the militia of Colonial soldiers—a body of armed citizens prepared to serve in times of emergency. The authority for maintaining militia groups was later written into the Constitution. Article 1, Section 8 authorizes Congress to call out "the Militia to execute the Laws of the Union, suppress insurrections and repel invasions." Article 2, Section 2 places the President in command of the National Guard in emergencies.

The oldest existing Guard unit is the 182nd Infantry of Massachusetts, founded as the Middlesex County militia regiment of 1636. The term *National Guard* made its first appearance in 1824 when New York militia groups adopted the name to honor General Lafayette, commander of the French *Garde Nationale,* during his visit to this country.

National Guard units have figured prominently in all the wars of the United States; they have also protected life and property against the havoc of peacetime disasters such as hurricanes, floods, forest fires, and blizzards.

The commemorative stamp pictures a National Guardsman ready for action. At the left we see an amphibious landing with air cover; at the right the National Guard is seen carrying out a flood rescue, one of its traditional peacetime tasks.

Outline Map of Ohio and State Seal

1018 · 3¢ brown · 1953

OHIO WAS the first state carved out of the Northwest Territory. There is an amusing story connected with its entry into the Union.

When Congress approved Ohio's constitution and boundaries in 1803, it neglected to pass a resolution establishing Ohio's statehood. To remedy this oversight, Representative George Bender, of Ohio, introduced a resolution in Congress in 1953 to admit Ohio as a state—as of March 1, 1803.

As a part of the Northwest Territory, Ohio benefited greatly from the wise provisions of the Ordinance of 1787 (stamp 795). The settlement of Ohio got under way in real earnest the following year (stamp 837). Six years later the Battle of Fallen Timbers broke the power of the Indians in the Ohio country.

The commemorative stamp pictures an outline map of Ohio together with the State Seal. The sixteen stars on the sides represent the first sixteen states. The large star at the top stands for Ohio, the seventeenth state admitted to the Union.

The buckeye leaf at the lower left reminds us that Ohio is the Buckeye State. The buckeye is a variety of horse chestnut found in great numbers in the Ohio Valley. This tree was named for the pale scar on its dark nut. The Indians saw a fanciful resemblance between this scar and a deer's eye; hence, the name.

314

Washington Pioneers

1019 · 3¢ green · 1953

THE EARLY history of the present state of Washington has been swallowed up in the history of Oregon. The Washington region, originally a part of the Oregon country, was the subject of a long boundary dispute between the United States and Great Britain.

Captain Robert Gray gave the United States its basic claim to the region when he sailed up the Pacific coast and explored the mouth of the Columbia River in 1792. In 1805 the Lewis and Clark expedition reached the same location after its rugged overland journey. This reinforced the American claim, as did the founding of the fur-trading post at Astoria. Early settlers owed much to the kindness of John McLoughlin (stamp 964).

In 1836 Marcus Whitman and other heroic missionaries started west over the Oregon Trail. The settlement of the boundary dispute in 1846 greatly stimulated the arrival of new immigrants and led to the formation of Washington Territory in 1853.

At the left of the commemorative stamp we see an ox-drawn covered wagon on its way west; at the right, weary pioneers who have at last reached their goal look out on an impressive expanse of lake, with forested shores and snow-capped mountains on the horizon.

315

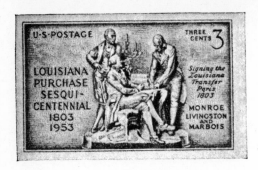

Signing of the Treaty

1020 · 3¢ maroon · 1953

IN 1801 President Jefferson instructed Robert Livingston, his minister to France, to purchase New Orleans and an adjoining strip of land (see stamp 323). For a long time Livingston met with exasperating evasion. Suddenly, Napoleon Bonaparte's officials told Livingston he could have the vast Louisiana territory for a mere fifteen million dollars.

Napoleon, on the point of declaring war on England, feared he might lose the whole territory to England with no compensation whatever. Furthermore, he needed money for the war, and the sale of Louisiana would satisfy his immediate needs. There was another angle that appealed to the crafty Napoleon. The deal might create bad feeling between America and England; so much the better for France.

Livingston and James Monroe (Jefferson's special envoy) agreed to accept the astounding offer, even though they were going far beyond their authority. Rightly feeling that Jefferson would back them up, they concluded the decisive negotiations with François de Barbé-Marbois, Napoleon's friendly finance minister.

On May 2, 1803, as they signed the Louisiana Purchase treaty, Livingston exclaimed exultantly, "From this day the United States take their place among the powers of the first rank!"

50th Anniversary of the Kittyhawk Flight

C 47 · 6¢ red · 1953

THE WRIGHT brothers began their experiments with flight by building gliders. To get the information they needed, they constructed a wind tunnel from a discarded box and a weather vane. They produced gusts of wind with a fan powered by a gas engine.

To test their gliders, they selected the bleak dunes of Kittyhawk, North Carolina, on the advice of the United States Weather Bureau. The wind currents were stable; the slightly hilly ground was good for take-offs; the soft sand would cushion abrupt landings.

After gliding six hundred feet in a one-minute flight at Kittyhawk in September, 1902, the Wrights were ready for powered flight. They built their own biplane, with wings forty feet long and six feet apart. The one hundred and fifty pound engine was to the right of center on the lower wing; the pilot lay on the left side for balance. The two propellers were directly in back of the wings.

On December 17, 1903, this homemade plane flew one hundred and twenty feet, staying in the air for twelve seconds. This flight, the first successful powered flight in history, began the Air Age. During the week the commemorative stamp was issued, an American rocket plane flew sixteen hundred miles in an hour.

Commodore Matthew Calbraith Perry
(1794-1858)

1021 · 5¢ green · 1953

UP TO 1853 the Japanese refused to have anything to do with Westerners, either commercially or culturally. With occasional slight exceptions, they barred their ports for centuries to any Western ships. Portuguese traders and missionaries were tolerated for a time, and then driven away and Christianity ruthlessly stamped out. However, the Dutch were permitted to maintain a small trading post at Nagasaki.

Toward the end of 1852 Commodore Matthew Calbraith Perry sailed from Norfolk, Virginia, with a fleet of four ships. His mission was to open Japanese ports to American shipping, and he was instructed not to use force.

On July 8, 1853, Perry anchored in the outer bay of Yedo (now Tokyo) and sent word ashore that he had letters for the Emperor from President Fillmore. A week later Perry went ashore with an escort of three hundred Marines and delivered his letters to two nobles of the palace. On his return the following year, Perry had a friendly reception and signed a treaty of peace, amity, and commerce.

A portrait of Commodore Perry appears in the upper right of the commemorative stamp. The main part of the design is given over to a moonlight view of the American fleet riding at anchor outside Yedo Bay.

75th Anniversary

1022 · 3¢ violet · 1953

WHEN THE American Bar Association was founded in 1878, its chief objective was to raise the standards of education for the legal profession.

The Bar Association has also inspired a number of notable legal reforms. The most important one was the creation of the United States Circuit and District Courts in 1891 to ease the strain on the Supreme Court's calendar.

By adopting canons of professional ethics in 1908 and canons of judicial ethics in 1924, the Bar Association performed a valuable service for both professions and for the community as a whole.

The striking commemorative stamp illustrates part of an impressive frieze for the Supreme Court chamber. It includes allegorical figures representing Wisdom, Justice, Divine Inspiration, and Truth. This stamp, which was issued in honor of the seventy-fifth anniversary of the American Bar Association, carries the appropriate slogan: "Liberty under Law."

The frieze is the work of Adolph A. Weinman, a distinguished sculptor who studied with Saint-Gaudens and produced some remarkably fine work for public buildings throughout the country. Weinman was also the designer of the "Mercury" dime, one of our handsomest coins.

Roosevelt Family Home

1023 · 3¢ green · 1953

FROM THE very start of his colorful political career, Theodore Roosevelt (1858-1919) was a crusader for badly needed reforms. He attacked slums, corrupt politics, the spoils system, and other evils.

Roosevelt's "Rough Rider" expedition (see stamp 973) made him a national hero and led to his nomination for Vice-President in 1900. A year later the assassination of President McKinley brought Roosevelt to the White House as the youngest of all the Presidents.

Roosevelt pursued a vigorous foreign policy, especially in making possible the construction of the Panama Canal (see stamps 398 and 856). He also fought valiantly to conserve America's forests and other natural resources and to reclaim millions of acres of wasteland in the West. In politics and out, Roosevelt was a man of superb vitality and constantly preached "the strenuous life."

In 1911 Roosevelt split the Republican party to found the Progressive ("Bull Moose") movement. The failure of his bid for the Presidency ended his political career.

The commemorative stamp pictures the Roosevelt family home at Oyster Bay, Long Island, which became a national shrine in 1953.

25th Anniversary

1024 · 3¢ blue · 1953

THE FUTURE FARMERS OF AMERICA is a national organization of farm boys studying vocational agriculture in rural high schools. At the time this stamp appeared, there were three hundred and fifty thousand Future Farmers in nine thousand chapters.

Ten per cent of our present farmers are alumni of this organization, which has the fourfold motto:

> Learning to do;
> Doing to learn;
> Earning to live;
> Living to serve.

The commemorative stamp shows a farm scene with rolling hills in the background. In the foreground we see a farm boy standing under a tree as he looks at fields and crops. There are shrubs at his left, while a bird perches on a barbed-wire fence to his right. On the back of the youngster's jacket we see the FFA emblem. This is a cross-section view of an ear of corn, with an American eagle on top. Corn, a crop native to the New World, is particularly suitable as a symbol of American farming.

The circle contains three other symbols. To the ancient Greeks, Minerva's owl represented wisdom and knowledge. The plow stands for labor and tillage of the soil. The rising sun is the familiar sign for progress and the dawn of a new day.

50th Anniversary

1025 · 3¢ violet · 1953

THE MOTOR truck got its real start in 1903 when the Automobile Club of America demonstrated that "trucks could be successfully used in commerce at less cost and to greater advantage than horse-drawn vehicles."

The development of fine highways, beginning in 1920, and the introduction of the trailer in 1921, made possible an enormous increase in the use of trucks. The trailer gives trucks a flexibility and versatility capable of endless variation. This has made it feasible, for example, to use trucks to carry food, transport mail, remove garbage, fight fires, and bring portable libraries to rural areas.

By 1953 the United States had almost ten million trucks and trailers. The industry had become the nation's largest industrial employer, providing one out of every ten jobs, with an annual outlay of twenty-seven billion dollars for pay rolls and materials. In 1953 trucks were moving three-quarters of the country's freight tonnage.

The commemorative stamp shows a truck against a background of a farm scene to the left and a city skyline on the right. Along the roads linking these two areas we see trucks fulfilling their task of maintaining communication between farm, factory, store, and home.

322

General George S. Patton, Jr.
(1885-1945)

1026 · 3¢ violet · 1953

GENERAL GEORGE S. PATTON, JR., was one of the most colorful figures in American military history. As the Army's leading specialist in mechanized warfare, Patton played an important part in the North African campaign of 1942-1943. "Old Blood and Guts," as Patton was known to his men, commanded the forces that defeated the renowned Afrika Korps of General Rommel, the "Desert Fox."

After this triumph, Patton led the Seventh Army in the invasion of Sicily, in July, 1943. After thirty-eight days of whirlwind fighting, he had the island under Allied control. Yet Patton always remained a stickler for smart appearance. A typical order read: "Every man who is old enough will shave once a day."

In August, 1944, Patton began the remarkable armored invasion that took the four hundred and fifty thousand men of the Third Army through France, Luxembourg, Germany, Czechoslovakia, and Austria. Soon, Patton's men were roaring along the roads five hundred miles ahead of their base of supplies. Before they were through, they killed or wounded half a million enemy troops and captured another half million.

Six months after the war was over, Patton was mortally hurt in an automobile accident. "It's a hell of a way to die!" was his characteristic comment on his tragic end.

Views of New Amsterdam and New York

1027 · 3¢ violet · 1953

IN 1647 New Amsterdam had about eight hundred settlers. Peter Stuyvesant, the governor, was conscientious and devoted to the colony's welfare. Unfortunately, he was also stubborn and quarrelsome. He spent much of his time in struggling with the English in Connecticut and the Swedes in Delaware.

Some of Stuyvesant's decrees were excellent. He saw to it, for example, that pigs were equipped with nose rings instead of being allowed to wander at will on the streets of New Amsterdam. Nevertheless, his dictatorial ways incensed the Dutch burghers. They were already sufficiently chafed by the restrictions imposed by the West India Company. Their place of residence and the kind of crops to be planted were imposed from above. Dealings with outsiders were forbidden.

Finally, in order to calm the growing dissension, Stuyvesant granted New Amsterdam a charter in February, 1653. This document restrained the governor's authority, liberalized the government, and provided for the election of a town council and other officials.

The commemorative stamp shows a Dutch vessel of the period in New Amsterdam harbor. The low-lying settlement, complete with windmill, appears against the towering skyline of modern New York.

Pioneers in
Desert Country

1028 · 3¢ brown · 1953

IN 1853, when James Gadsden was American minister to Mexico, he negotiated the purchase of 45,535 square miles of Mexican territory for $10,000,000. This long, fairly narrow strip of land now forms the southern border of New Mexico and Arizona.

Gadsden, an ardent Southern patriot and a knowledgeable railroad man, foresaw that a railroad passing through this strip could link the Pacific region with the Southern Atlantic seaboard. This would enable Southern ports to ship the products of the Pacific area to Europe.

In this way, Gadsden reasoned, the South could snatch the profits of a vast commercial empire from its Northern rivals. Gadsden's judgment was at least partially upheld by the later construction of the Southern Pacific line along his favored route.

In 1953 the area of the purchase supported an estimated 350,000 people. The three Arizona counties that lie wholly within the Gadsden region had a mining income of $50,000,000 that year, as well as $150,000,000 in bank deposits, and substantial holdings in livestock and cotton. It is all a far cry from the scene depicted on the commemorative stamp, which shows pioneers advancing grimly through a forbidding, cactus-studded landscape.

Low Memorial Library

1029 · 3¢ blue · 1954

In 1754 the Reverend Samuel Johnson founded King's College near Trinity Church in New York. The school, chartered by George II, had eight pupils. The administration of King's College was staunchly loyalist. Yet Alexander Hamilton, one of its early students, became a leader of the American Revolution.

During the Revolution King's College became Columbia College. The college grew very slowly; as late as the 1850's it had 89 students and six professors. In 1954 Columbia was the fourth largest university in the United States, with a student body of 25,000 and a faculty of 3,300. It had 25 colleges, a physical plant of 71 buildings, and an endowment of over $110,000,000.

Columbia owed its phenomenal growth to the fruitful work of three notable presidents: Frederick Augustus Barnard (1864-1889); Seth Low (1889-1901); and Nicholas Murray Butler (1902-1945), an incisive personality and a superb administrator.

In 1898 President Low personally contributed a million dollars to establish the magnificent Low Memorial Library. In 1954 Columbia's libraries housed about a million volumes.

The impressive commemorative stamp presents a view of Low Memorial Library. The bottom border contains the always timely motto: "Man's Right to Knowledge and the Free Use Thereof"—the theme of Columbia's bicentennial celebration.

"The Sower"

1060 · 3¢ violet · 1954

AFTER NEBRASKA became American territory as a result of the Louisiana Purchase in 1803, many explorers visited the region. They were followed by the fur traders, and Bellevue, Nebraska's first permanent settlement, started as a trading post. Later on, when the Oregon, California, and Mormon trails all passed through Nebraska, pioneers were attracted to its rich prairie soil.

According to the terms of the Missouri Compromise of 1820, Kansas and Nebraska should automatically have been organized as "free" territories, with slavery prohibited. Instead, the Kansas-Nebraska Bill, passed in 1854, gave them the option of adopting or declining slavery within their borders. Thus the whole bitter struggle was reopened.

The men who framed the bill thought that, though Nebraska would surely become a free territory, Kansas might become a slave territory. As indicated on page 328, their calculations turned out badly.

The commemorative stamp features *The Sower,* a bronze statue which rises 27 feet above the tower of the Nebraska State Capitol at Lincoln. The statue is the work of Lee Lawrie and was inspired by a famous painting by the French artist Jean François Millet.

Wagon Train
of Pioneers

1061 · 3¢ reddish gold · 1954

IN PREHISTORIC times Kansas was a great shallow sea, as evidenced by its salt deposits and chalk beds as well as fossils of sea animals. More recently this region was the stamping grounds of several Indian tribes—the Wichitas, the Pawnees, and the Kansas (for whom the state was named).

In 1803 Kansas, then part of the Louisiana Territory, passed into American hands. Only a small southeastern corner was successively claimed by Spain, Mexico, and Texas. Later Kansas became part of the Indian Territory reserved for the Five Civilized Indian Tribes (page 263).

However, with the increase of travel on the Santa Fe Trail, the coming of the Mexican War, and the discovery of gold in California, Kansas received a large influx of settlers. In 1854 Congress passed a law setting up Kansas as a territory (page 327). The resulting violent struggles between abolitionists and proslavery men gave the region the poignant nickname of "bleeding Kansas." In 1861 Kansas finally entered the Union as a free state.

The design of this stamp shows a wheat field with farm buildings in the background. Above we see a wagon train of pioneers in light silhouette.

George Eastman

(1854-1932)

1062 · 3¢ brown · 1954

GEORGE EASTMAN became a wealthy man by revolutionizing photography. By inventing the convenient and quick-acting dry-plate process he did away with the clumsy and time-consuming wet-plate process. To manufacture the new plates he set up his first plant at Rochester in 1880.

In 1888 Eastman introduced roll film and the Kodak. The first Kodaks sold for $25, but as he improved the camera he reduced the price until a far superior model was available for $2.00.

Eastman was also one of the pioneers of large-scale industrial research. In addition, he was an innovator in the use of intensive but completely reliable advertising.

After building up a fortune of $100,000,000, Eastman gave it away during his lifetime. Some of his money went into the profit-sharing plans, retirement annuities, life insurance policies, and disability benefits he established for his employees. He also gave millions to the Massachusetts Institute of Technology, the Eastman School of Music, the University of Rochester Medical School, and the Rochester Dental Dispensary. His explanation was simple: "It is more fun to give money than to will it. And that is why I give."

Landing of
Lewis and Clark

1063 · 3¢ dark brown · 1954

THE LEWIS AND CLARK EXPEDITION, described on page 32, is one of the enduring epics of American history. Each generation of Americans is enthralled by the thrills, the dangers, and the natural wonders of that three-year trip through uncharted territory. More immediately, the success of the expedition stimulated the spread of fur trapping to the streams of the Rocky Mountain region.

One of the most important members of the expedition was a young Indian woman named Sacajawea (Sack uh jah wé uh), "the Bird Woman." She was the wife of Toussaint Charbonneau, a French-Canadian trapper who acted as interpreter for the expedition.

Although Sacajawea brought along her newborn infant, Baptiste, she bore all the hardships of the trip uncomplainingly. Her knowledge of the Indian country was invaluable, and she helped secure the success of the expedition by winning over the Shoshone Indians to a friendly attitude toward the white strangers. Equally important, she persuaded the Indians to give the exhausted explorers horses to finish their trip to the Pacific.

During the course of the expedition Sacajawea was reunited with her own tribe, the Snake Indians, from whom she had been kidnaped as a little girl.

Charles Willson Peale

(1741-1827)

"The Artist in His Museum"

1064 · 3¢ rose brown · 1955

CHARLES WILLSON PEALE was one of those universal geniuses who were so plentiful in the eighteenth century. As one of the leading artists of his day, Peale painted many of the Founding Fathers. He was Washington's favorite painter, and did seven portraits of him. (Four of these were used in the 1932 Bicentennial issue—see Stamps 704, 706, 708, and 710.)

Peale was a soldier, a politician, and an administrator—and mechanic, an inventor, a silversmith, a millwright, a naturalist, and a watchmaker! He designed everything from false teeth to windmills, and found time to run a museum of natural history. Manasseh Cutler (see page 137) said that Peale's museum was like Noah's Ark—"only Peale's is much better!"

In 1805 Peale organized a group of Philadelphia's leading citizens to found the Pennsylvania Academy of the Fine Arts. One of the Academy's most precious paintings, by Peale himself, was used on the commemorative stamp. It shows the artist lifting the curtain of his museum. At the left is a stuffed turkey; at the right, the bones of a mastodon.

Peale painted this self-portrait when he was eighty-three years old.

First of the
Land-Grant Colleges
1065 · 3¢ green · 1955

Up to 1855, higher education in the United States was supplied, for the most part, to wealthy youngsters and to those who were training for such professions as law, medicine, and the ministry. In that year, however, there was a break with tradition when educational pioneers planned courses of study for prospective farmers and technicians.

In February, 1855, Michigan Agricultural College (later Michigan State College) and the Farmers' High School (which eventually became Pennsylvania State University) were chartered. Both institutions, starting on a small scale, have since flourished mightily.

Seven years later, during the Civil War, Representative Morrill of Vermont proposed a bill empowering the Federal government to help each state found a college "to teach such branches of learning as are related to the agricultural and mechanic arts." As a result, Congress passed the Morrill Act, under the terms of which the states received grants of Federal lands and then sold them to finance the new colleges, known as "land-grant colleges."

On the commemorative stamp we see symbols of agriculture, mining, chemistry, and engineering—the chief courses offered at the land-grant colleges.

50th Anniversary
1066 · 8¢ deep blue · 1955

ON FEBRUARY 23, 1905, a youthful Chicago lawyer named Paul P. Harris met with a mining engineer, a coal dealer, and a merchant tailor to form the first Rotary club. Their object was to unite men of varying religious and political faiths, and of different nationalities and occupations, into one organization.

The founders took the name of their club from *rota,* the Latin word for "wheel," because they rotated their weekly meetings at the business locations of the members. This was the origin of the well-known Rotary emblem, a gear wheel with six spokes, twenty-four cogs, and a slot in the hub.

At the time of its Golden Jubilee in 1955, Rotary International had 400,000 members and 8400 clubs in eighty-nine countries. Dedicated to the ideal of serving the community, Rotarians try to advance "international understanding, good will, and peace."

Rotary's most notable contribution to this cause is the Rotary Fellowships for Advanced Study, which enable brilliant students to attend universities outside their native land. By 1955, over six hundred students from fifty-seven countries had been financed by the endowment fund, which in 1955 amounted to almost four million dollars. Even Sinclair Lewis, at first a strong critic of Rotary, ended by praising it.

Members of the Armed Forces

1067 · 3¢ purple · 1955

THIS STAMP was issued on May 21, 1955, to honor members of the Armed Forces Reserve. The Marines, Coast Guard, Army, Navy, and Air Force are represented on the stamp, with an eagle and shield in the background.

Today the Reserve, which originated in the Minute Men of the Revolution, numbers millions of men. Though they are not in active service, their names are included on the roster of the armed forces. The National Guard, described on page 313, is part of the Army Reserve.

Under present conditions, a young man under 26 is drafted for two years of active training. Thereafter his name is kept on the Reserve rolls for another six years.

Maintenance of the Reserve has been made necessary by the unsettled world conditions that have prevailed since the end of World War II. The tension between the Western countries and the Iron Curtain countries, the unrest in colonial areas, and the atomic arms race have all contributed to the tension. Undeclared wars, such as the conflicts in Korea and Indochina, have resulted from the stresses and strains that may lead to sudden flare-ups in many parts of our uneasy globe. A lessening of international tensions would undoubtedly affect both the draft and the Reserve.

The Great Stone Face
(or The Old Man of the Mountains)

1068 · 3¢ green · 1955

AT FRANCONIA NOTCH in the White Mountains of New Hampshire, thousands of years of erosion by wind and water produced one of the great natural wonders of the world—a huge outcropping of rocks which outline a gigantic human face.

When Nathaniel Hawthorne published his beautiful story *The Great Stone Face* in 1850, he gave this natural wonder nation-wide fame. Here is the impressive way he described it: "There was the broad arch of the forehead, a hundred feet in height; the nose, with its long bridge; and the vast lips, which, if they could have spoken, would have rolled their thunder accents from one end of the valley to the other."

Although The Great Stone Face was discovered by workmen in 1805, it was of course known for centuries before that to the Indians of the region. The Indians were content to admire the rocks and weave picturesque legends about them. On the other hand, when the famous showman P. T. Barnum saw the rocks, he regretted that he could not cart them away for public exhibition—at a fee. Since his day some fifteen million tourists have come to Franconia Notch to marvel at The Old Man of the Mountains.

335

Map of the Great Lakes and Two Steamers

1069 · 3¢ blue · 1955

THE SOO CANAL at Sault Sainte Marie, Michigan, has been nick-named "the billion-dollar mile"—and with good reason. For this strategic waterway carries more traffic than the Suez Canal, and three times as much as the Panama Canal.

The importance of the Great Lakes for shipping thousands of cargoes of ore, coal, lumber, and grain has already been explained on pages 22-23. But it is worth knowing something about the building of the canal.

Originally traffic was hampered by the fact that the turbulent St. Mary's Rapids fall twenty feet from the level of Lake Superior to the level of Lake Huron. In 1852 Congress authorized the construction of a canal linking the two lakes.

Work on the canal started in 1853 and went on for two years. Much of it was done in freezing weather; the Indians were uncooperative; cholera carried off many of the workers; the canal walls collapsed; yet the canal opened on June 18, 1855.

The state of Michigan operated the Soo Canal until 1881, when the Federal government took over the locks, in order to maintain them and make necessary additions as the volume of traffic grew. Since 1855 the annual freight tonnage carried through the canal has increased from 14,500 the first year to 130,000,000 in 1955.

Atomic Energy Encircling the Hemispheres

1070 · 3¢ deep blue · 1955

WHEN THE first atomic bomb was exploded by nuclear fission at Los Alamos, New Mexico, on July 16, 1945, at a temperature of 100,000,000 degrees Fahrenheit, it created a sight that was "unprecedented, magnificent, beautiful, stupendous, and terrifying." Later on, the first wartime use of the bomb brought about Japan's immediate surrender. Since then hydrogen bombs, operating on the nuclear fusion principle, have been built in ever larger and deadlier forms.

Yet the nuclear scientists have presented man with many benefits, too. Nuclear reactors promise to give us the cheapest and most efficient fuel known. The radioisotopes produced in reactors are valuable in fighting cancer and other diseases. Better crops, food preservation, and many new and valuable industrial techniques have been made possible by splitting the uranium atom.

In the course of an address on July 28, 1955, marking the issue of this stamp, President Eisenhower said, "Every discovery we have made, even the use of fire to warm our bodies, to cook our food, has also been used as one of the devastating weapons of war to bring destruction to enemies." Whether the atom will be used for good or evil remains the gravest problem confronting the world today.

Plan of the Fortress

1071 · 3¢ light brown · 1955

WHEN YOU look at a map of New York State, you can see that Lake Champlain and Lake George form natural waterways for north-south invasion routes. Between the two lakes, which are not connected, there was once a portage path for carrying canoes. Hence the name "Ticonderoga," in Indian language "the place between two lakes." This path naturally took on great strategic importance.

Originally the Iroquois and Algonquin Indians fought over the portage path. In the eighteenth century it became a prize in the wars between England and France.

Finally in 1755 Marquis de Montcalm, the able French commander, built a great stone fortress on the shores of Lake Champlain to control the invasion route. The bastion bristled with cannon and was large enough to house three thousand soldiers and ample military supplies. Yet Fort "Ti" never lived up to its mighty reputation, for the British stormed it in 1759, and in 1775 the Americans seized it without a struggle.

The commemorative stamp features a boldly outlined plan of the fort on which are superimposed a cannon, cannon balls, a powder keg, and the formidable figure of Ethan Allen (see page 198).

338

Andrew W. Mellon

(1855-1937)

1072 · 3¢ maroon · 1955

THOUGH ANDREW MELLON was a prominent figure in many types of business, he is best remembered for his work in organizing the gigantic Aluminum Corporation of America. Ever since it was founded, Alcoa has steadily pursued the goals of creating new aluminum products and improving its manufacturing processes.

In 1913, together with his brother Richard, Mellon founded the Mellon Institute of Industrial Research, which has done valuable work in pure science as well as in industrial research. In 1955 the Institute combined forces with the Trudeau Foundation to fight the ravages of tuberculosis.

In his later years Mellon turned to public life, serving as Secretary of the Treasury from 1921 to 1932 and Ambassador to Great Britain from 1932 to 1933.

Through his association of many years with Lord Duveen, the famous art dealer, Mellon built up one of the finest art collections in the world. In 1937 he presented his art treasures to the nation and also donated funds for the construction of the National Gallery of Art to house them. The design of the commemorative stamp is copied from a portrait in the Founders' Room of the museum.

250th Anniversary of Franklin's Birth

1073 · 3¢ vermilion · 1956

BENJAMIN FRANKLIN has justifiably been called a universal genius. He was equally successful as a journalist, printer, publisher, scientist, inventor, politician, educator, postmaster, philosopher, diplomat, and as an avid organizer of community projects. His inventions include bifocal glasses, the Franklin stove, and the glass "harmonica" with a keyboard of 24 perfectly tuned musical glasses.

It was in 1752 that Franklin performed the most famous of his experiments. Here is how he described it in his autobiography: "A hemp cord conducted the electricity to a key near his hand, and from this he received the shock which proved the truth of his theory that lightning and electricity are the same."

This experiment aroused so much interest that it inspired a painting by Benjamin West entitled *Franklin Taking Electricity from the Sky*. The design for the commemorative stamp is based on West's painting.

Throughout his long life Franklin remained an enthusiastic believer in the benefits of science. When a friend was told about the first man-carrying balloon, he glumly asked Franklin, "What good is it?" To this Franklin replied, doubtless with a twinkle in his eye, "What good is a baby?"

SOURCES OF STAMP DESIGNS

(This section contains a partial listing of works of art on which various commemorative stamps are based. Special information is provided on the Famous Americans and Overrun Countries series.)

PAGE	SCOTT CATALOG NUMBER	
1	230	After a painting by William H. Powell.
2	231	After the painting by Vanderlyn in the Rotunda of the Capitol in Washington, D.C.
2	232	After a Spanish engraving.
3	233	After a Spanish engraving.
4	234	After the painting by Vaclav Brozik in the Metropolitan Museum of Art.
5	235	After a panel in the bronze doors by Randolph Rogers in the Capitol in Washington, D.C.
6	236	After a painting by Francisco Jover.
7	237	After the painting by Luigi Gregori at the University of Notre Dame.
7	238	After the painting by R. Balaca in Madrid.
8	239	After a painting by R. Maso.
9	240	After the painting by A. G. Heaton in the Capitol in Washington, D.C.
10	241	After the painting by Muñoz Degrain in Madrid.
11	242	After the painting by Luetze in Germantown, Pa.
11	243	After a painting by Francisco Jover.
12	244	Portrait of Isabella after a painting in Madrid. Portrait of Columbus after a painting by Lotto.
12	245	After the cast for the Columbian Exposition Commemorative Half Dollar.
13	285	After the painting by Lamprecht, now at Marquette College in Milwaukee.
14	286	After a photograph.

Page	Scott Catalog Number	
15	287	After an engraving in Schoolcraft's *History of the Indian Tribes*.
16	288	After an old engraving.
17	289	After a drawing by Frederic Remington.
18	290	After a painting by A. G. Heaton.
19	291	After a drawing by Frederic Remington.
20	292	After a painting by J. MacWhirter.
21	293	After a photograph.
33	328	After a painting in the Virginia State Library.
36	367	After the Saint-Gaudens statue in Chicago.
51	617	After a drawing in the Cambridge Public Library.
52	618	After the painting by Henry Sandham in the town hall of Lexington.
53	619	After Daniel Chester French's statue in Concord, Mass.
57	628	After a memorial statue unveiled in Washington, D.C. in 1926.
58	629	After a painting by E. F. Ward.
68	651	After a painting by Frederick C. Yohn.
71	680	After the memorial group on the Fallen Timbers monument.
75	688	After the statue of Colonel George Washington on the site of the Battle of Braddock's Field.
77	690	After an etching by H. B. Hall.
80	704	After a miniature painted by Charles Willson Peale in 1777; now in the Metropolitan Museum of Art.
81	705	After a profile bust made by Jean Antoine Houdon in 1785; now at Mount Vernon.
82	706	After a portrait painted by Charles Willson Peale at Mount Vernon in 1772; now at Washington and Lee University.
83	707	After a portrait painted by Gilbert Stuart at Germantown, Pa. in 1796; now in the Boston Museum of Fine Arts.

Page	Scott Catalog Number	
145	836	After a painting by Stanley M. Arthurs.
146	837	After the statue by Gutzon Borglum at Marietta, Ohio.
155	859	All the stamps in the Authors' group feature a closed book, a scroll, a quill pen, and an inkwell at the base of the portrait.
160	864	All the stamps in the Poets' group feature a reproduction of the winged horse Pegasus, symbol of the poetic imagination.
165	869	All the stamps in the Educators' group feature the Lamp of Knowledge at the base of the portrait.
170	874	Each of the stamps in the Scientists' group carries a symbol of the science with which the subject was associated. Thus, the Audubon stamp has a picture of a bird; the Long stamp shows a chemist's retort; the Reed stamp bears the wand of Esculapius, symbol of the medical profession.
175	879	All the stamps in the Composers' group feature a spray of laurel and the Pipes of Pan.
180	884	All the stamps in the Artists' group feature an artist's palette with brushes and a stonecutter's maul with chisels.
185	889	All the stamps in the Inventors' group feature a cogwheel, uplifted wings, and a lightning flash. These stand for power, flight, and electricity.
191	895	After the painting *Springtime* by Sandro Botticelli.
194	898	After a painting by Gerald Cassidy.
197	902	After the "Emancipation" statue by Thomas Ball in Lincoln Park, Washington, D.C.
199	904	After the mural by Gilbert White in the State Capitol at Frankfort.
200	905	After a poster by Mark O'Dea.
203	908	After a plaster cast by Paul Manship.
204-212	909-921	The stamps of this series use the flags of the over-

344

		run countries as the main element of the design. Several of the stamps are in two colors, most are in three. This is in addition to the main frame, which is in purple on every stamp. All the stamps have identical side panels: on the left a phoenix, the mythical bird that symbolizes rebirth from the ashes of destruction; on the right a female figure is seen breaking the chains of oppression and slavery.
224	929	After a photograph by Joseph Rosenthal.
225	934	After a photograph by Peter Carroll.
236	945	This stamp bears the same power symbols that appear on the stamps of the Inventors' group of the Famous Americans Series.
238	947	The Franklin portrait is after a drawing by James B. Longacre. The Washington portrait is after a painting by Gilbert Stuart.
239	949	After the painting *The Doctor* by Sir Luke Fildes in the National Gallery in London.
243	953	This stamp, like stamp 875, features a chemist's retort.
251	960	This stamp bears the same symbols that appear on the stamps of the Authors' group of the Famous Americans Series.
256	965	This stamp follows the pattern of the Famous Americans Series, with the scales symbolizing Justice.
264	973	After a statue in Prescott, Arizona.
271	980	This stamp bears the same symbols that appear on the stamps of the Authors' group of the Famous Americans Series.
278	986	This stamp bears the same symbols that appear on the stamps of the Poets' group of the Famous Americans Series.

SCOTT CATALOG		
PAGE	NUMBER	
300	1004	After the painting *Birth of Our Nation's Flag* by Charles H. Weisgerber.
310	1014	After a painting by Edward Laning in the New York Public Library.
316	1020	After a sculptured plaque by Karl Bitter in St. Louis.
319	1022	After the Supreme Court frieze by Adolph A. Weinman.
327	1060	After the statue *The Sower* by Lee Lawrie, at the Nebraska State Capitol, based on the painting by Jean François Millet.
330	1063	The figures of Lewis and Clark are drawn from a monument at Charlottesville, Va., by Charles Keck. The figure of Sacajawea is drawn from the statue at Bismarck, N.D.
331	1064	After the painting *The Artist in His Museum* by Charles Willson Peale in the Pennsylvania Academy of the Fine Arts.
338	1072	After a portrait of Andrew Mellon by Oswald Birley in the Founders' Room of the National Gallery of Art at Washington, D.C.
339	1073	After the painting *Franklin Taking Electricity from the Sky* by Benjamin West.

INDEX

Items in capitals and small capitals refer to commemorative stamps.

347

Items in capitals and small capitals refer to commemorative stamps.

Items in capitals and small capitals refer to commemorative stamps.

Items in capitals and small capitals refer to commemorative stamps.

Items in capitals and small capitals refer to commemorative stamps.

Items in capitals and small capitals refer to commemorative stamps.

Items in capitals and small capitals refer to commemorative stamps.

Items in capitals and small capitals refer to commemorative stamps.

Items in capitals and small capitals refer to commemorative stamps.

Items in capitals and small capitals refer to commemorative stamps.

Items in capitals and small capitals refer to commemorative stamps.

Items in capitals and small capitals refer to commemorative stamps.